Pride and Prejudice and Zombies

The Graphic Novel

Pride and Prejudice and Zombies

The Graphic Novel

Jane Austen and Seth Grahame-Smith

ADAPTED BY TONY LEE • ILLUSTRATED BY CLIFF RICHARDS

TITAN BOOKS

Pride and Prejudice and Zombies
ISBN: 9781848566941

Published by Titan Books
A division of Titan Publishing Group Ltd.
144 Southwark St
London, SE1 0UP

Adapted from **Pride and Prejudice and Zombies**
by Jane Austen and Seth Grahame-Smith, published in 2009
by Quirk Books, Philadelphia, copyright © 2009 by Quirk Productions, Inc.
www.quirkclassics.com

A CIP catalogue record for this title is available from the British Library.

First edition: April 2010

1 3 5 7 9 10 8 6 4 2

Printed in Italy

What did you think of this book? We love to hear from our readers.
Please email us at: readerfeedback@titanemail.com, or write to us at the above address.

To receive advance information, news, competitions, and exclusive Titan offers online,
please register by clicking the "sign up" button on our website: www.titanbooks.com

Pride and Prejudice
and Zombies

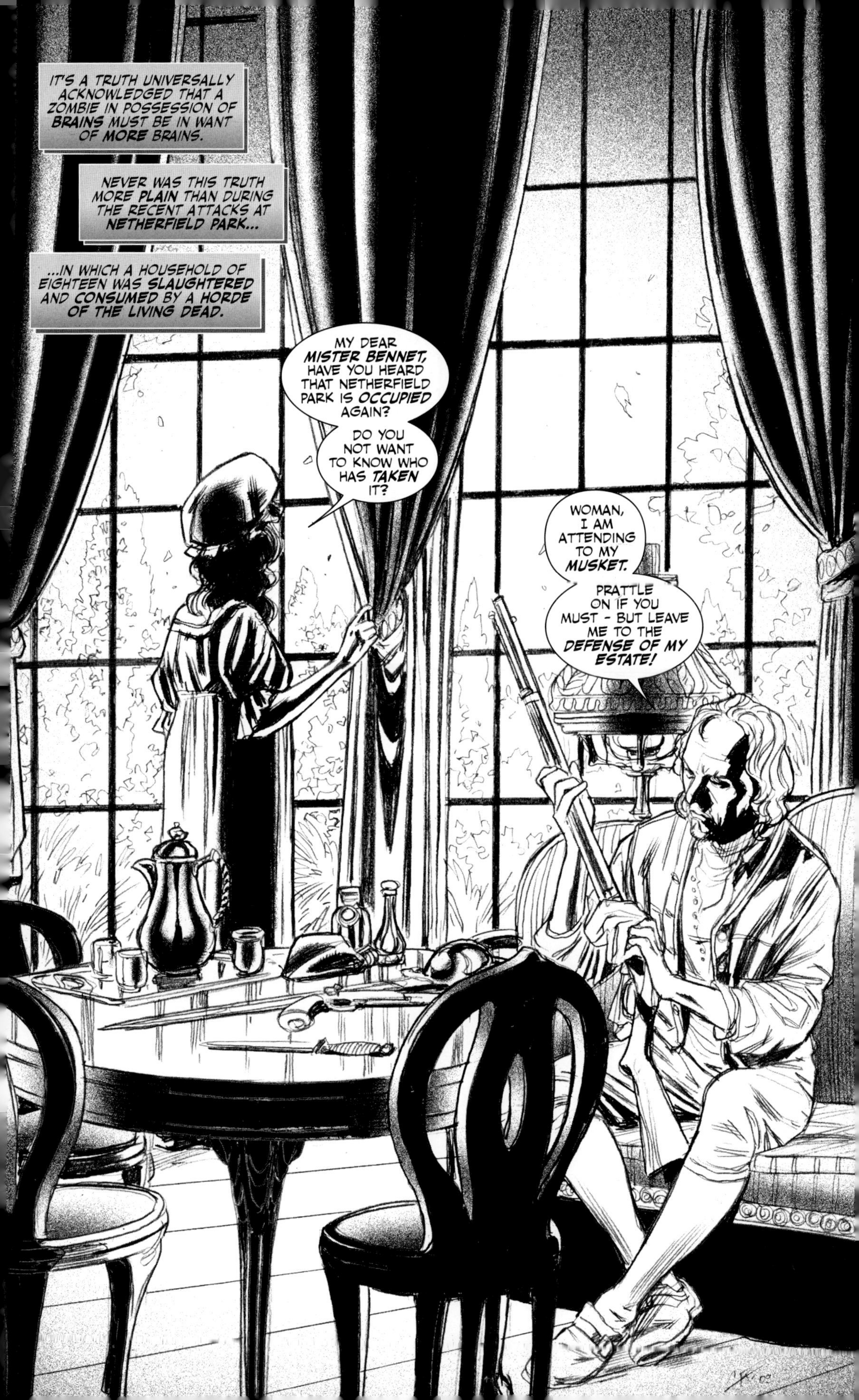
IT'S A TRUTH UNIVERSALLY ACKNOWLEDGED THAT A ZOMBIE IN POSSESSION OF BRAINS MUST BE IN WANT OF MORE BRAINS.
NEVER WAS THIS TRUTH MORE PLAIN THAN DURING THE RECENT ATTACKS AT NETHERFIELD PARK...
...IN WHICH A HOUSEHOLD OF EIGHTEEN WAS SLAUGHTERED AND CONSUMED BY A HORDE OF THE LIVING DEAD.
MY DEAR MISTER BENNET, HAVE YOU HEARD THAT NETHERFIELD PARK IS OCCUPIED AGAIN?
DO YOU NOT WANT TO KNOW WHO HAS TAKEN IT?
WOMAN, I AM ATTENDING TO MY MUSKET.
PRATTLE ON IF YOU MUST - BUT LEAVE ME TO THE DEFENSE OF MY ESTATE!

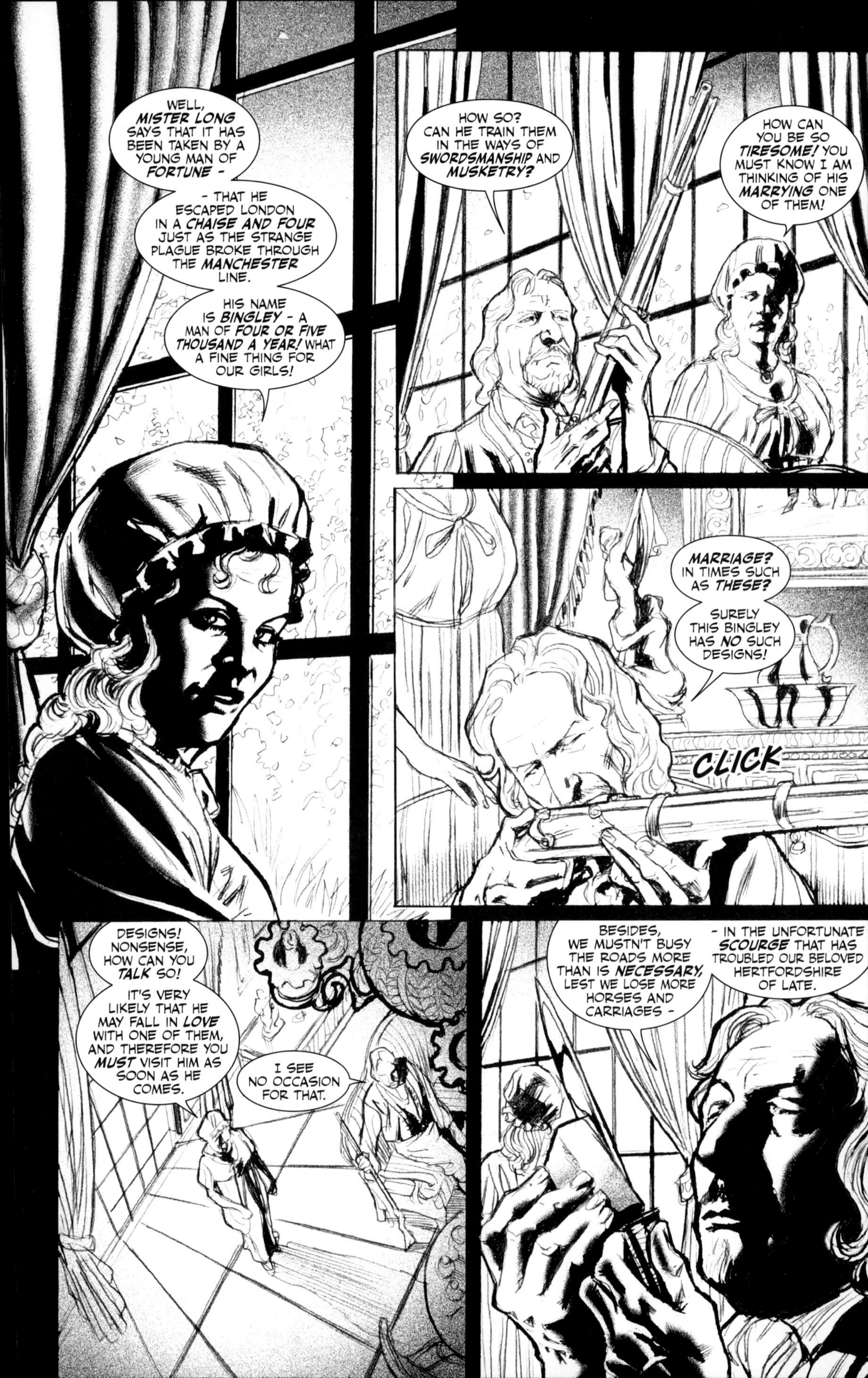
WELL, MISTER LONG SAYS THAT IT HAS BEEN TAKEN BY A YOUNG MAN OF FORTUNE -
- THAT HE ESCAPED LONDON IN A CHAISE AND FOUR JUST AS THE STRANGE PLAGUE BROKE THROUGH THE MANCHESTER LINE.
HIS NAME IS BINGLEY - A MAN OF FOUR OR FIVE THOUSAND A YEAR! WHAT A FINE THING FOR OUR GIRLS!
HOW SO? CAN HE TRAIN THEM IN THE WAYS OF SWORDSMANSHIP AND MUSKETRY?
HOW CAN YOU BE SO TIRESOME! YOU MUST KNOW I AM THINKING OF HIS MARRYING ONE OF THEM!
MARRIAGE? IN TIMES SUCH AS THESE?
SURELY THIS BINGLEY HAS NO SUCH DESIGNS!
CLICK
DESIGNS! NONSENSE, HOW CAN YOU TALK SO!
IT'S VERY LIKELY THAT HE MAY FALL IN LOVE WITH ONE OF THEM, AND THEREFORE YOU MUST VISIT HIM AS SOON AS HE COMES.
I SEE NO OCCASION FOR THAT.
BESIDES, WE MUSTN'T BUSY THE ROADS MORE THAN IS NECESSARY, LEST WE LOSE MORE HORSES AND CARRIAGES -
- IN THE UNFORTUNATE SCOURGE THAT HAS TROUBLED OUR BELOVED HERTFORDSHIRE OF LATE.

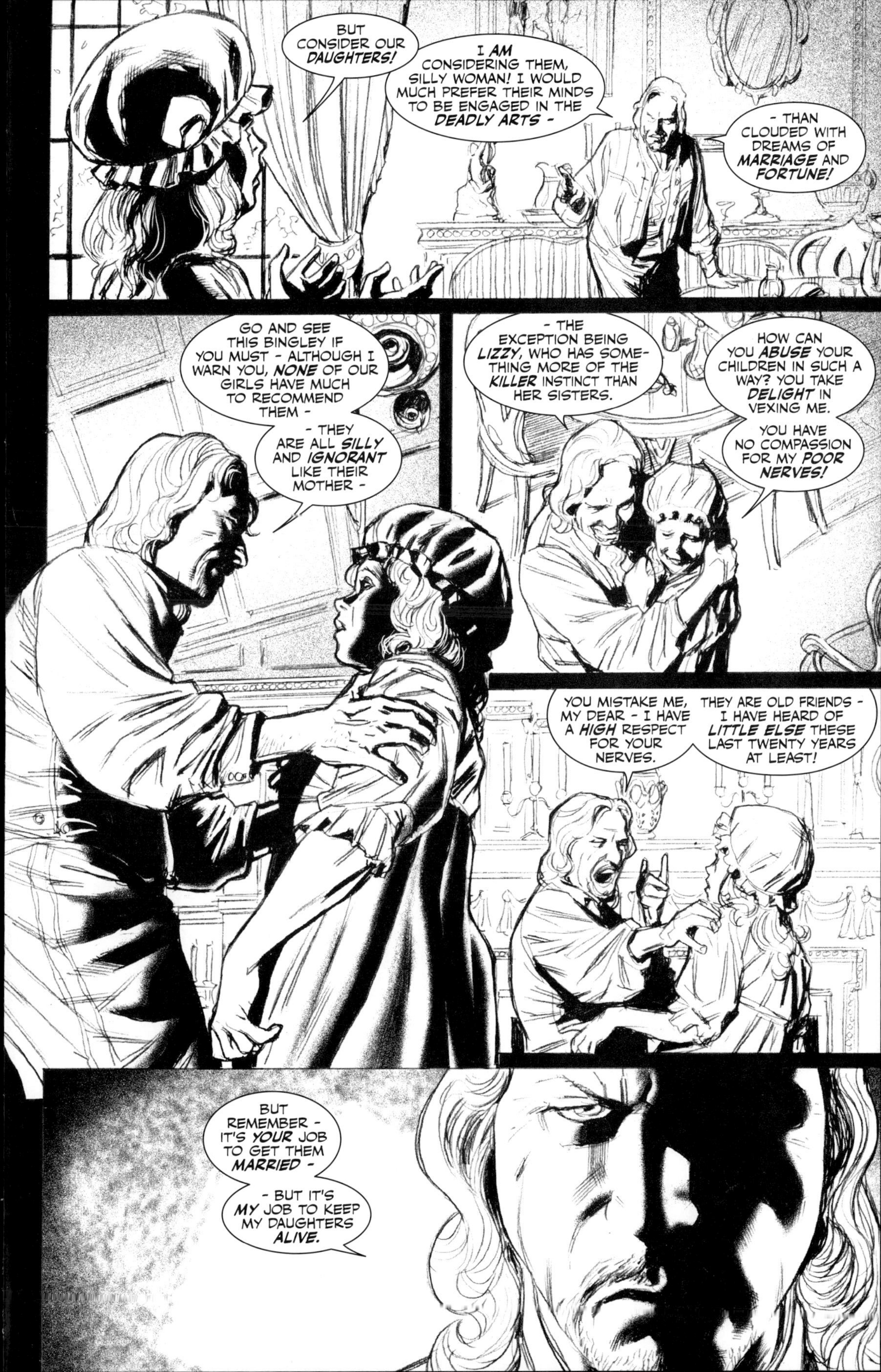
BUT CONSIDER OUR DAUGHTERS!
I AM CONSIDERING THEM, SILLY WOMAN! I WOULD MUCH PREFER THEIR MINDS TO BE ENGAGED IN THE DEADLY ARTS -
- THAN CLOUDED WITH DREAMS OF MARRIAGE AND FORTUNE!
GO AND SEE THIS BINGLEY IF YOU MUST - ALTHOUGH I WARN YOU, NONE OF OUR GIRLS HAVE MUCH TO RECOMMEND THEM -
- THEY ARE ALL SILLY AND IGNORANT LIKE THEIR MOTHER -
- THE EXCEPTION BEING LIZZY, WHO HAS SOMETHING MORE OF THE KILLER INSTINCT THAN HER SISTERS.
HOW CAN YOU ABUSE YOUR CHILDREN IN SUCH A WAY? YOU TAKE DELIGHT IN VEXING ME.
YOU HAVE NO COMPASSION FOR MY POOR NERVES!
YOU MISTAKE ME, MY DEAR - I HAVE A HIGH RESPECT FOR YOUR NERVES.
THEY ARE OLD FRIENDS - I HAVE HEARD OF LITTLE ELSE THESE LAST TWENTY YEARS AT LEAST!
BUT REMEMBER - IT'S YOUR JOB TO GET THEM MARRIED -
- BUT IT'S MY JOB TO KEEP MY DAUGHTERS ALIVE.

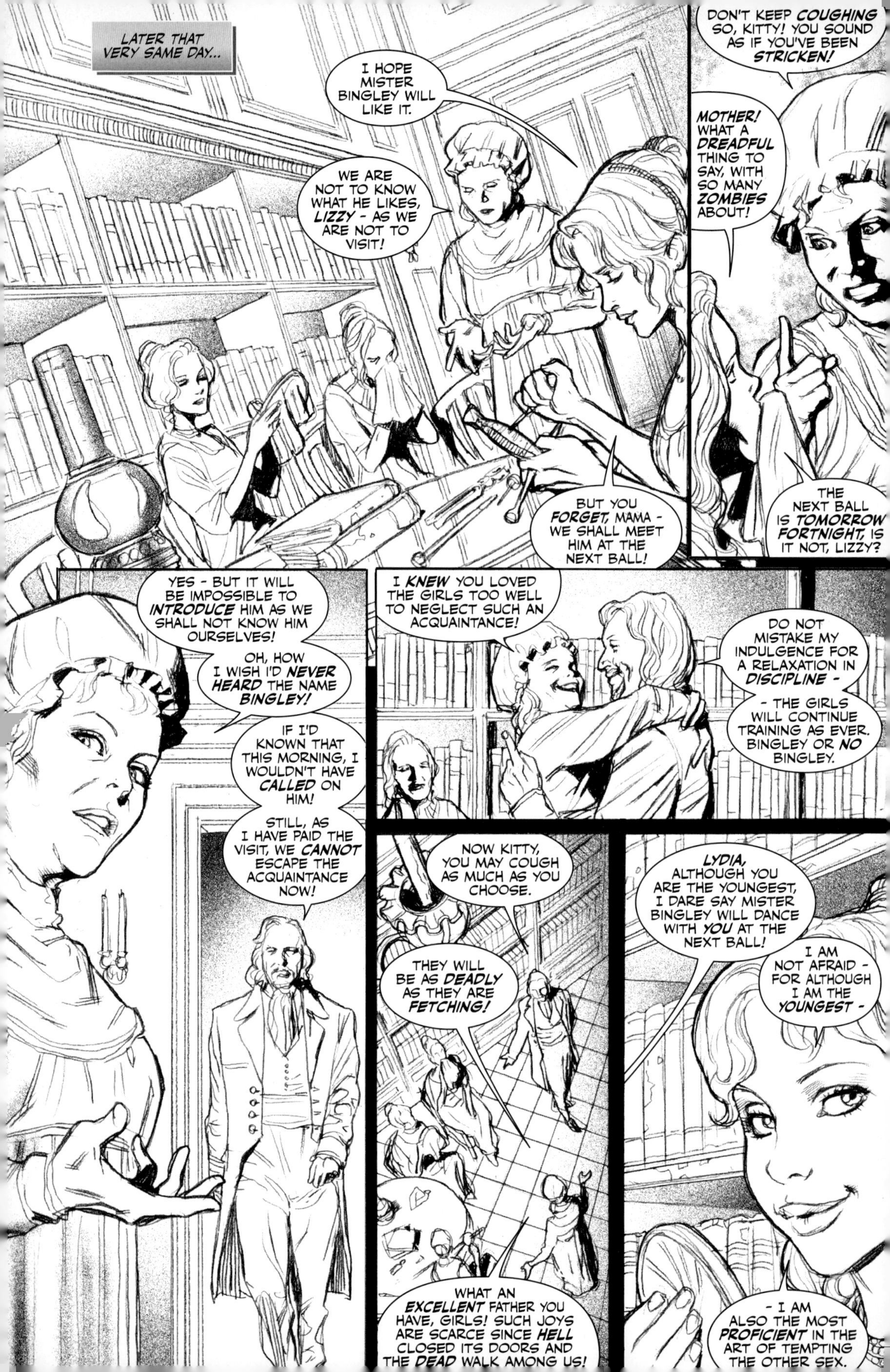
LATER THAT VERY SAME DAY...
I HOPE MISTER BINGLEY WILL LIKE IT.
WE ARE NOT TO KNOW WHAT HE LIKES, LIZZY - AS WE ARE NOT TO VISIT!
BUT YOU FORGET, MAMA - WE SHALL MEET HIM AT THE NEXT BALL!
DON'T KEEP COUGHING SO, KITTY! YOU SOUND AS IF YOU'VE BEEN STRICKEN!
MOTHER! WHAT A DREADFUL THING TO SAY, WITH SO MANY ZOMBIES ABOUT!
THE NEXT BALL IS TOMORROW FORTNIGHT, IS IT NOT, LIZZY?
YES - BUT IT WILL BE IMPOSSIBLE TO INTRODUCE HIM AS WE SHALL NOT KNOW HIM OURSELVES!
OH, HOW I WISH I'D NEVER HEARD THE NAME BINGLEY!
IF I'D KNOWN THAT THIS MORNING, I WOULDN'T HAVE CALLED ON HIM!
STILL, AS I HAVE PAID THE VISIT, WE CANNOT ESCAPE THE ACQUAINTANCE NOW!
I KNEW YOU LOVED THE GIRLS TOO WELL TO NEGLECT SUCH AN ACQUAINTANCE!
DO NOT MISTAKE MY INDULGENCE FOR A RELAXATION IN DISCIPLINE -
- THE GIRLS WILL CONTINUE TRAINING AS EVER. BINGLEY OR NO BINGLEY.
NOW KITTY, YOU MAY COUGH AS MUCH AS YOU CHOOSE.
THEY WILL BE AS DEADLY AS THEY ARE FETCHING!
WHAT AN EXCELLENT FATHER YOU HAVE, GIRLS! SUCH JOYS ARE SCARCE SINCE HELL CLOSED ITS DOORS AND THE DEAD WALK AMONG US!
LYDIA, ALTHOUGH YOU ARE THE YOUNGEST, I DARE SAY MISTER BINGLEY WILL DANCE WITH YOU AT THE NEXT BALL!
I AM NOT AFRAID - FOR ALTHOUGH I AM THE YOUNGEST -
- I AM ALSO THE MOST PROFICIENT IN THE ART OF TEMPTING THE OTHER SEX.

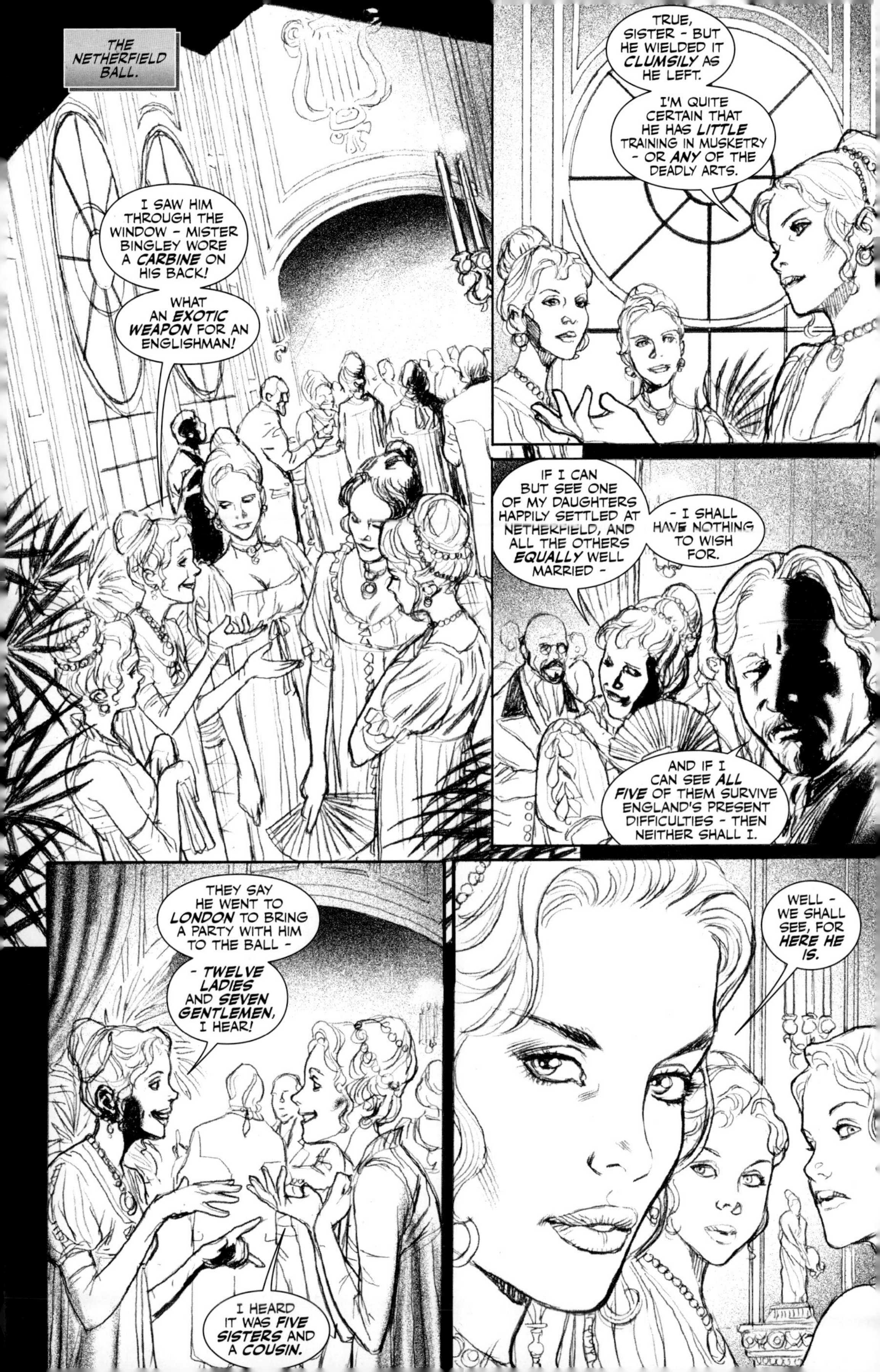
THE NETHERFIELD BALL.
I SAW HIM THROUGH THE WINDOW - MISTER BINGLEY WORE A CARBINE ON HIS BACK!
WHAT AN EXOTIC WEAPON FOR AN ENGLISHMAN!
TRUE, SISTER - BUT HE WIELDED IT CLUMSILY AS HE LEFT.
I'M QUITE CERTAIN THAT HE HAS LITTLE TRAINING IN MUSKETRY - OR ANY OF THE DEADLY ARTS.
IF I CAN BUT SEE ONE OF MY DAUGHTERS HAPPILY SETTLED AT NETHERFIELD, AND ALL THE OTHERS EQUALLY WELL MARRIED -
- I SHALL HAVE NOTHING TO WISH FOR.
AND IF I CAN SEE ALL FIVE OF THEM SURVIVE ENGLAND'S PRESENT DIFFICULTIES - THEN NEITHER SHALL I.
THEY SAY HE WENT TO LONDON TO BRING A PARTY WITH HIM TO THE BALL -
- TWELVE LADIES AND SEVEN GENTLEMEN, I HEAR!
I HEARD IT WAS FIVE SISTERS AND A COUSIN.
WELL - WE SHALL SEE, FOR HERE HE IS.

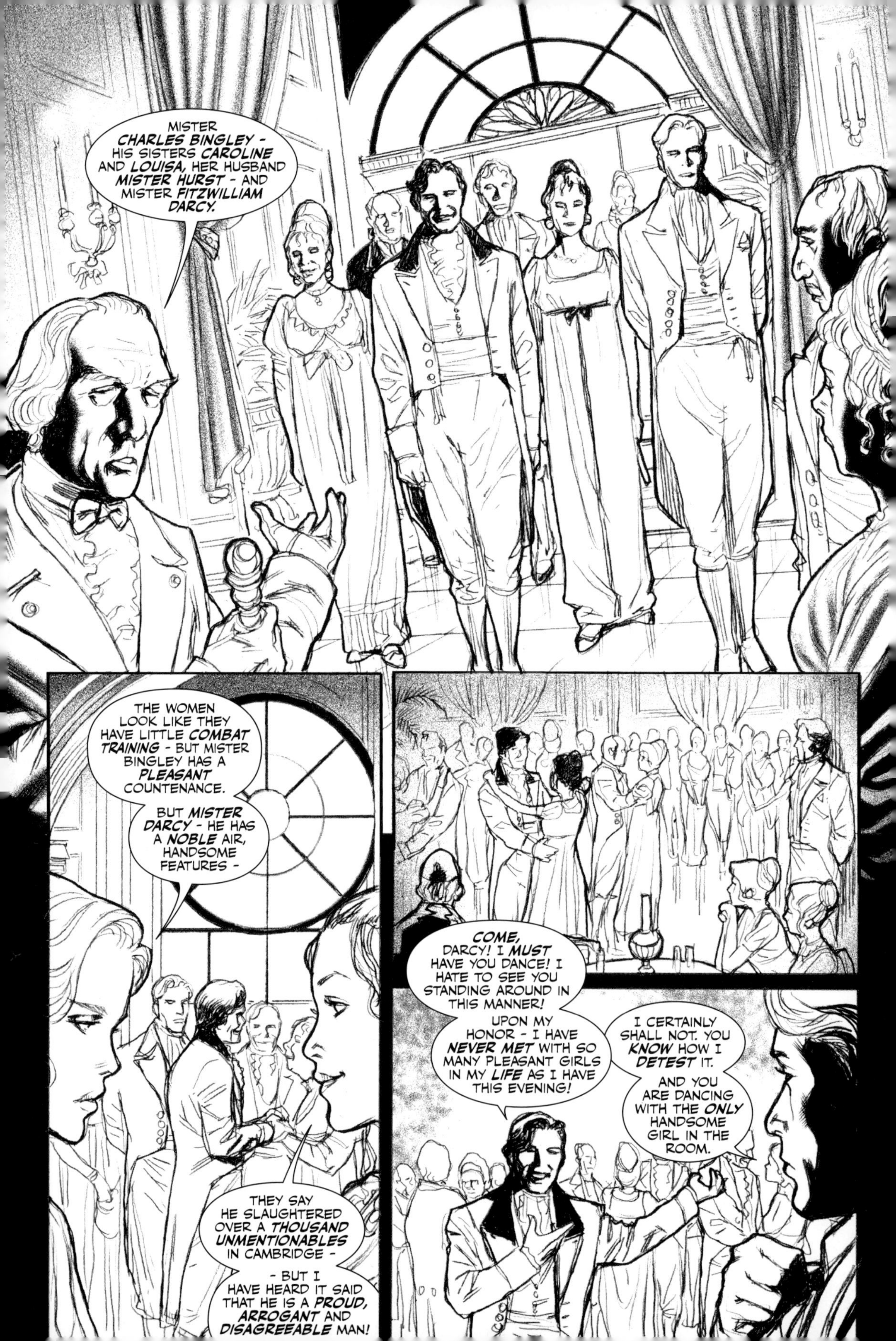
MISTER CHARLES BINGLEY - HIS SISTERS CAROLINE AND LOUISA, HER HUSBAND MISTER HURST - AND MISTER FITZWILLIAM DARCY.
THE WOMEN LOOK LIKE THEY HAVE LITTLE COMBAT TRAINING - BUT MISTER BINGLEY HAS A PLEASANT COUNTENANCE.
BUT MISTER DARCY - HE HAS A NOBLE AIR, HANDSOME FEATURES -
THEY SAY HE SLAUGHTERED OVER A THOUSAND UNMENTIONABLES IN CAMBRIDGE -
- BUT I HAVE HEARD IT SAID THAT HE IS A PROUD, ARROGANT AND DISAGREEABLE MAN!
COME, DARCY! I MUST HAVE YOU DANCE! I HATE TO SEE YOU STANDING AROUND IN THIS MANNER!
I CERTAINLY SHALL NOT. YOU KNOW HOW I DETEST IT.
AND YOU ARE DANCING WITH THE ONLY HANDSOME GIRL IN THE ROOM.
UPON MY HONOR - I HAVE NEVER MET WITH SO MANY PLEASANT GIRLS IN MY LIFE AS I HAVE THIS EVENING!

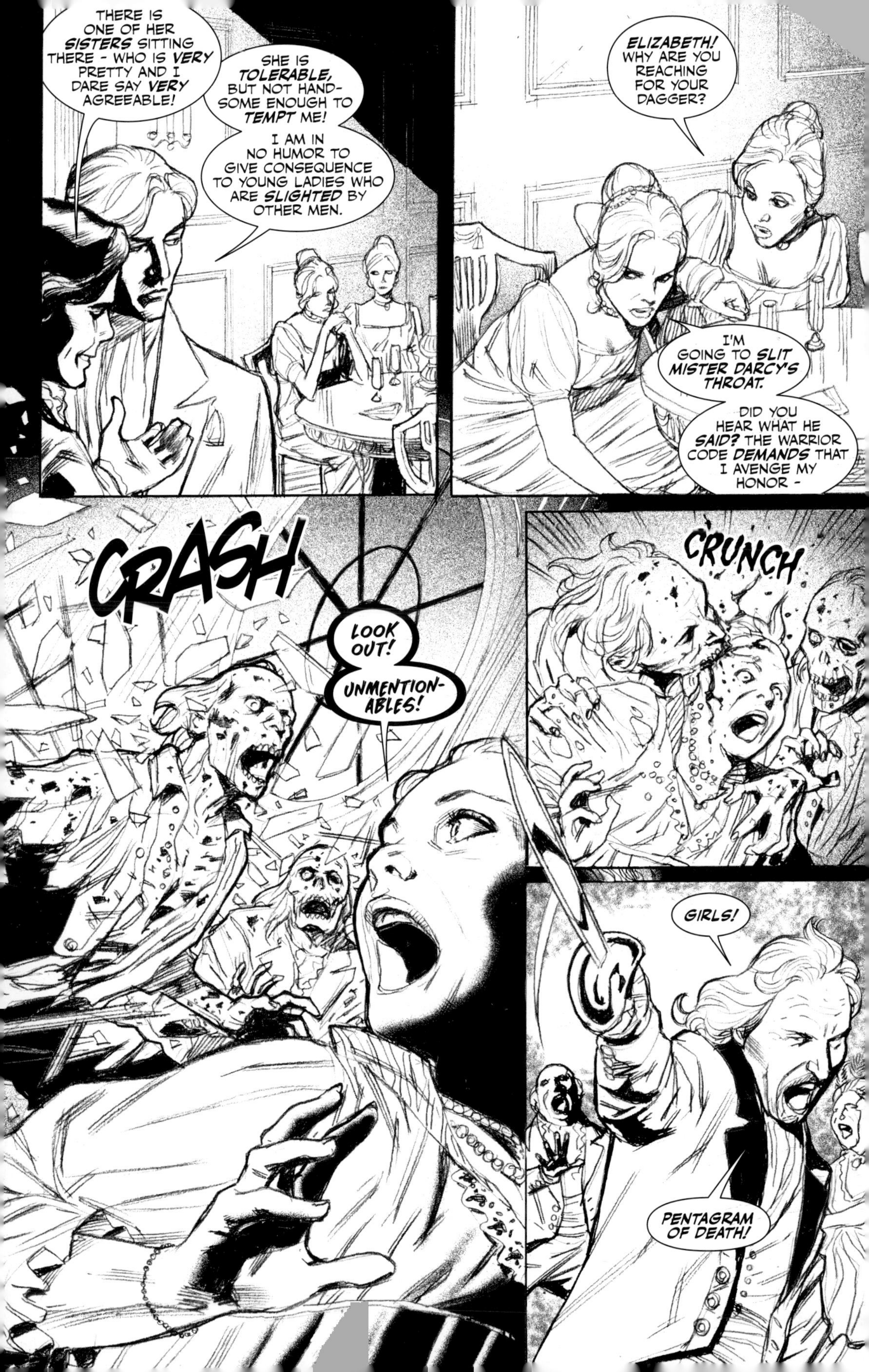
THERE IS ONE OF HER SISTERS SITTING THERE - WHO IS VERY PRETTY AND I DARE SAY VERY AGREEABLE!
SHE IS TOLERABLE, BUT NOT HAND-SOME ENOUGH TO TEMPT ME!
I AM IN NO HUMOR TO GIVE CONSEQUENCE TO YOUNG LADIES WHO ARE SLIGHTED BY OTHER MEN.
ELIZABETH! WHY ARE YOU REACHING FOR YOUR DAGGER?
I'M GOING TO SLIT MISTER DARCY'S THROAT.
DID YOU HEAR WHAT HE SAID? THE WARRIOR CODE DEMANDS THAT I AVENGE MY HONOR -
CRASH
LOOK OUT!
UNMENTION-ABLES!
CRUNCH
GIRLS!
PENTAGRAM OF DEATH!

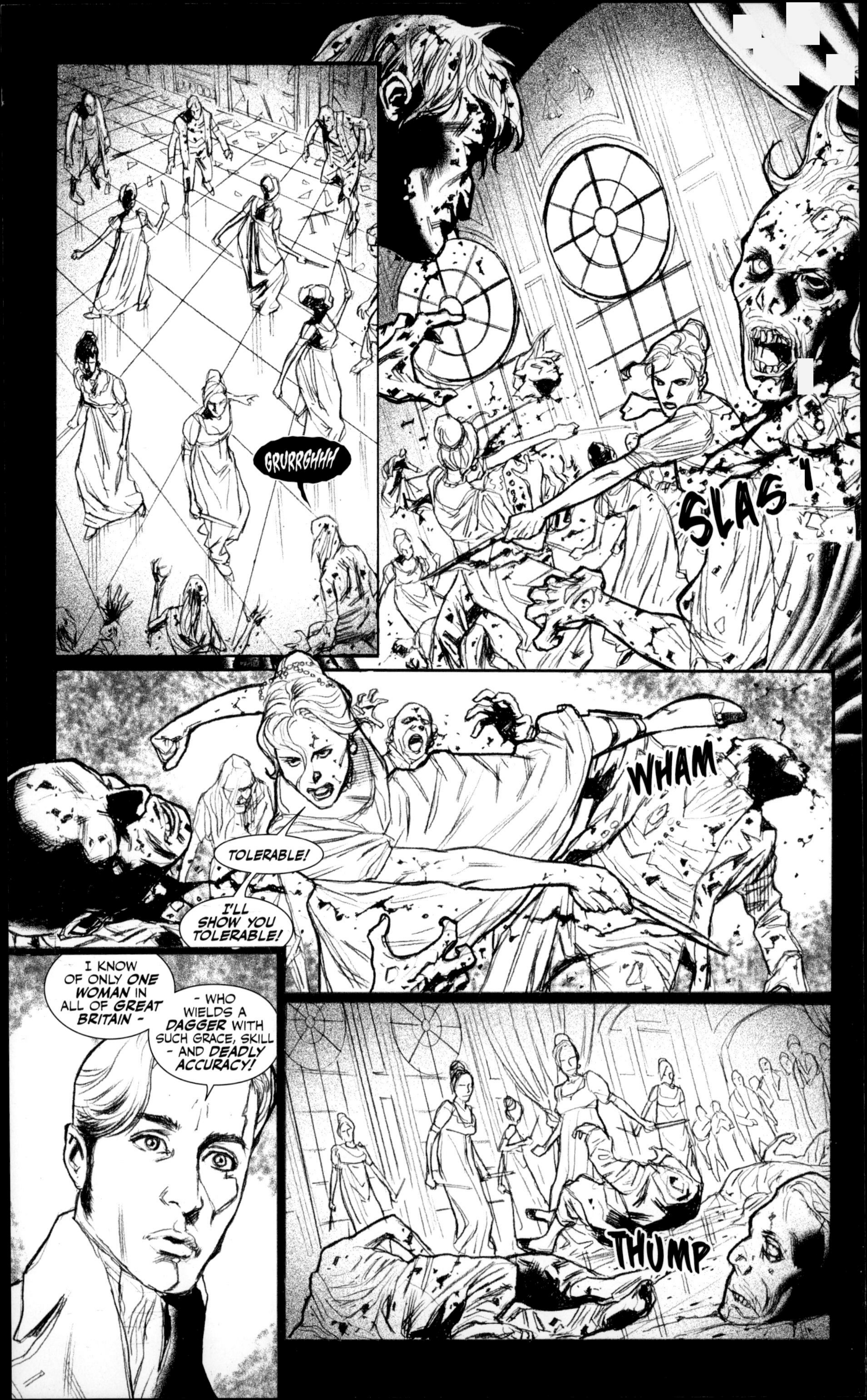
GRURRGHHH
SLAS
WHAM
TOLERABLE!
I'LL SHOW YOU TOLERABLE!
I KNOW OF ONLY ONE WOMAN IN ALL OF GREAT BRITAIN -
- WHO WIELDS A DAGGER WITH SUCH GRACE, SKILL - AND DEADLY ACCURACY!
THUMP

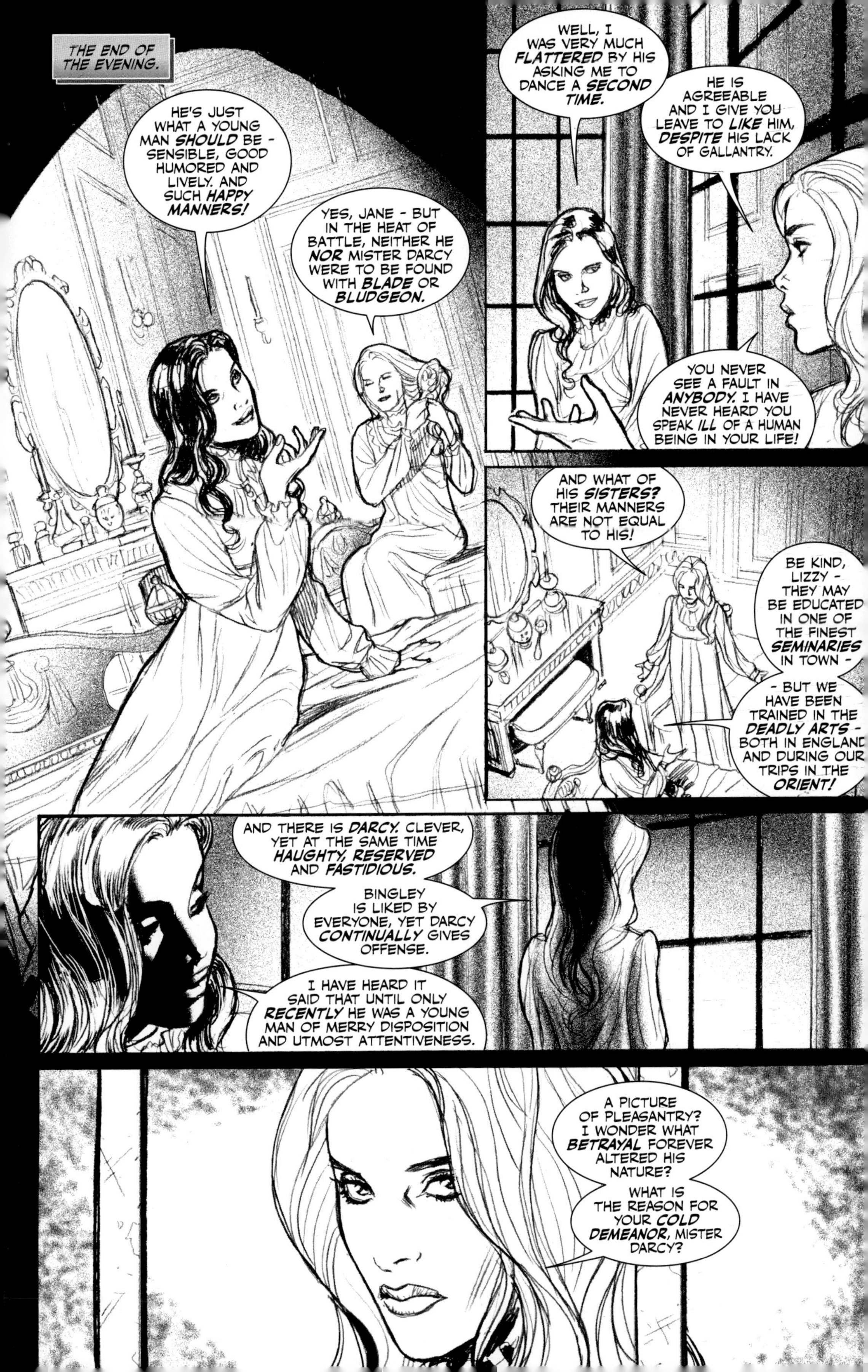
THE END OF THE EVENING.
HE'S JUST WHAT A YOUNG MAN SHOULD BE - SENSIBLE, GOOD HUMORED AND LIVELY. AND SUCH HAPPY MANNERS!
YES, JANE - BUT IN THE HEAT OF BATTLE, NEITHER HE NOR MISTER DARCY WERE TO BE FOUND WITH BLADE OR BLUDGEON.
WELL, I WAS VERY MUCH FLATTERED BY HIS ASKING ME TO DANCE A SECOND TIME.
HE IS AGREEABLE AND I GIVE YOU LEAVE TO LIKE HIM, DESPITE HIS LACK OF GALLANTRY.
YOU NEVER SEE A FAULT IN ANYBODY. I HAVE NEVER HEARD YOU SPEAK ILL OF A HUMAN BEING IN YOUR LIFE!
AND WHAT OF HIS SISTERS? THEIR MANNERS ARE NOT EQUAL TO HIS!
BE KIND, LIZZY - THEY MAY BE EDUCATED IN ONE OF THE FINEST SEMINARIES IN TOWN -
- BUT WE HAVE BEEN TRAINED IN THE DEADLY ARTS - BOTH IN ENGLAND AND DURING OUR TRIPS IN THE ORIENT!
AND THERE IS DARCY. CLEVER, YET AT THE SAME TIME HAUGHTY, RESERVED AND FASTIDIOUS.
BINGLEY IS LIKED BY EVERYONE, YET DARCY CONTINUALLY GIVES OFFENSE.
I HAVE HEARD IT SAID THAT UNTIL ONLY RECENTLY HE WAS A YOUNG MAN OF MERRY DISPOSITION AND UTMOST ATTENTIVENESS.
A PICTURE OF PLEASANTRY? I WONDER WHAT BETRAYAL FOREVER ALTERED HIS NATURE?
WHAT IS THE REASON FOR YOUR COLD DEMEANOR, MISTER DARCY?

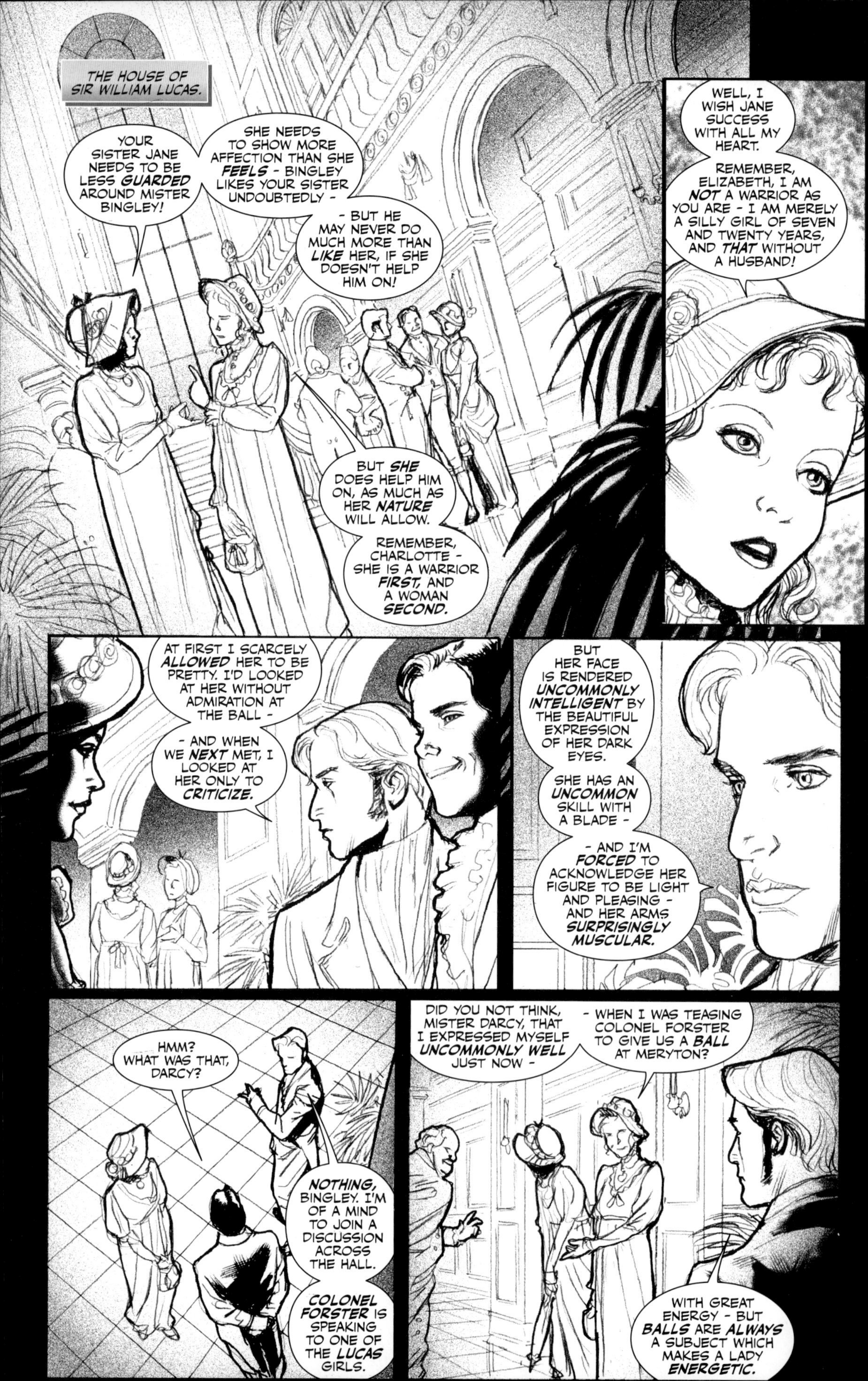
THE HOUSE OF SIR WILLIAM LUCAS.
YOUR SISTER JANE NEEDS TO BE LESS GUARDED AROUND MISTER BINGLEY!
SHE NEEDS TO SHOW MORE AFFECTION THAN SHE FEELS - BINGLEY LIKES YOUR SISTER UNDOUBTEDLY -
- BUT HE MAY NEVER DO MUCH MORE THAN LIKE HER, IF SHE DOESN'T HELP HIM ON!
BUT SHE DOES HELP HIM ON, AS MUCH AS HER NATURE WILL ALLOW.
REMEMBER, CHARLOTTE - SHE IS A WARRIOR FIRST, AND A WOMAN SECOND.
WELL, I WISH JANE SUCCESS WITH ALL MY HEART.
REMEMBER, ELIZABETH, I AM NOT A WARRIOR AS YOU ARE - I AM MERELY A SILLY GIRL OF SEVEN AND TWENTY YEARS, AND THAT WITHOUT A HUSBAND!
AT FIRST I SCARCELY ALLOWED HER TO BE PRETTY. I'D LOOKED AT HER WITHOUT ADMIRATION AT THE BALL -
- AND WHEN WE NEXT MET, I LOOKED AT HER ONLY TO CRITICIZE.
BUT HER FACE IS RENDERED UNCOMMONLY INTELLIGENT BY THE BEAUTIFUL EXPRESSION OF HER DARK EYES.
SHE HAS AN UNCOMMON SKILL WITH A BLADE -
- AND I'M FORCED TO ACKNOWLEDGE HER FIGURE TO BE LIGHT AND PLEASING - AND HER ARMS SURPRISINGLY MUSCULAR.
HMM? WHAT WAS THAT, DARCY?
NOTHING, BINGLEY. I'M OF A MIND TO JOIN A DISCUSSION ACROSS THE HALL.
COLONEL FORSTER IS SPEAKING TO ONE OF THE LUCAS GIRLS.
DID YOU NOT THINK, MISTER DARCY, THAT I EXPRESSED MYSELF UNCOMMONLY WELL JUST NOW -
- WHEN I WAS TEASING COLONEL FORSTER TO GIVE US A BALL AT MERYTON?
WITH GREAT ENERGY - BUT BALLS ARE ALWAYS A SUBJECT WHICH MAKES A LADY ENERGETIC.

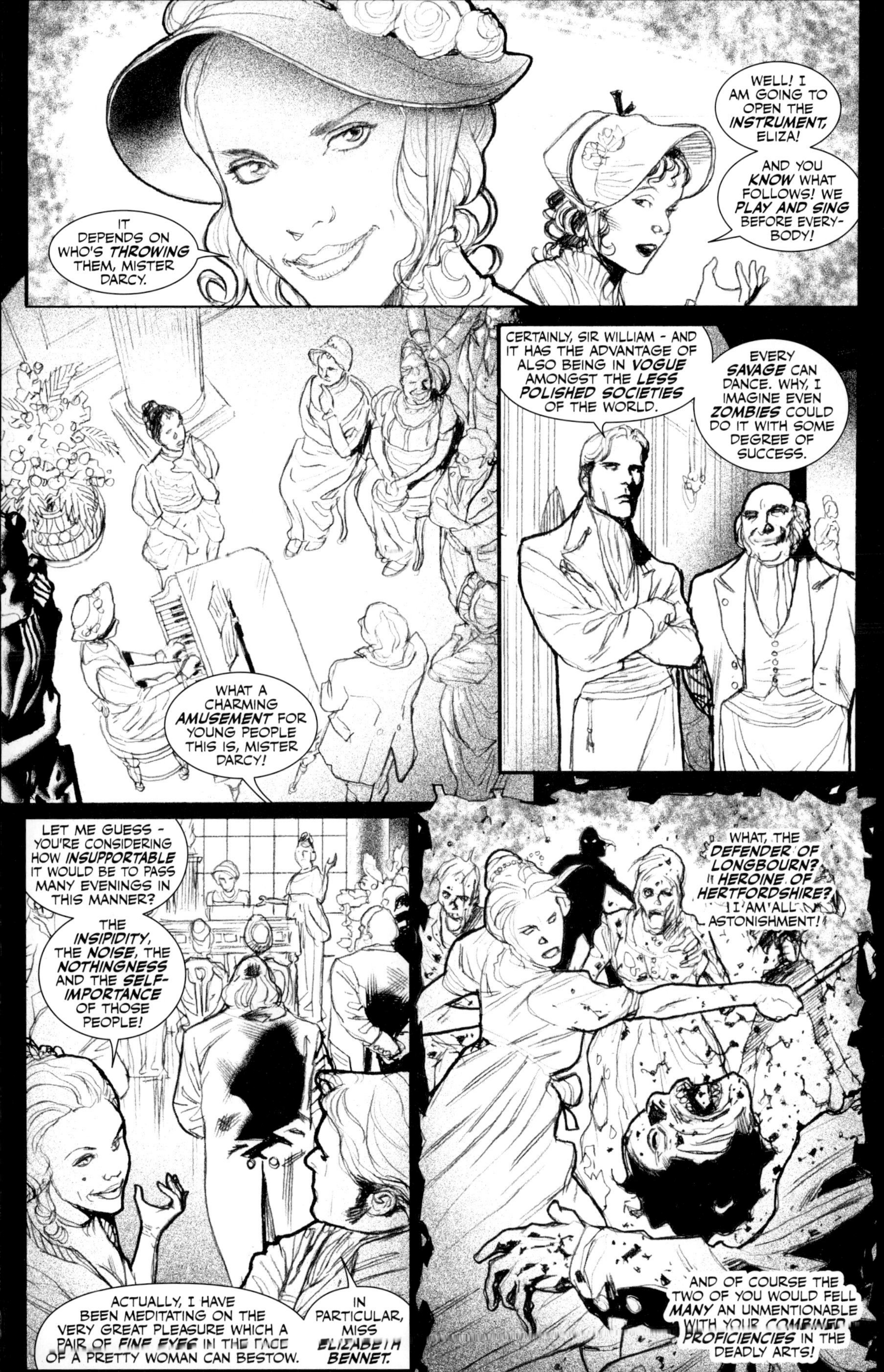
IT DEPENDS ON WHO'S *THROWING* THEM, MISTER DARCY.
WELL! I AM GOING TO OPEN THE *INSTRUMENT,* ELIZA!
AND YOU *KNOW* WHAT FOLLOWS! WE *PLAY AND SING* BEFORE EVERY-BODY!
WHAT A CHARMING *AMUSEMENT* FOR YOUNG PEOPLE THIS IS, MISTER DARCY!
CERTAINLY, SIR WILLIAM - AND IT HAS THE ADVANTAGE OF ALSO BEING IN *VOGUE* AMONGST THE *LESS POLISHED SOCIETIES* OF THE WORLD.
EVERY *SAVAGE* CAN DANCE. WHY, I IMAGINE EVEN *ZOMBIES* COULD DO IT WITH SOME DEGREE OF SUCCESS.
LET ME GUESS - YOU'RE CONSIDERING HOW *INSUPPORTABLE* IT WOULD BE TO PASS MANY EVENINGS IN THIS MANNER?
THE *INSIPIDITY*, THE *NOISE*, THE *NOTHINGNESS* AND THE *SELF-IMPORTANCE* OF THOSE PEOPLE!
ACTUALLY, I HAVE BEEN MEDITATING ON THE VERY GREAT PLEASURE WHICH A PAIR OF *FINE EYES* IN THE FACE OF A PRETTY WOMAN CAN BESTOW.
IN PARTICULAR, MISS *ELIZABETH BENNET.*
WHAT, THE *DEFENDER OF LONGBOURN? HEROINE OF HERTFORDSHIRE?* I AM ALL ASTONISHMENT!
AND OF COURSE THE TWO OF YOU WOULD FELL *MANY* AN UNMENTIONABLE WITH YOUR *COMBINED PROFICIENCIES* IN THE DEADLY ARTS!

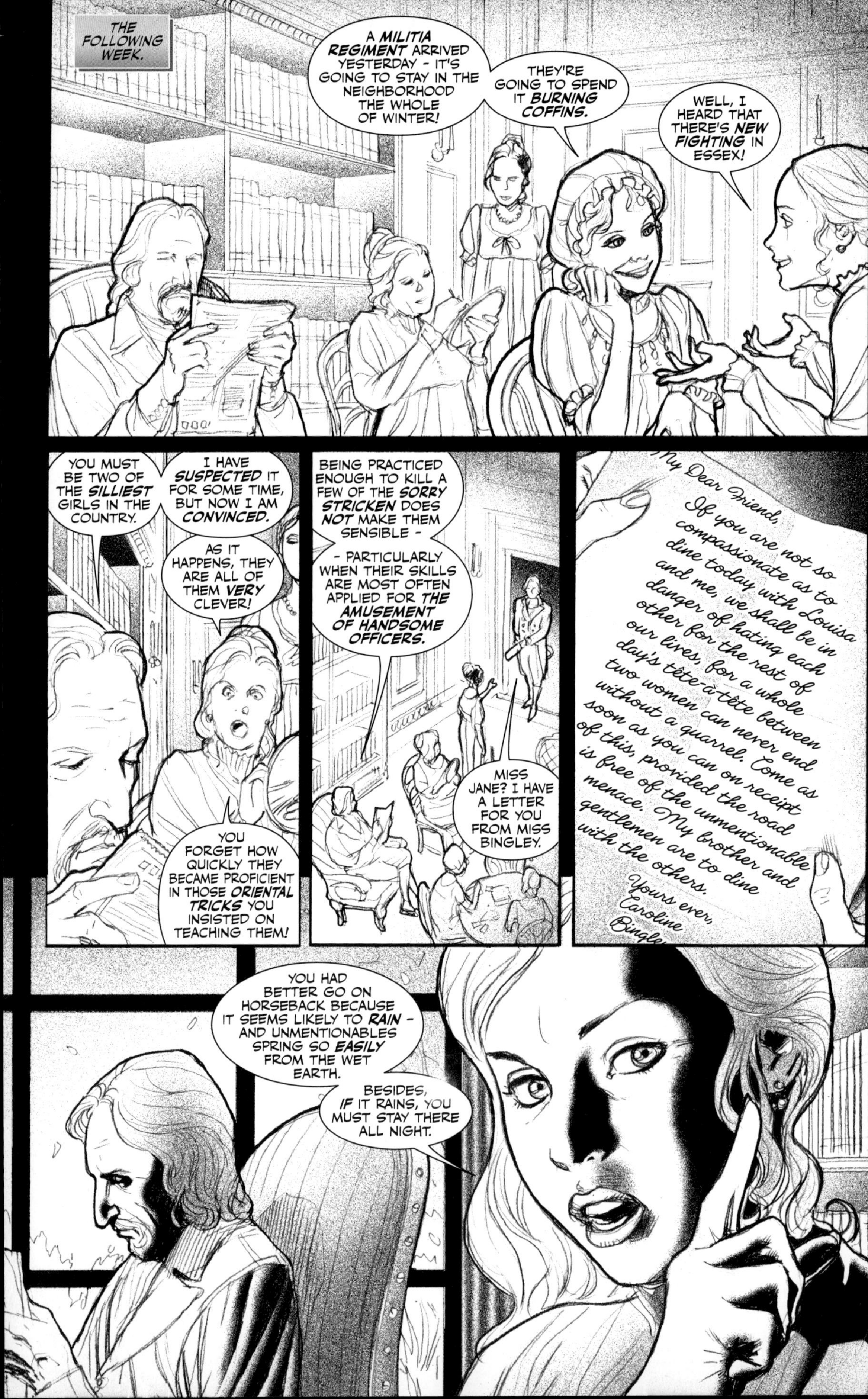
THE FOLLOWING WEEK.
A MILITIA REGIMENT ARRIVED YESTERDAY - IT'S GOING TO STAY IN THE NEIGHBORHOOD THE WHOLE OF WINTER!
THEY'RE GOING TO SPEND IT BURNING COFFINS.
WELL, I HEARD THAT THERE'S NEW FIGHTING IN ESSEX!
YOU MUST BE TWO OF THE SILLIEST GIRLS IN THE COUNTRY.
I HAVE SUSPECTED IT FOR SOME TIME, BUT NOW I AM CONVINCED.
AS IT HAPPENS, THEY ARE ALL OF THEM VERY CLEVER!
YOU FORGET HOW QUICKLY THEY BECAME PROFICIENT IN THOSE ORIENTAL TRICKS YOU INSISTED ON TEACHING THEM!
BEING PRACTICED ENOUGH TO KILL A FEW OF THE SORRY STRICKEN DOES NOT MAKE THEM SENSIBLE -
- PARTICULARLY WHEN THEIR SKILLS ARE MOST OFTEN APPLIED FOR THE AMUSEMENT OF HANDSOME OFFICERS.
MISS JANE? I HAVE A LETTER FOR YOU FROM MISS BINGLEY.
My Dear Friend,
If you are not so compassionate as to dine today with Louisa and me, we shall be in danger of hating each other for the rest of our lives, for a whole day's tête-à-tête between two women can never end without a quarrel. Come as soon as you can on receipt of this, provided the road is free of the unmentionable menace. My brother and gentlemen are to dine with the others.
Yours ever,
Caroline
YOU HAD BETTER GO ON HORSEBACK BECAUSE IT SEEMS LIKELY TO RAIN - AND UNMENTIONABLES SPRING SO EASILY FROM THE WET EARTH.
BESIDES, IF IT RAINS, YOU MUST STAY THERE ALL NIGHT.

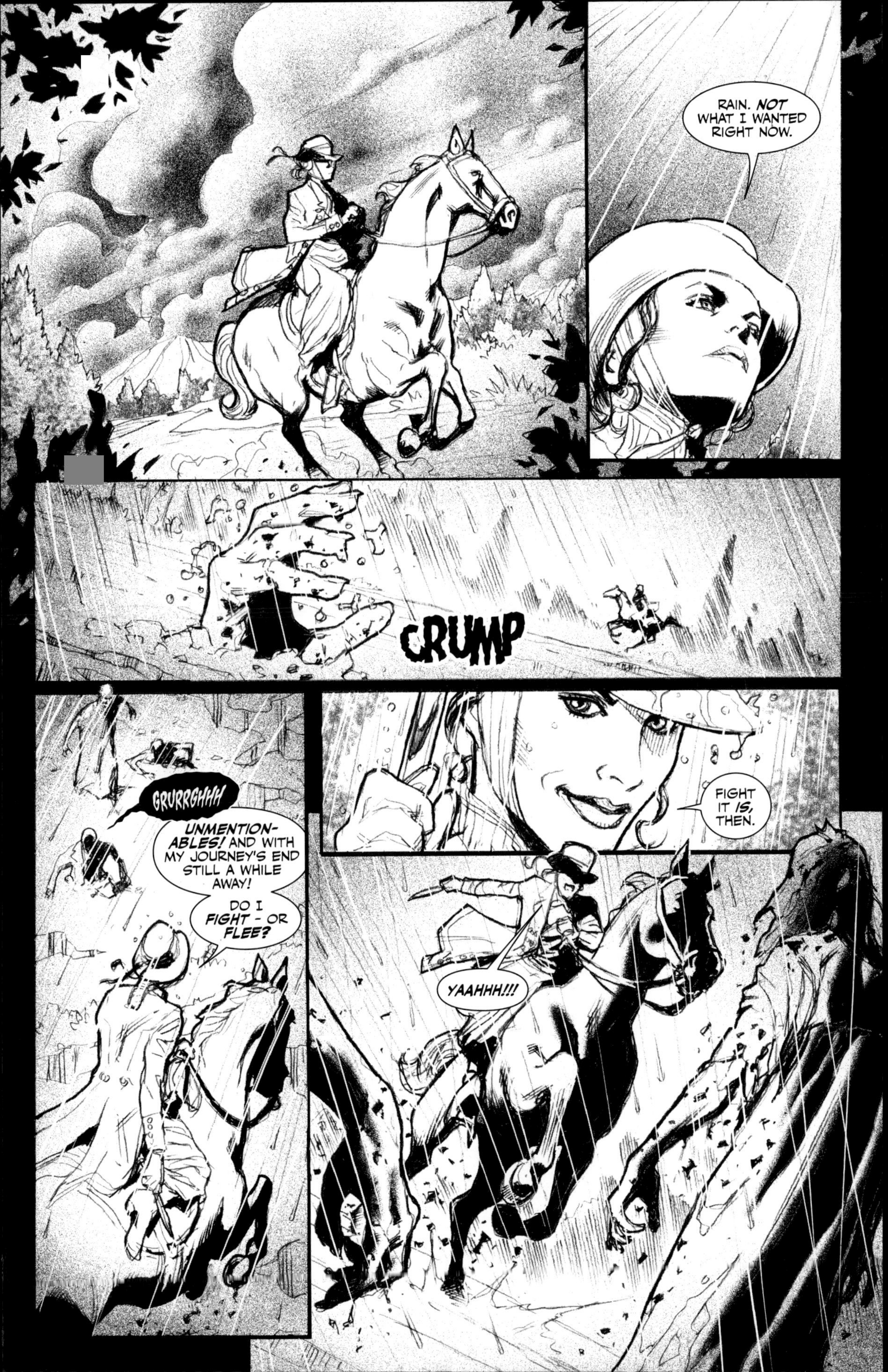
RAIN. NOT WHAT I WANTED RIGHT NOW.
CRUMP
GRURRGHHH
UNMENTION-ABLES! AND WITH MY JOURNEY'S END STILL A WHILE AWAY!
DO I FIGHT - OR FLEE?
FIGHT IT IS, THEN.
YAAHHH!!!

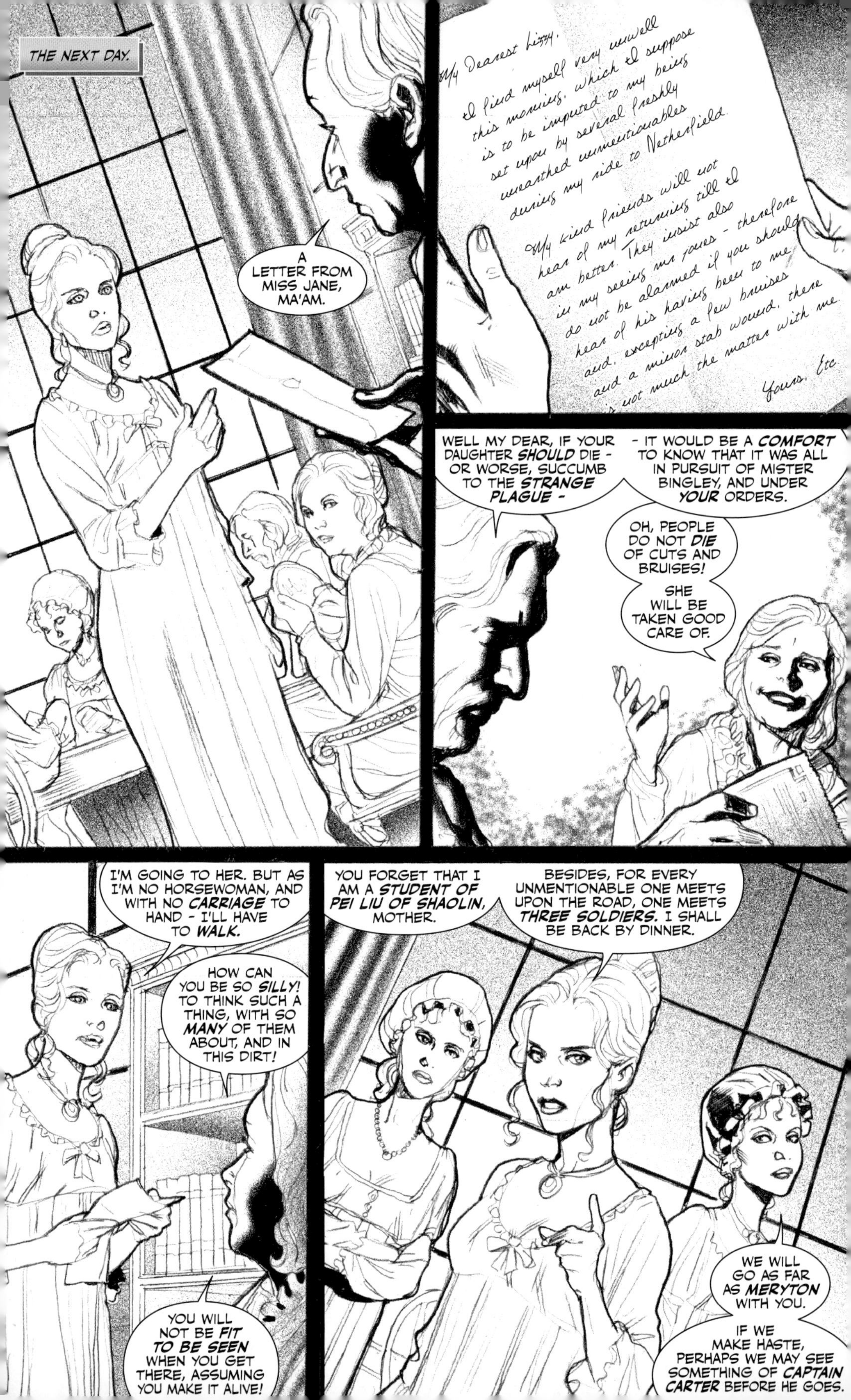
THE NEXT DAY.
A LETTER FROM MISS JANE, MA'AM.
My Dearest Lizzy,
I find myself very unwell this morning, which I suppose is to be imputed to my being set upon by several freshly unearthed unmentionables during my ride to Netherfield.
My kind friends will not hear of my returning till I am better. They insist also in my seeing Mr Jones - therefore do not be alarmed if you should hear of his having been to me and, excepting a few bruises and a minor stab wound, there is not much the matter with me.
Yours, Etc.
WELL MY DEAR, IF YOUR DAUGHTER SHOULD DIE - OR WORSE, SUCCUMB TO THE STRANGE PLAGUE -
- IT WOULD BE A COMFORT TO KNOW THAT IT WAS ALL IN PURSUIT OF MISTER BINGLEY, AND UNDER YOUR ORDERS.
OH, PEOPLE DO NOT DIE OF CUTS AND BRUISES!
SHE WILL BE TAKEN GOOD CARE OF.
I'M GOING TO HER. BUT AS I'M NO HORSEWOMAN, AND WITH NO CARRIAGE TO HAND - I'LL HAVE TO WALK.
HOW CAN YOU BE SO SILLY! TO THINK SUCH A THING, WITH SO MANY OF THEM ABOUT, AND IN THIS DIRT!
YOU WILL NOT BE FIT TO BE SEEN WHEN YOU GET THERE, ASSUMING YOU MAKE IT ALIVE!
YOU FORGET THAT I AM A STUDENT OF PEI LIU OF SHAOLIN, MOTHER.
BESIDES, FOR EVERY UNMENTIONABLE ONE MEETS UPON THE ROAD, ONE MEETS THREE SOLDIERS. I SHALL BE BACK BY DINNER.
WE WILL GO AS FAR AS MERYTON WITH YOU.
IF WE MAKE HASTE, PERHAPS WE MAY SEE SOMETHING OF CAPTAIN CARTER BEFORE HE GOES.

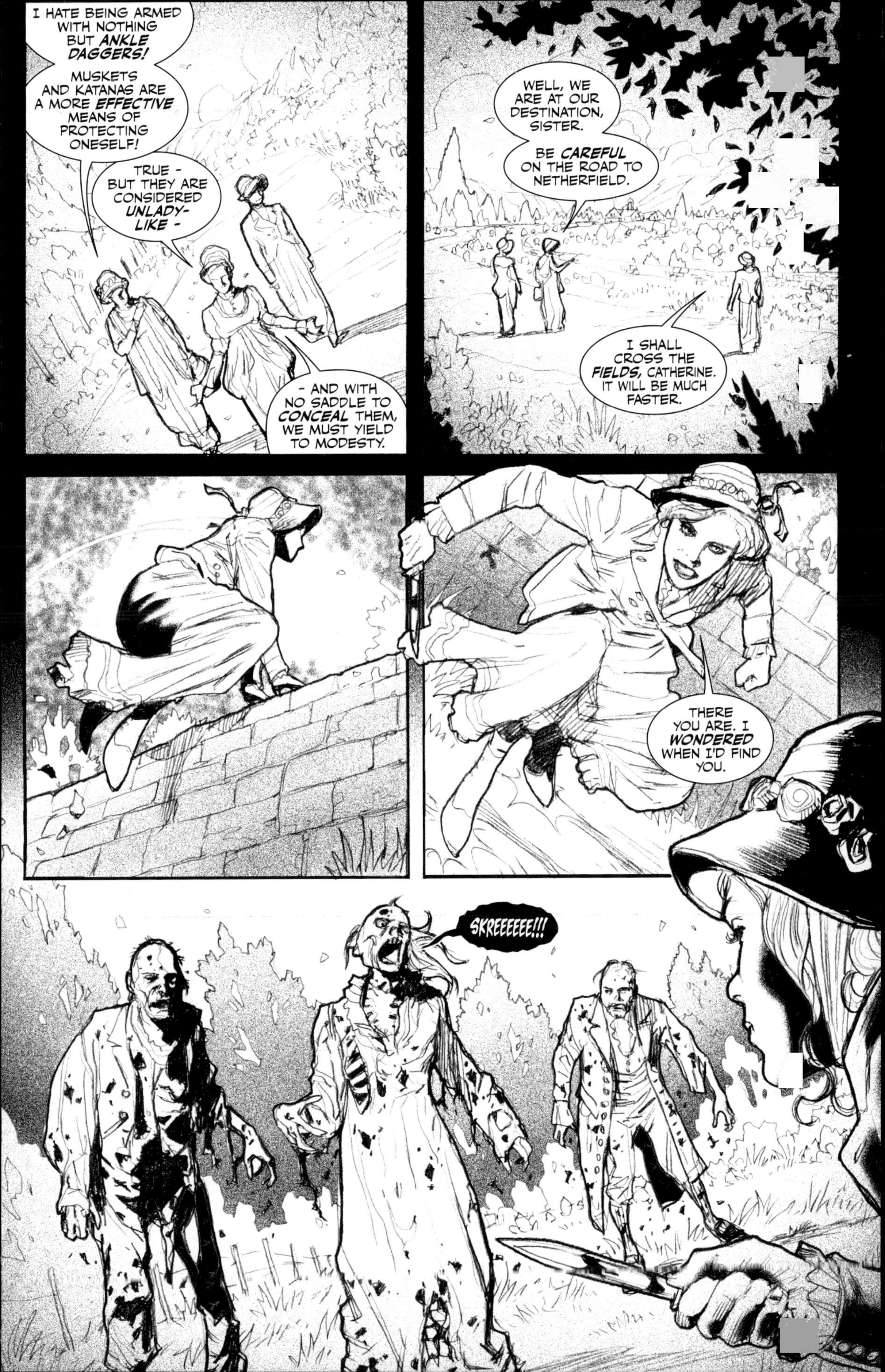
I HATE BEING ARMED WITH NOTHING BUT *ANKLE DAGGERS!*
MUSKETS AND KATANAS ARE A MORE *EFFECTIVE* MEANS OF PROTECTING ONESELF!
TRUE - BUT THEY ARE CONSIDERED *UNLADY-LIKE* -
- AND WITH NO SADDLE TO *CONCEAL* THEM, WE MUST YIELD TO MODESTY.
WELL, WE ARE AT OUR DESTINATION, SISTER.
BE *CAREFUL* ON THE ROAD TO NETHERFIELD.
I SHALL CROSS THE *FIELDS,* CATHERINE. IT WILL BE MUCH FASTER.
THERE YOU ARE. I *WONDERED* WHEN I'D FIND YOU.
SKREEEEEE!!!

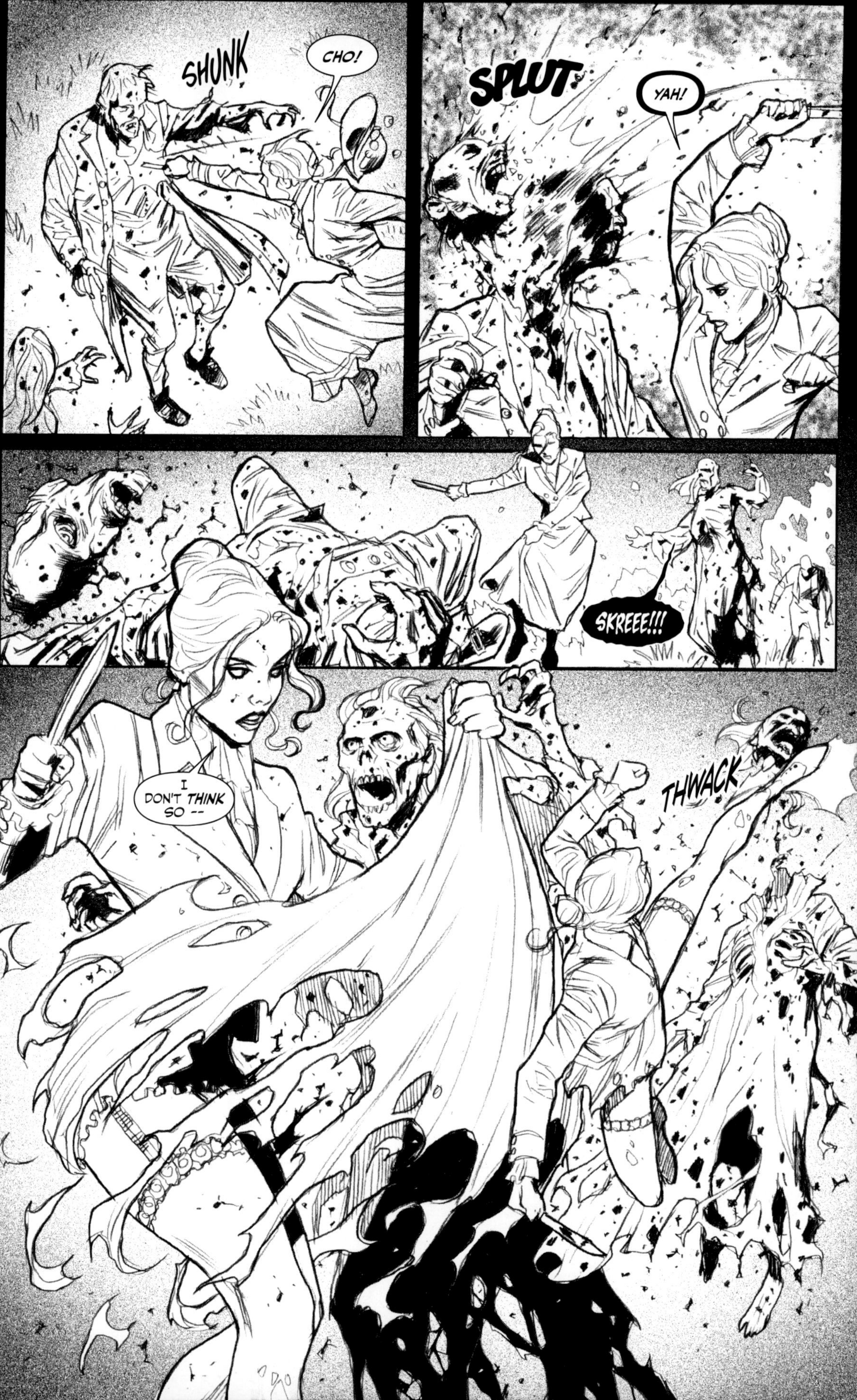
SHUNK
CHO!
SPLUT
YAH!
SKREEE!!!
I DON'T THINK SO --
THWACK

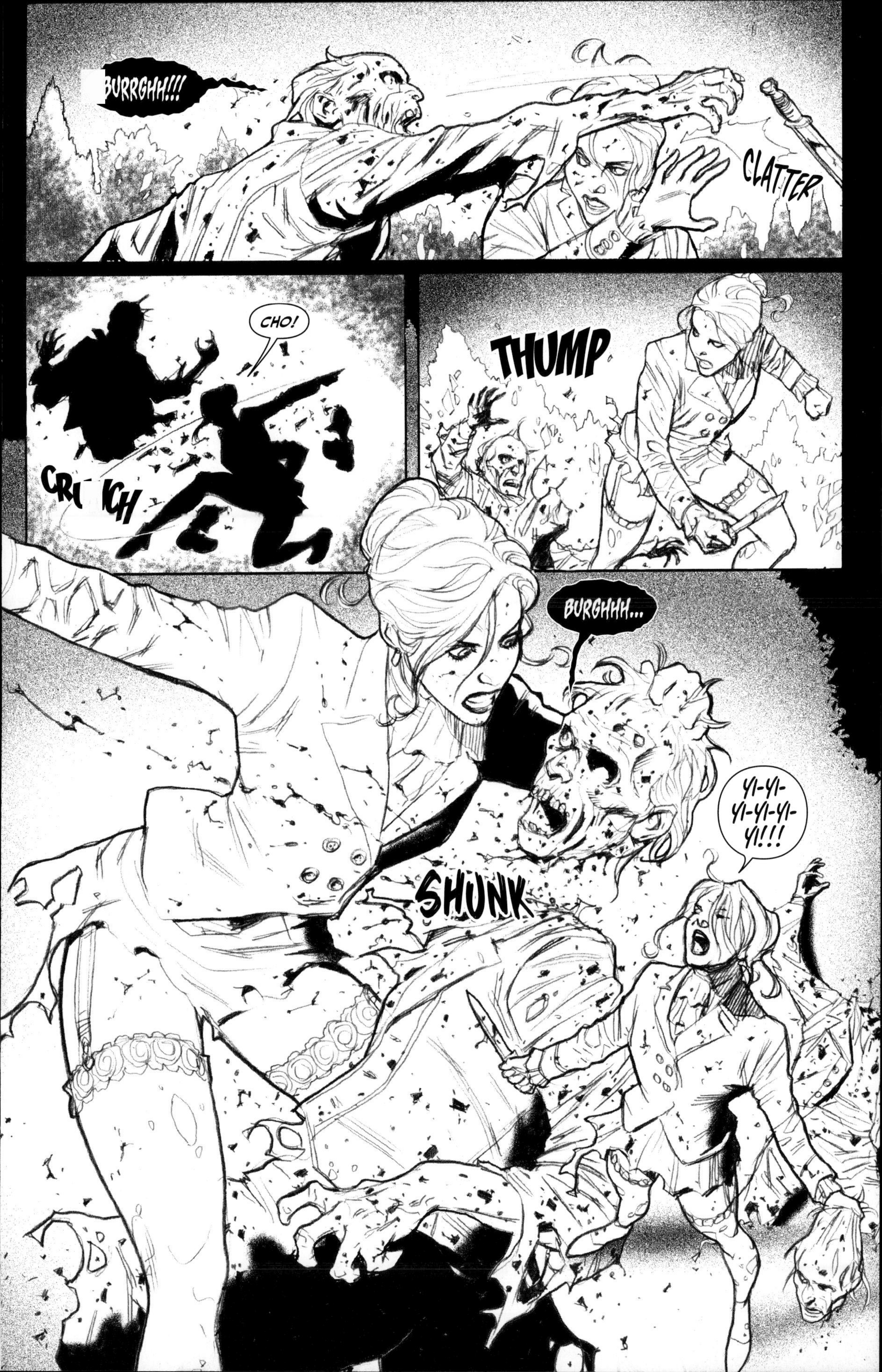
BURRGHH!!!
CLATTER
CHO!
CRUNCH
THUMP
BURGHHH...
SHUNK
YI-YI-
YI-YI-YI-
YI!!!

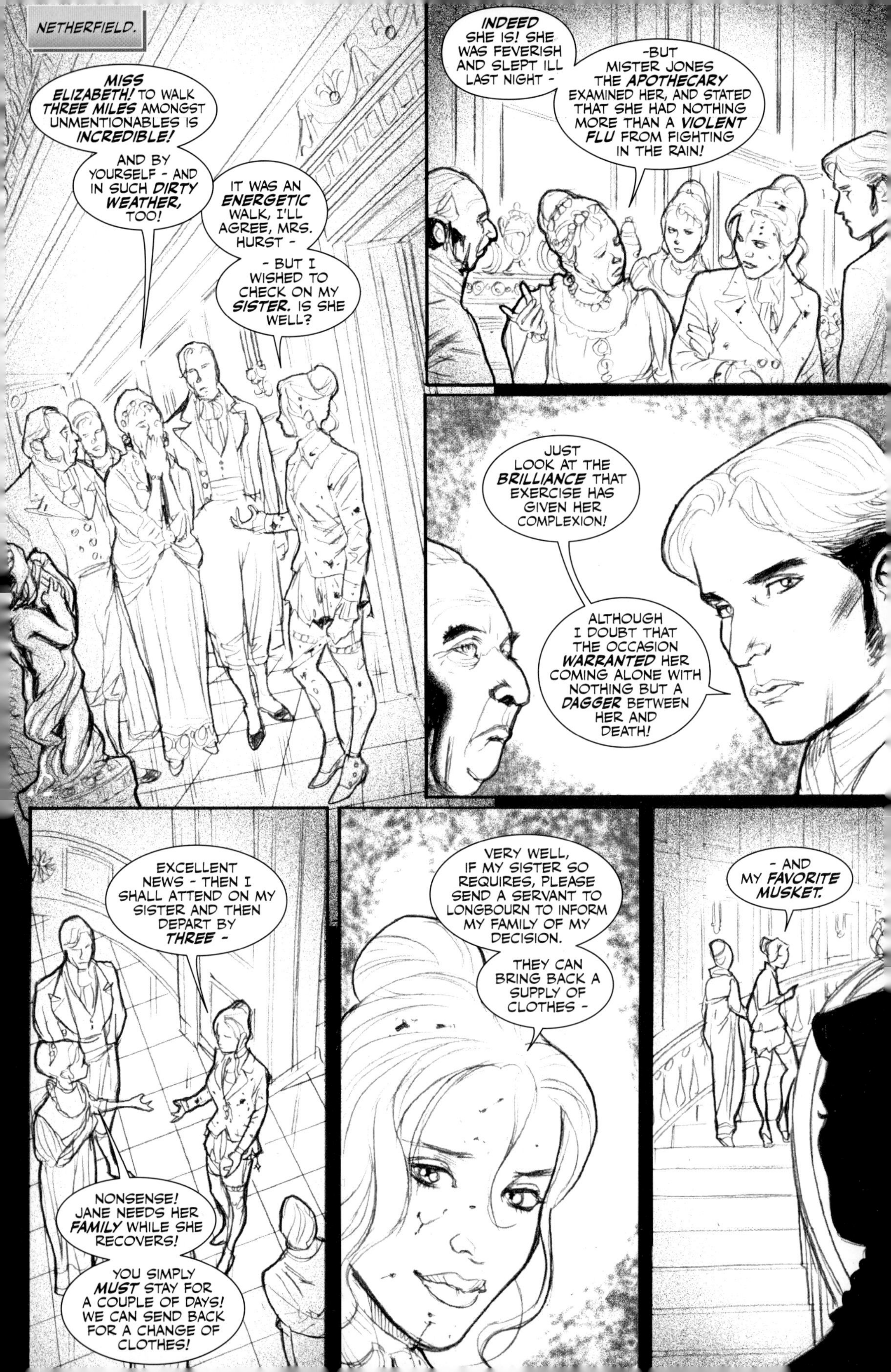
NETHERFIELD.
MISS ELIZABETH! TO WALK THREE MILES AMONGST UNMENTIONABLES IS INCREDIBLE!
AND BY YOURSELF - AND IN SUCH DIRTY WEATHER, TOO!
IT WAS AN ENERGETIC WALK, I'LL AGREE, MRS. HURST -
- BUT I WISHED TO CHECK ON MY SISTER. IS SHE WELL?
INDEED SHE IS! SHE WAS FEVERISH AND SLEPT ILL LAST NIGHT -
-BUT MISTER JONES THE APOTHECARY EXAMINED HER, AND STATED THAT SHE HAD NOTHING MORE THAN A VIOLENT FLU FROM FIGHTING IN THE RAIN!
JUST LOOK AT THE BRILLIANCE THAT EXERCISE HAS GIVEN HER COMPLEXION!
ALTHOUGH I DOUBT THAT THE OCCASION WARRANTED HER COMING ALONE WITH NOTHING BUT A DAGGER BETWEEN HER AND DEATH!
EXCELLENT NEWS - THEN I SHALL ATTEND ON MY SISTER AND THEN DEPART BY THREE -
NONSENSE! JANE NEEDS HER FAMILY WHILE SHE RECOVERS!
YOU SIMPLY MUST STAY FOR A COUPLE OF DAYS! WE CAN SEND BACK FOR A CHANGE OF CLOTHES!
VERY WELL, IF MY SISTER SO REQUIRES, PLEASE SEND A SERVANT TO LONGBOURN TO INFORM MY FAMILY OF MY DECISION.
THEY CAN BRING BACK A SUPPLY OF CLOTHES -
- AND MY FAVORITE MUSKET.

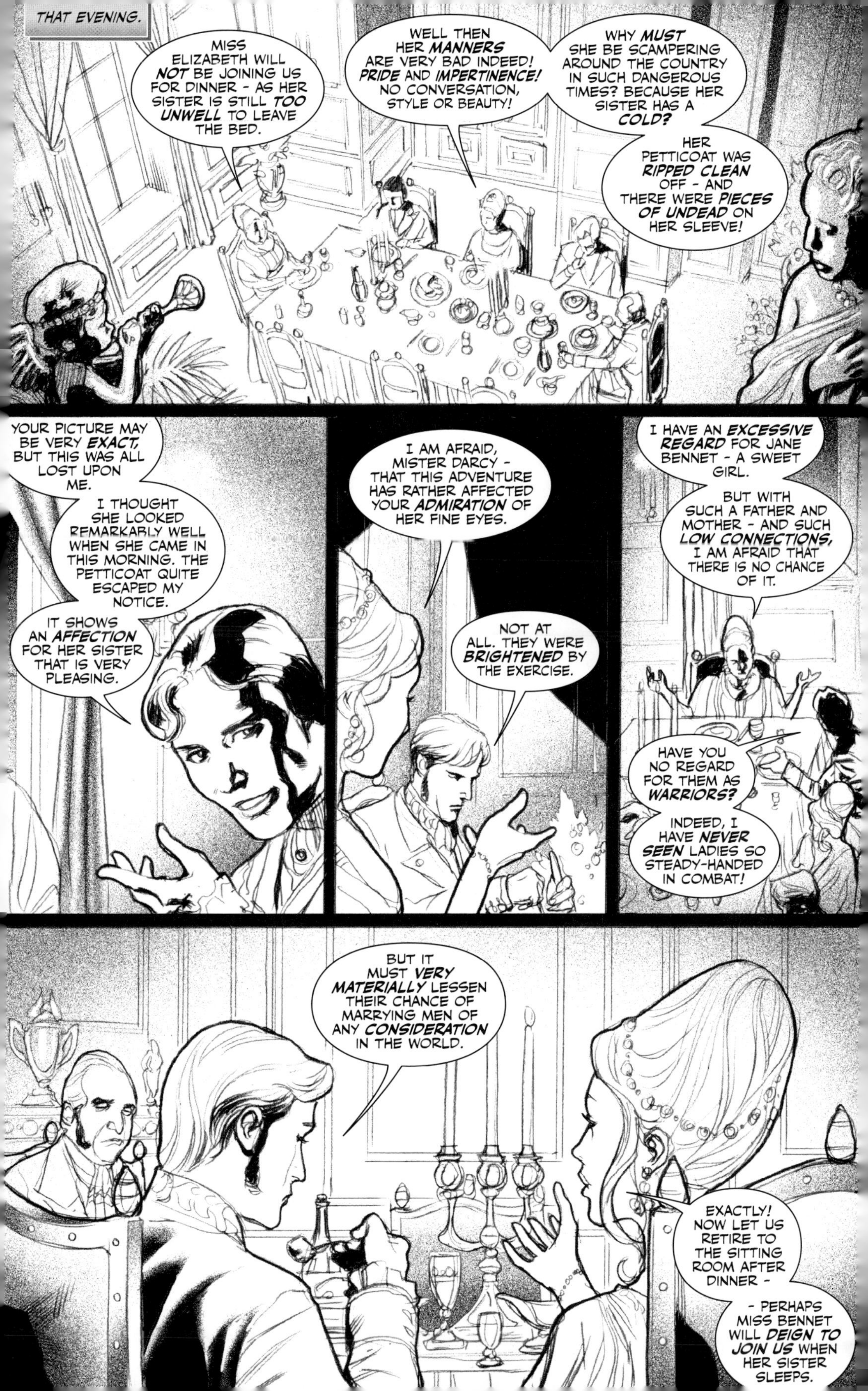
THAT EVENING.
MISS ELIZABETH WILL NOT BE JOINING US FOR DINNER - AS HER SISTER IS STILL TOO UNWELL TO LEAVE THE BED.
WELL THEN HER MANNERS ARE VERY BAD INDEED! PRIDE AND IMPERTINENCE! NO CONVERSATION, STYLE OR BEAUTY!
WHY MUST SHE BE SCAMPERING AROUND THE COUNTRY IN SUCH DANGEROUS TIMES? BECAUSE HER SISTER HAS A COLD?
HER PETTICOAT WAS RIPPED CLEAN OFF - AND THERE WERE PIECES OF UNDEAD ON HER SLEEVE!
YOUR PICTURE MAY BE VERY EXACT, BUT THIS WAS ALL LOST UPON ME.
I THOUGHT SHE LOOKED REMARKABLY WELL WHEN SHE CAME IN THIS MORNING. THE PETTICOAT QUITE ESCAPED MY NOTICE.
IT SHOWS AN AFFECTION FOR HER SISTER THAT IS VERY PLEASING.
I AM AFRAID, MISTER DARCY - THAT THIS ADVENTURE HAS RATHER AFFECTED YOUR ADMIRATION OF HER FINE EYES.
NOT AT ALL. THEY WERE BRIGHTENED BY THE EXERCISE.
I HAVE AN EXCESSIVE REGARD FOR JANE BENNET - A SWEET GIRL.
BUT WITH SUCH A FATHER AND MOTHER - AND SUCH LOW CONNECTIONS, I AM AFRAID THAT THERE IS NO CHANCE OF IT.
HAVE YOU NO REGARD FOR THEM AS WARRIORS?
INDEED, I HAVE NEVER SEEN LADIES SO STEADY-HANDED IN COMBAT!
BUT IT MUST VERY MATERIALLY LESSEN THEIR CHANCE OF MARRYING MEN OF ANY CONSIDERATION IN THE WORLD.
EXACTLY! NOW LET US RETIRE TO THE SITTING ROOM AFTER DINNER -
- PERHAPS MISS BENNET WILL DEIGN TO JOIN US WHEN HER SISTER SLEEPS.

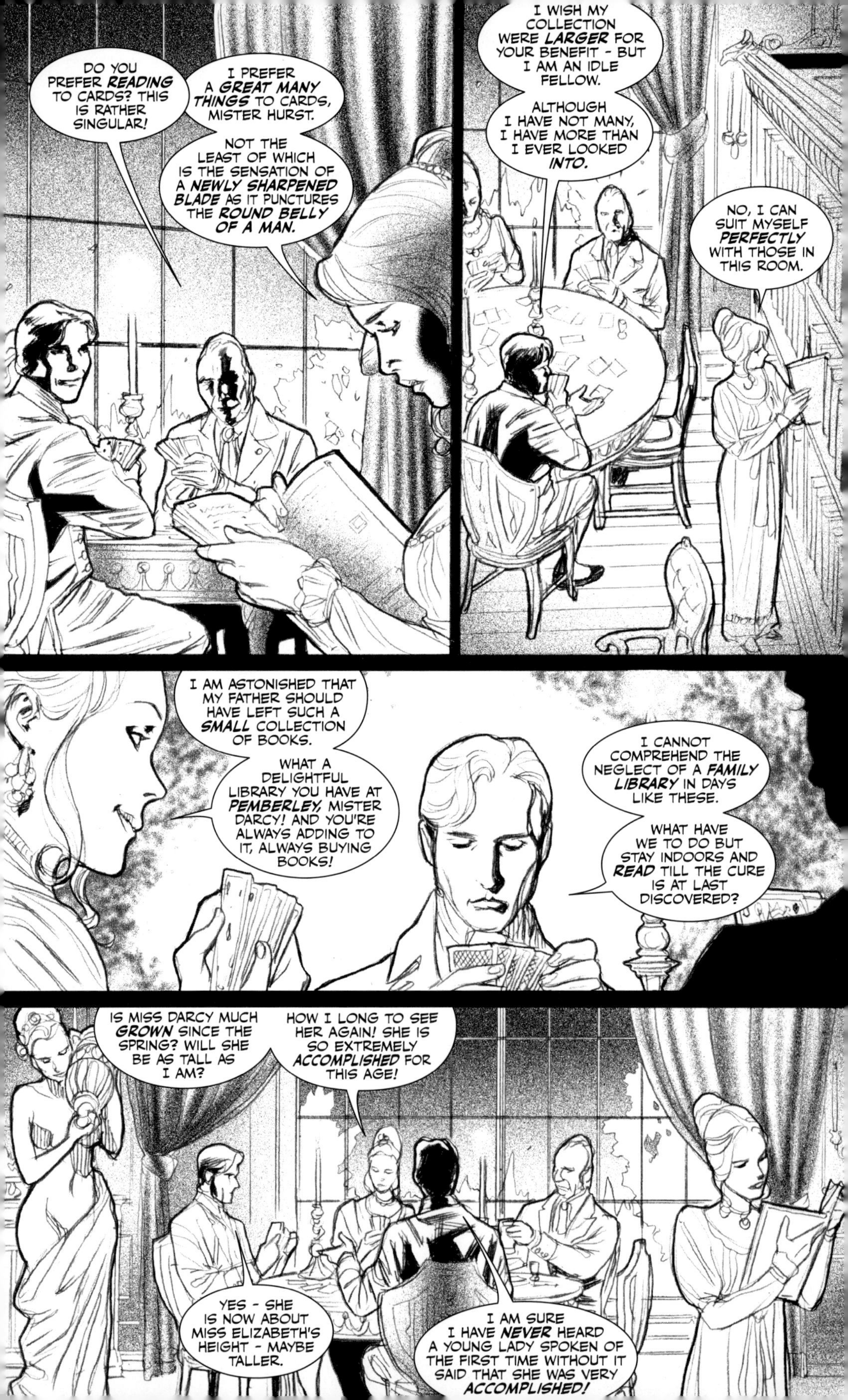
DO YOU PREFER *READING* TO CARDS? THIS IS RATHER SINGULAR!
I PREFER A *GREAT MANY THINGS* TO CARDS, MISTER HURST.
NOT THE LEAST OF WHICH IS THE SENSATION OF A *NEWLY SHARPENED BLADE* AS IT PUNCTURES THE *ROUND BELLY OF A MAN.*
I WISH MY COLLECTION WERE *LARGER* FOR YOUR BENEFIT - BUT I AM AN IDLE FELLOW.
ALTHOUGH I HAVE NOT MANY, I HAVE MORE THAN I EVER LOOKED *INTO.*
NO, I CAN SUIT MYSELF *PERFECTLY* WITH THOSE IN THIS ROOM.
I AM ASTONISHED THAT MY FATHER SHOULD HAVE LEFT SUCH A *SMALL* COLLECTION OF BOOKS.
WHAT A DELIGHTFUL LIBRARY YOU HAVE AT *PEMBERLEY,* MISTER DARCY! AND YOU'RE ALWAYS ADDING TO IT, ALWAYS BUYING BOOKS!
I CANNOT COMPREHEND THE NEGLECT OF A *FAMILY LIBRARY* IN DAYS LIKE THESE.
WHAT HAVE WE TO DO BUT STAY INDOORS AND *READ* TILL THE CURE IS AT LAST DISCOVERED?
IS MISS DARCY MUCH *GROWN* SINCE THE SPRING? WILL SHE BE AS TALL AS I AM?
HOW I LONG TO SEE HER AGAIN! SHE IS SO EXTREMELY *ACCOMPLISHED* FOR THIS AGE!
YES - SHE IS NOW ABOUT MISS ELIZABETH'S HEIGHT - MAYBE TALLER.
I AM SURE I HAVE *NEVER* HEARD A YOUNG LADY SPOKEN OF THE FIRST TIME WITHOUT IT SAID THAT SHE WAS VERY *ACCOMPLISHED!*

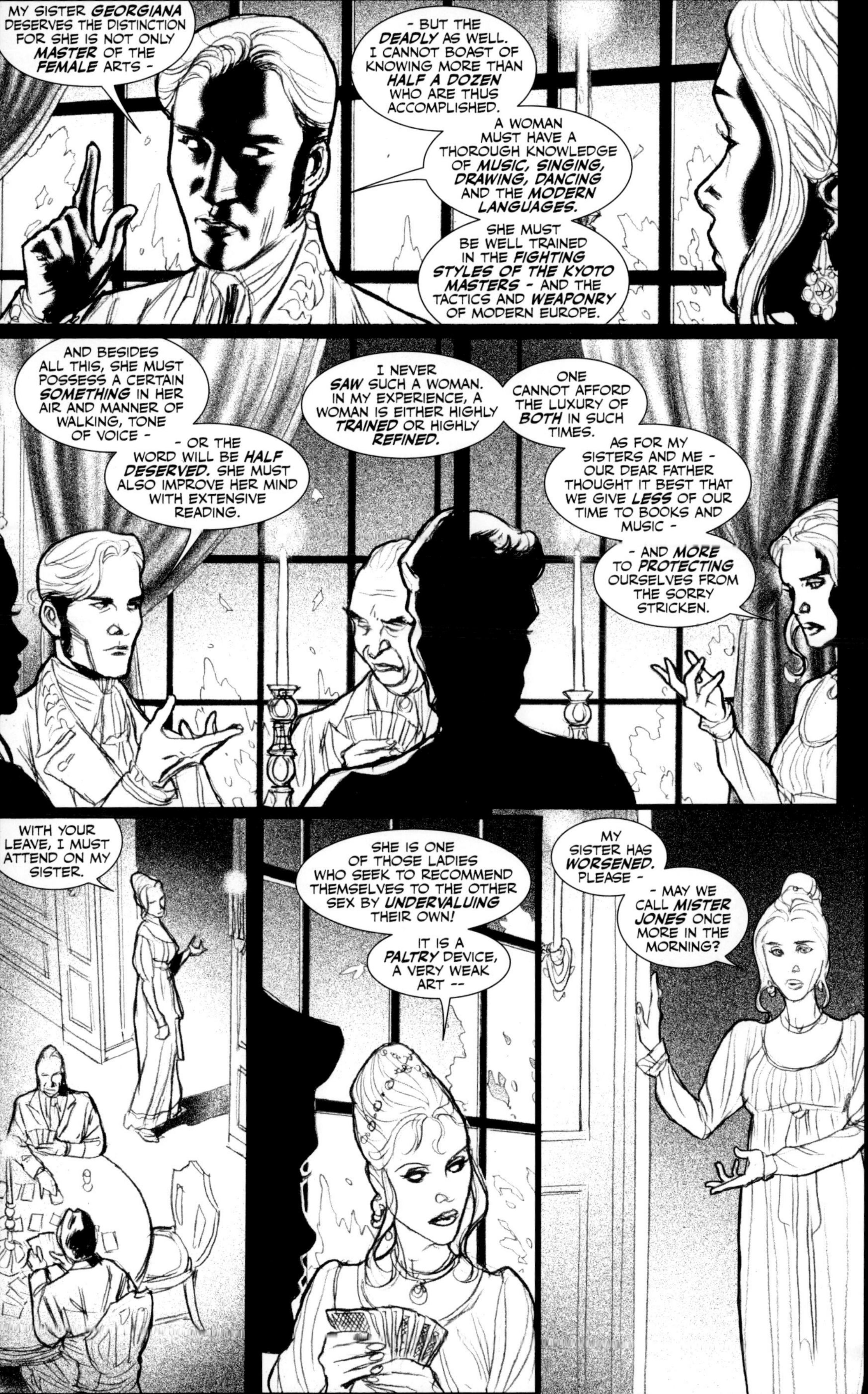
MY SISTER GEORGIANA DESERVES THE DISTINCTION FOR SHE IS NOT ONLY MASTER OF THE FEMALE ARTS -
- BUT THE DEADLY AS WELL. I CANNOT BOAST OF KNOWING MORE THAN HALF A DOZEN WHO ARE THUS ACCOMPLISHED.
A WOMAN MUST HAVE A THOROUGH KNOWLEDGE OF MUSIC, SINGING, DRAWING, DANCING AND THE MODERN LANGUAGES.
SHE MUST BE WELL TRAINED IN THE FIGHTING STYLES OF THE KYOTO MASTERS - AND THE TACTICS AND WEAPONRY OF MODERN EUROPE.
AND BESIDES ALL THIS, SHE MUST POSSESS A CERTAIN SOMETHING IN HER AIR AND MANNER OF WALKING, TONE OF VOICE -
- OR THE WORD WILL BE HALF DESERVED. SHE MUST ALSO IMPROVE HER MIND WITH EXTENSIVE READING.
I NEVER SAW SUCH A WOMAN. IN MY EXPERIENCE, A WOMAN IS EITHER HIGHLY TRAINED OR HIGHLY REFINED.
ONE CANNOT AFFORD THE LUXURY OF BOTH IN SUCH TIMES.
AS FOR MY SISTERS AND ME - OUR DEAR FATHER THOUGHT IT BEST THAT WE GIVE LESS OF OUR TIME TO BOOKS AND MUSIC -
- AND MORE TO PROTECTING OURSELVES FROM THE SORRY STRICKEN.
WITH YOUR LEAVE, I MUST ATTEND ON MY SISTER.
SHE IS ONE OF THOSE LADIES WHO SEEK TO RECOMMEND THEMSELVES TO THE OTHER SEX BY UNDERVALUING THEIR OWN!
IT IS A PALTRY DEVICE, A VERY WEAK ART --
MY SISTER HAS WORSENED. PLEASE -
- MAY WE CALL MISTER JONES ONCE MORE IN THE MORNING?

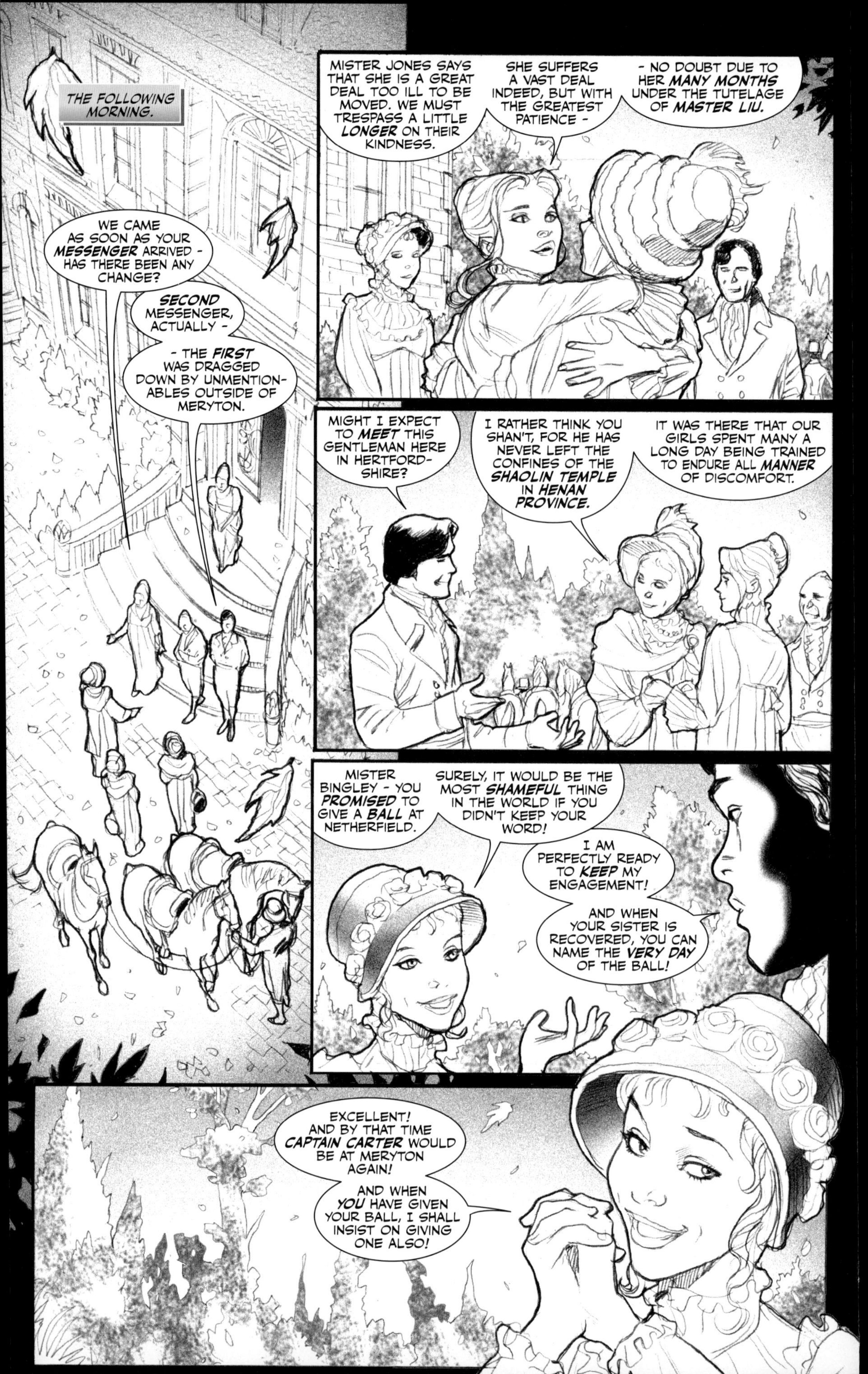
THE FOLLOWING MORNING.
WE CAME AS SOON AS YOUR MESSENGER ARRIVED - HAS THERE BEEN ANY CHANGE?
SECOND MESSENGER, ACTUALLY -
- THE FIRST WAS DRAGGED DOWN BY UNMENTIONABLES OUTSIDE OF MERYTON.
MISTER JONES SAYS THAT SHE IS A GREAT DEAL TOO ILL TO BE MOVED. WE MUST TRESPASS A LITTLE LONGER ON THEIR KINDNESS.
SHE SUFFERS A VAST DEAL INDEED, BUT WITH THE GREATEST PATIENCE -
- NO DOUBT DUE TO HER MANY MONTHS UNDER THE TUTELAGE OF MASTER LIU.
MIGHT I EXPECT TO MEET THIS GENTLEMAN HERE IN HERTFORDSHIRE?
I RATHER THINK YOU SHAN'T, FOR HE HAS NEVER LEFT THE CONFINES OF THE SHAOLIN TEMPLE IN HENAN PROVINCE.
IT WAS THERE THAT OUR GIRLS SPENT MANY A LONG DAY BEING TRAINED TO ENDURE ALL MANNER OF DISCOMFORT.
MISTER BINGLEY - YOU PROMISED TO GIVE A BALL AT NETHERFIELD.
SURELY, IT WOULD BE THE MOST SHAMEFUL THING IN THE WORLD IF YOU DIDN'T KEEP YOUR WORD!
I AM PERFECTLY READY TO KEEP MY ENGAGEMENT!
AND WHEN YOUR SISTER IS RECOVERED, YOU CAN NAME THE VERY DAY OF THE BALL!
EXCELLENT! AND BY THAT TIME CAPTAIN CARTER WOULD BE AT MERYTON AGAIN!
AND WHEN YOU HAVE GIVEN YOUR BALL, I SHALL INSIST ON GIVING ONE ALSO!

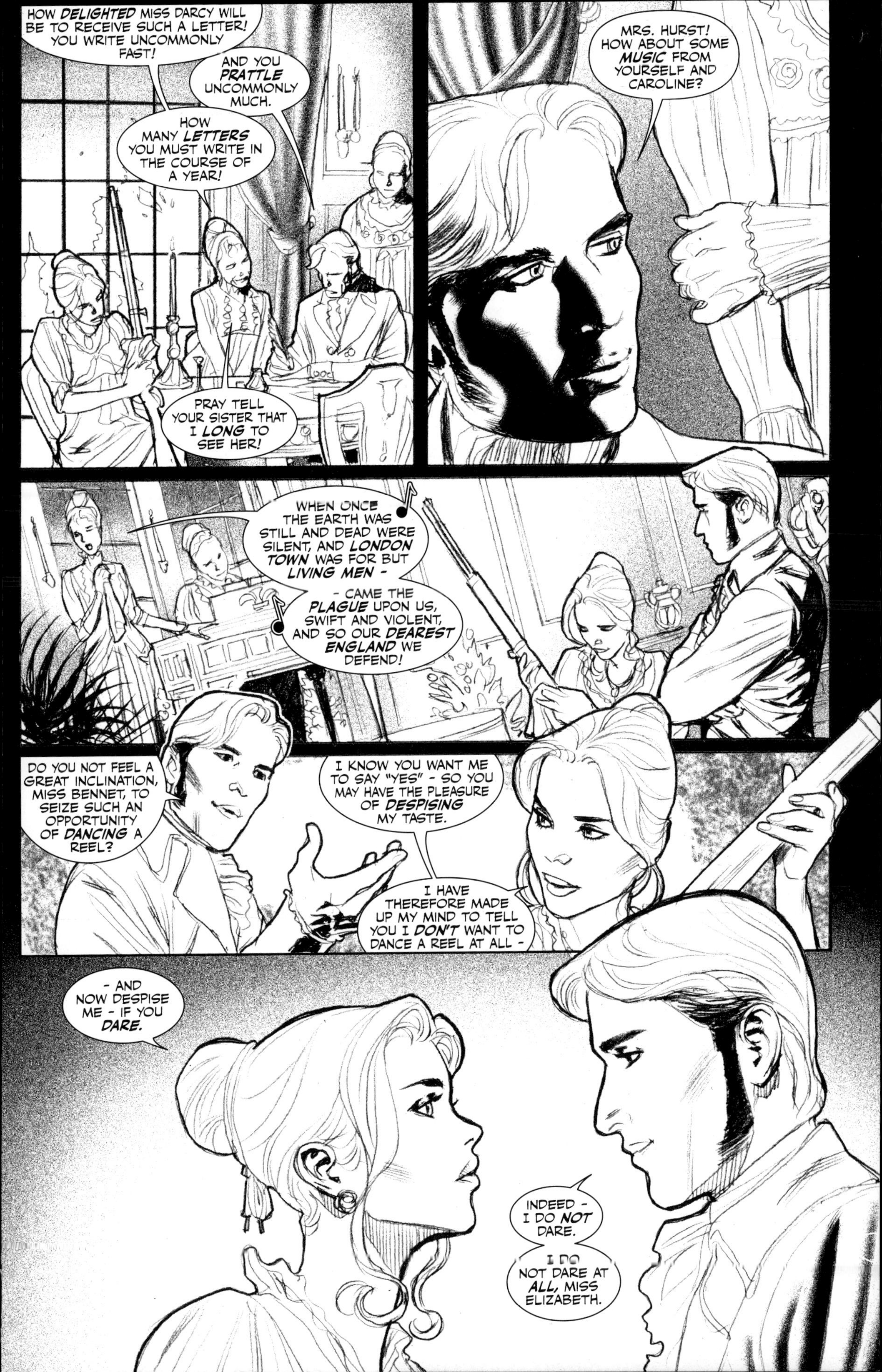
HOW DELIGHTED MISS DARCY WILL BE TO RECEIVE SUCH A LETTER! YOU WRITE UNCOMMONLY FAST!
AND YOU PRATTLE UNCOMMONLY MUCH.
HOW MANY LETTERS YOU MUST WRITE IN THE COURSE OF A YEAR!
PRAY TELL YOUR SISTER THAT I LONG TO SEE HER!
MRS. HURST! HOW ABOUT SOME MUSIC FROM YOURSELF AND CAROLINE?
WHEN ONCE THE EARTH WAS STILL AND DEAD WERE SILENT, AND LONDON TOWN WAS FOR BUT LIVING MEN -
- CAME THE PLAGUE UPON US, SWIFT AND VIOLENT, AND SO OUR DEAREST ENGLAND WE DEFEND!
DO YOU NOT FEEL A GREAT INCLINATION, MISS BENNET, TO SEIZE SUCH AN OPPORTUNITY OF DANCING A REEL?
I KNOW YOU WANT ME TO SAY "YES" - SO YOU MAY HAVE THE PLEASURE OF DESPISING MY TASTE.
I HAVE THEREFORE MADE UP MY MIND TO TELL YOU I DON'T WANT TO DANCE A REEL AT ALL -
- AND NOW DESPISE ME - IF YOU DARE.
INDEED - I DO NOT DARE.
I DO NOT DARE AT ALL, MISS ELIZABETH.

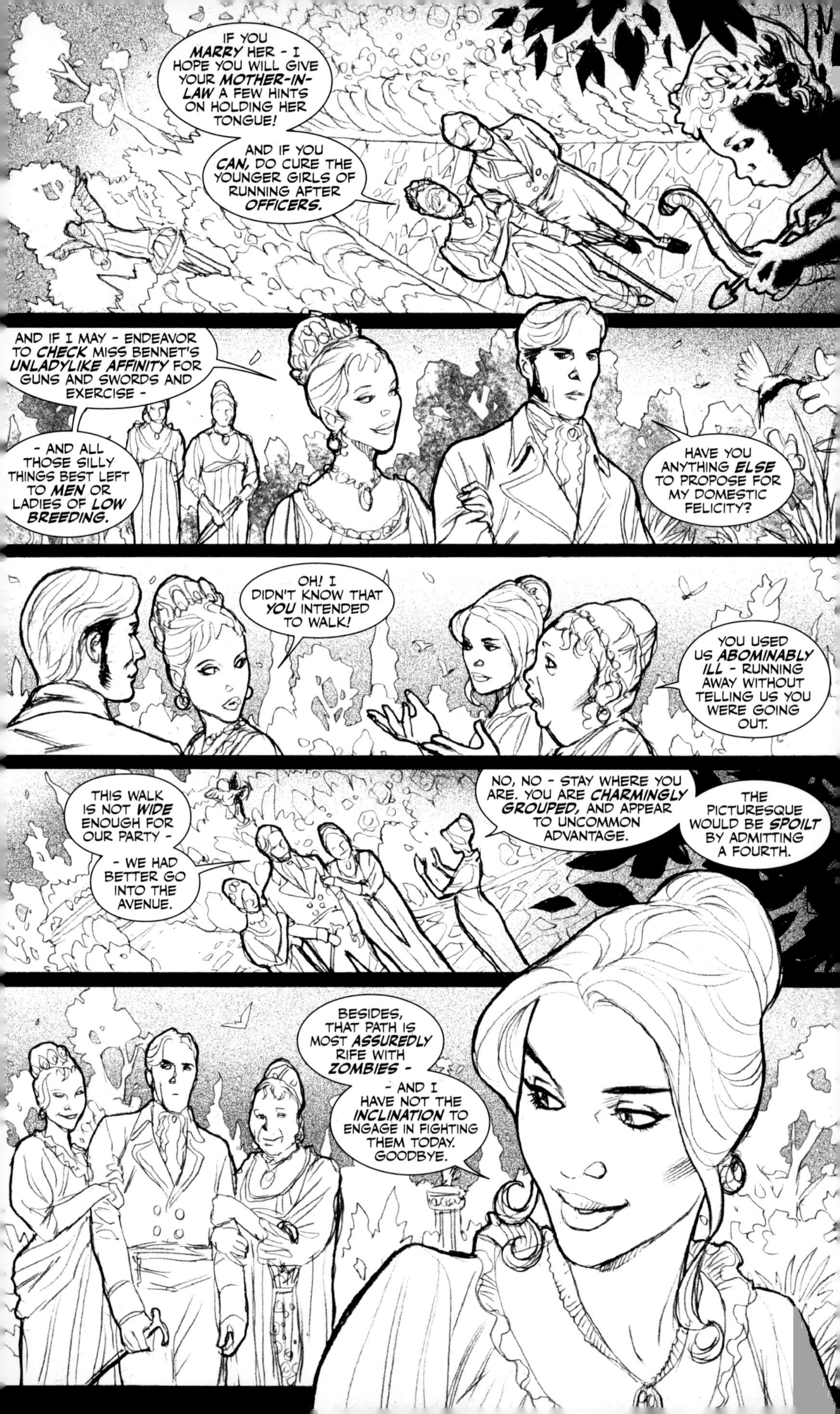
IF YOU MARRY HER - I HOPE YOU WILL GIVE YOUR MOTHER-IN-LAW A FEW HINTS ON HOLDING HER TONGUE!
AND IF YOU CAN, DO CURE THE YOUNGER GIRLS OF RUNNING AFTER OFFICERS.
AND IF I MAY - ENDEAVOR TO CHECK MISS BENNET'S UNLADYLIKE AFFINITY FOR GUNS AND SWORDS AND EXERCISE -
- AND ALL THOSE SILLY THINGS BEST LEFT TO MEN OR LADIES OF LOW BREEDING.
HAVE YOU ANYTHING ELSE TO PROPOSE FOR MY DOMESTIC FELICITY?
OH! I DIDN'T KNOW THAT YOU INTENDED TO WALK!
YOU USED US ABOMINABLY ILL - RUNNING AWAY WITHOUT TELLING US YOU WERE GOING OUT.
THIS WALK IS NOT WIDE ENOUGH FOR OUR PARTY -
- WE HAD BETTER GO INTO THE AVENUE.
NO, NO - STAY WHERE YOU ARE. YOU ARE CHARMINGLY GROUPED, AND APPEAR TO UNCOMMON ADVANTAGE.
THE PICTURESQUE WOULD BE SPOILT BY ADMITTING A FOURTH.
BESIDES, THAT PATH IS MOST ASSUREDLY RIFE WITH ZOMBIES -
- AND I HAVE NOT THE INCLINATION TO ENGAGE IN FIGHTING THEM TODAY. GOODBYE.

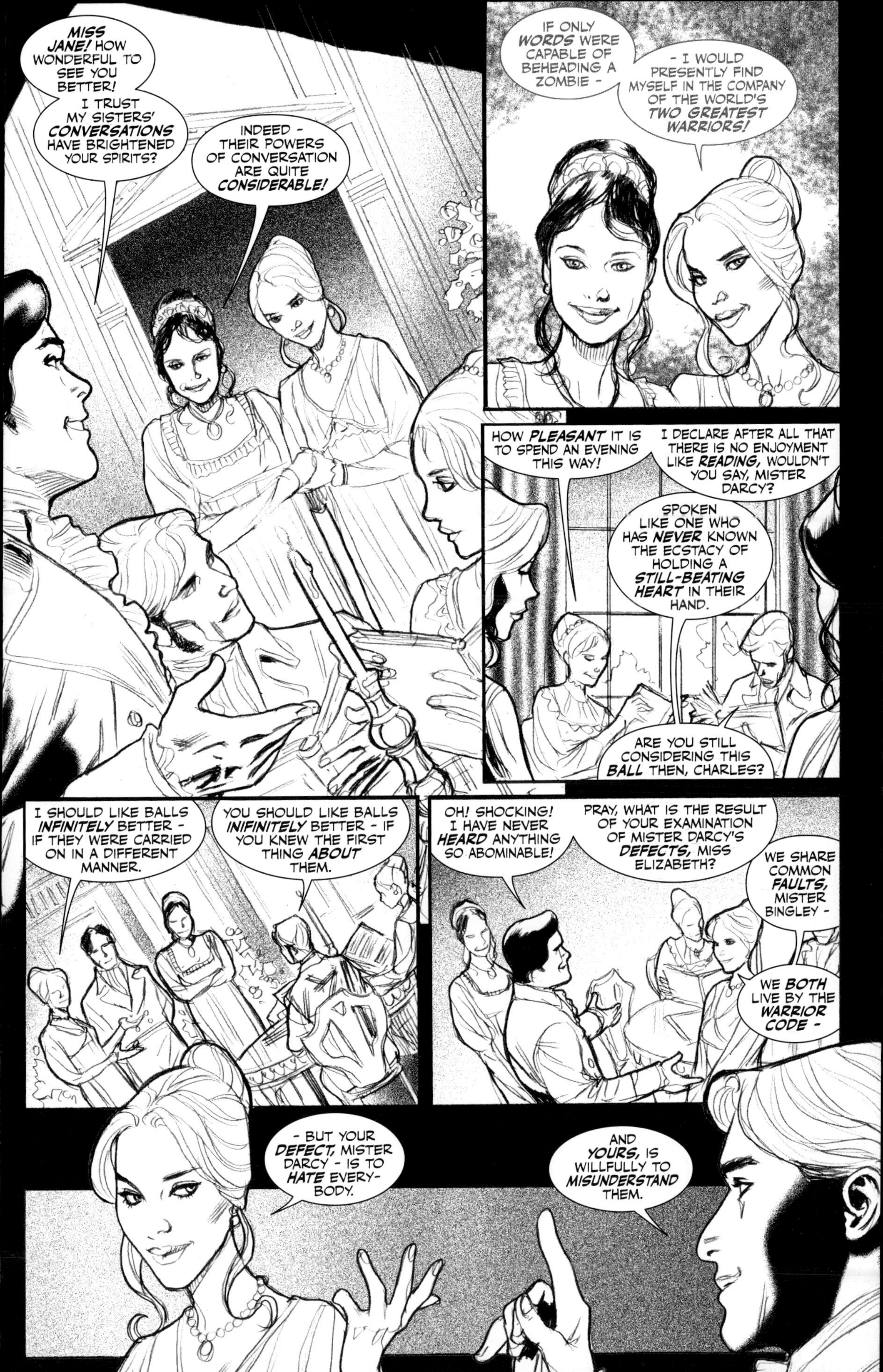
MISS JANE! HOW WONDERFUL TO SEE YOU BETTER!
I TRUST MY SISTERS' CONVERSATIONS HAVE BRIGHTENED YOUR SPIRITS?
INDEED - THEIR POWERS OF CONVERSATION ARE QUITE CONSIDERABLE!
IF ONLY WORDS WERE CAPABLE OF BEHEADING A ZOMBIE -
- I WOULD PRESENTLY FIND MYSELF IN THE COMPANY OF THE WORLD'S TWO GREATEST WARRIORS!
HOW PLEASANT IT IS TO SPEND AN EVENING THIS WAY!
I DECLARE AFTER ALL THAT THERE IS NO ENJOYMENT LIKE READING, WOULDN'T YOU SAY, MISTER DARCY?
SPOKEN LIKE ONE WHO HAS NEVER KNOWN THE ECSTACY OF HOLDING A STILL-BEATING HEART IN THEIR HAND.
ARE YOU STILL CONSIDERING THIS BALL THEN, CHARLES?
I SHOULD LIKE BALLS INFINITELY BETTER - IF THEY WERE CARRIED ON IN A DIFFERENT MANNER.
YOU SHOULD LIKE BALLS INFINITELY BETTER - IF YOU KNEW THE FIRST THING ABOUT THEM.
OH! SHOCKING! I HAVE NEVER HEARD ANYTHING SO ABOMINABLE!
PRAY, WHAT IS THE RESULT OF YOUR EXAMINATION OF MISTER DARCY'S DEFECTS, MISS ELIZABETH?
WE SHARE COMMON FAULTS, MISTER BINGLEY -
WE BOTH LIVE BY THE WARRIOR CODE -
- BUT YOUR DEFECT, MISTER DARCY - IS TO HATE EVERY-BODY.
AND YOURS, IS WILLFULLY TO MISUNDERSTAND THEM.

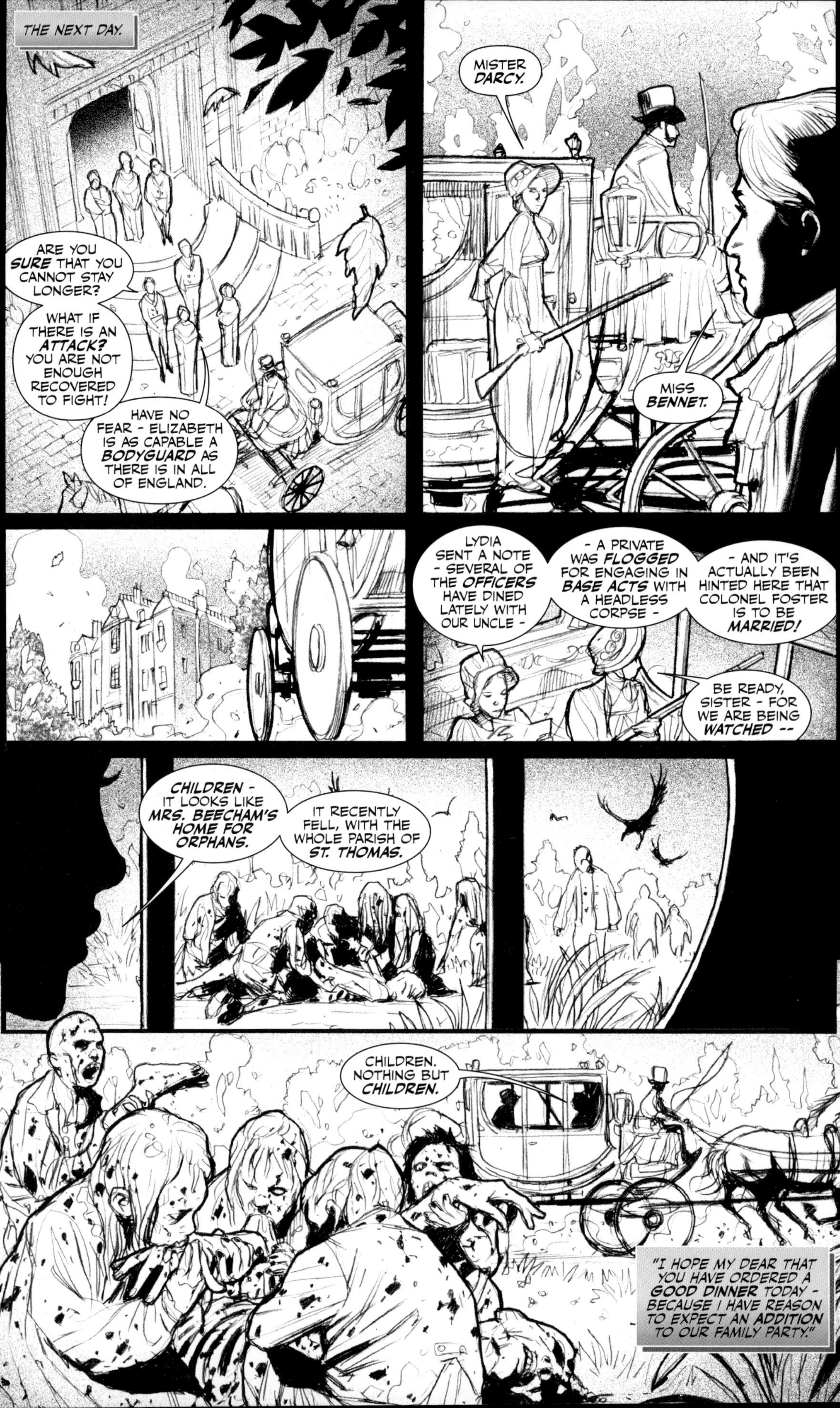
THE NEXT DAY.
ARE YOU SURE THAT YOU CANNOT STAY LONGER?
WHAT IF THERE IS AN ATTACK? YOU ARE NOT ENOUGH RECOVERED TO FIGHT!
HAVE NO FEAR - ELIZABETH IS AS CAPABLE A BODYGUARD AS THERE IS IN ALL OF ENGLAND.
MISTER DARCY.
MISS BENNET.
LYDIA SENT A NOTE - SEVERAL OF THE OFFICERS HAVE DINED LATELY WITH OUR UNCLE -
- A PRIVATE WAS FLOGGED FOR ENGAGING IN BASE ACTS WITH A HEADLESS CORPSE -
- AND IT'S ACTUALLY BEEN HINTED HERE THAT COLONEL FOSTER IS TO BE MARRIED!
BE READY, SISTER - FOR WE ARE BEING WATCHED --
CHILDREN - IT LOOKS LIKE MRS. BEECHAM'S HOME FOR ORPHANS.
IT RECENTLY FELL, WITH THE WHOLE PARISH OF ST. THOMAS.
CHILDREN. NOTHING BUT CHILDREN.
"I HOPE MY DEAR THAT YOU HAVE ORDERED A GOOD DINNER TODAY - BECAUSE I HAVE REASON TO EXPECT AN ADDITION TO OUR FAMILY PARTY."

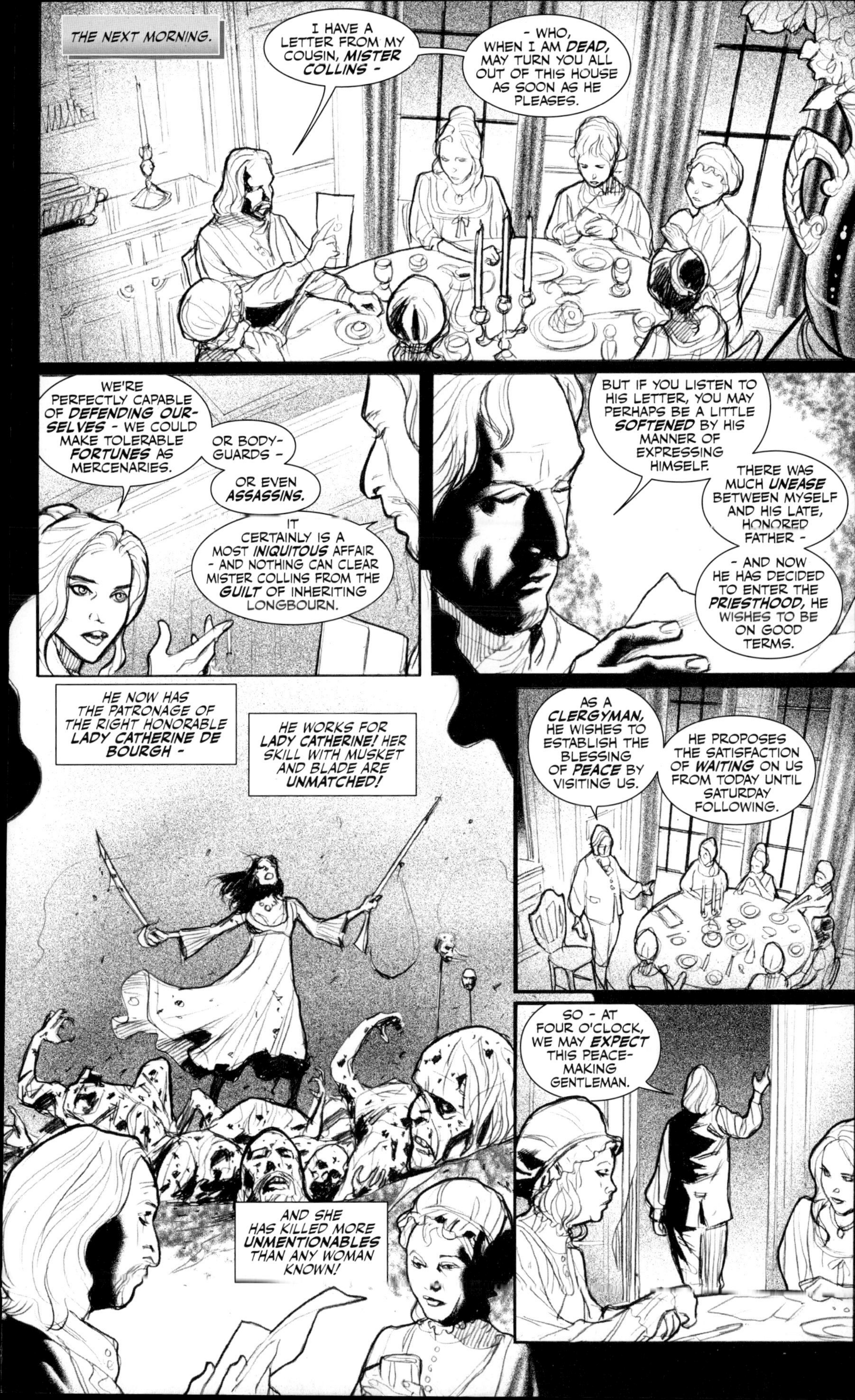
THE NEXT MORNING.
I HAVE A LETTER FROM MY COUSIN, MISTER COLLINS -
- WHO, WHEN I AM DEAD, MAY TURN YOU ALL OUT OF THIS HOUSE AS SOON AS HE PLEASES.
WE'RE PERFECTLY CAPABLE OF DEFENDING OURSELVES - WE COULD MAKE TOLERABLE FORTUNES AS MERCENARIES.
OR BODY-GUARDS -
- OR EVEN ASSASSINS.
IT CERTAINLY IS A MOST INIQUITOUS AFFAIR - AND NOTHING CAN CLEAR MISTER COLLINS FROM THE GUILT OF INHERITING LONGBOURN.
BUT IF YOU LISTEN TO HIS LETTER, YOU MAY PERHAPS BE A LITTLE SOFTENED BY HIS MANNER OF EXPRESSING HIMSELF.
THERE WAS MUCH UNEASE BETWEEN MYSELF AND HIS LATE, HONORED FATHER -
- AND NOW HE HAS DECIDED TO ENTER THE PRIESTHOOD, HE WISHES TO BE ON GOOD TERMS.
HE NOW HAS THE PATRONAGE OF THE RIGHT HONORABLE LADY CATHERINE DE BOURGH -
HE WORKS FOR LADY CATHERINE! HER SKILL WITH MUSKET AND BLADE ARE UNMATCHED!
AND SHE HAS KILLED MORE UNMENTIONABLES THAN ANY WOMAN KNOWN!
AS A CLERGYMAN, HE WISHES TO ESTABLISH THE BLESSING OF PEACE BY VISITING US.
HE PROPOSES THE SATISFACTION OF WAITING ON US FROM TODAY UNTIL SATURDAY FOLLOWING.
SO - AT FOUR O'CLOCK, WE MAY EXPECT THIS PEACE-MAKING GENTLEMAN.

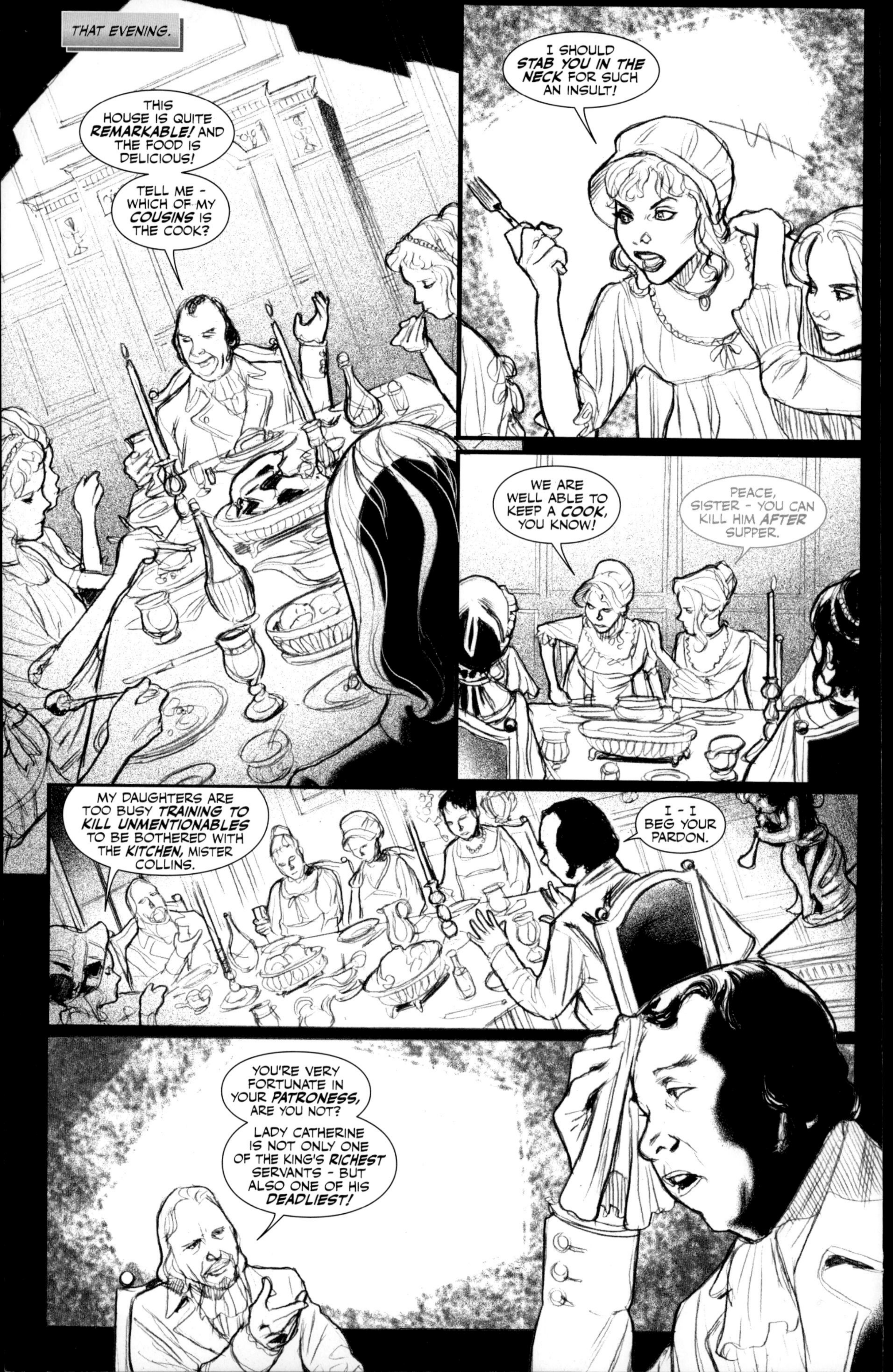
THAT EVENING.
THIS HOUSE IS QUITE REMARKABLE! AND THE FOOD IS DELICIOUS!
TELL ME - WHICH OF MY COUSINS IS THE COOK?
I SHOULD STAB YOU IN THE NECK FOR SUCH AN INSULT!
WE ARE WELL ABLE TO KEEP A COOK, YOU KNOW!
PEACE, SISTER - YOU CAN KILL HIM AFTER SUPPER.
MY DAUGHTERS ARE TOO BUSY TRAINING TO KILL UNMENTIONABLES TO BE BOTHERED WITH THE KITCHEN, MISTER COLLINS.
I - I BEG YOUR PARDON.
YOU'RE VERY FORTUNATE IN YOUR PATRONESS, ARE YOU NOT?
LADY CATHERINE IS NOT ONLY ONE OF THE KING'S RICHEST SERVANTS - BUT ALSO ONE OF HIS DEADLIEST!

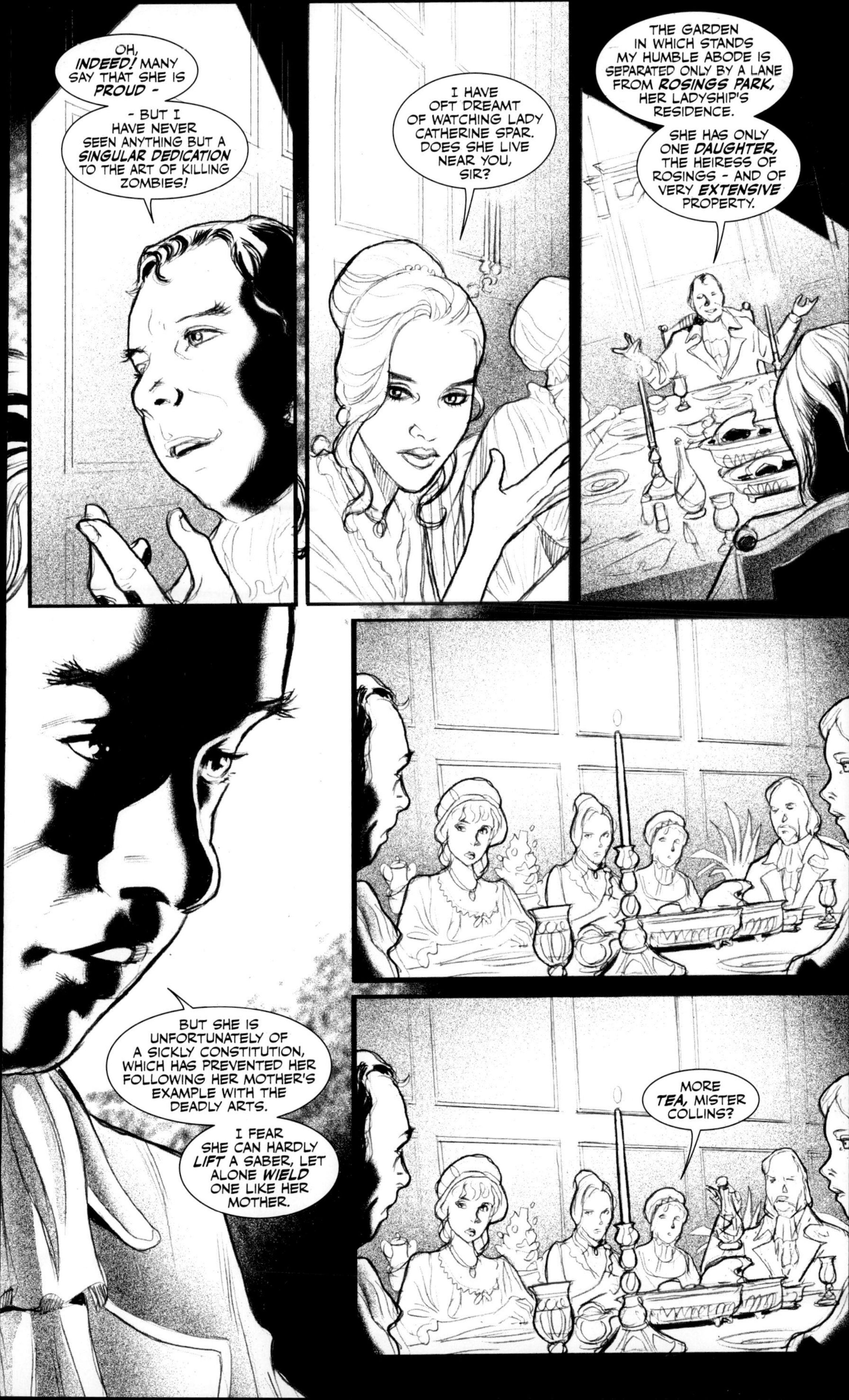
OH, INDEED! MANY SAY THAT SHE IS PROUD -
- BUT I HAVE NEVER SEEN ANYTHING BUT A SINGULAR DEDICATION TO THE ART OF KILLING ZOMBIES!
I HAVE OFT DREAMT OF WATCHING LADY CATHERINE SPAR. DOES SHE LIVE NEAR YOU, SIR?
THE GARDEN IN WHICH STANDS MY HUMBLE ABODE IS SEPARATED ONLY BY A LANE FROM ROSINGS PARK, HER LADYSHIP'S RESIDENCE.
SHE HAS ONLY ONE DAUGHTER, THE HEIRESS OF ROSINGS - AND OF VERY EXTENSIVE PROPERTY.
BUT SHE IS UNFORTUNATELY OF A SICKLY CONSTITUTION, WHICH HAS PREVENTED HER FOLLOWING HER MOTHER'S EXAMPLE WITH THE DEADLY ARTS.
I FEAR SHE CAN HARDLY LIFT A SABER, LET ALONE WIELD ONE LIKE HER MOTHER.
MORE TEA, MISTER COLLINS?

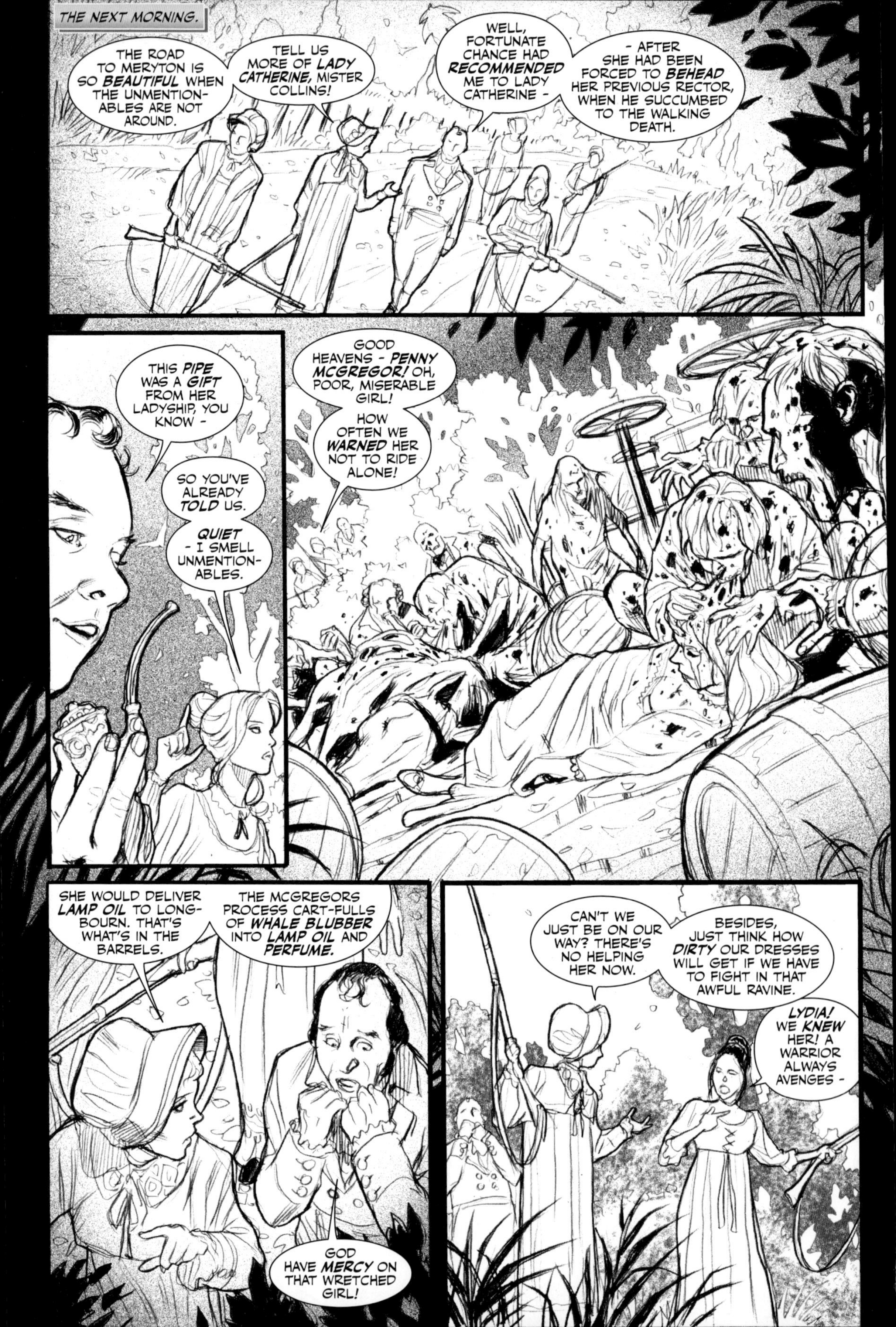
THE NEXT MORNING.
THE ROAD TO MERYTON IS SO BEAUTIFUL WHEN THE UNMENTIONABLES ARE NOT AROUND.
TELL US MORE OF LADY CATHERINE, MISTER COLLINS!
WELL, FORTUNATE CHANCE HAD RECOMMENDED ME TO LADY CATHERINE -
- AFTER SHE HAD BEEN FORCED TO BEHEAD HER PREVIOUS RECTOR, WHEN HE SUCCUMBED TO THE WALKING DEATH.
THIS PIPE WAS A GIFT FROM HER LADYSHIP, YOU KNOW -
SO YOU'VE ALREADY TOLD US.
QUIET - I SMELL UNMENTIONABLES.
GOOD HEAVENS - PENNY MCGREGOR! OH, POOR, MISERABLE GIRL!
HOW OFTEN WE WARNED HER NOT TO RIDE ALONE!
SHE WOULD DELIVER LAMP OIL TO LONGBOURN. THAT'S WHAT'S IN THE BARRELS.
THE MCGREGORS PROCESS CART-FULLS OF WHALE BLUBBER INTO LAMP OIL AND PERFUME.
GOD HAVE MERCY ON THAT WRETCHED GIRL!
CAN'T WE JUST BE ON OUR WAY? THERE'S NO HELPING HER NOW.
BESIDES, JUST THINK HOW DIRTY OUR DRESSES WILL GET IF WE HAVE TO FIGHT IN THAT AWFUL RAVINE.
LYDIA! WE KNEW HER! A WARRIOR ALWAYS AVENGES -

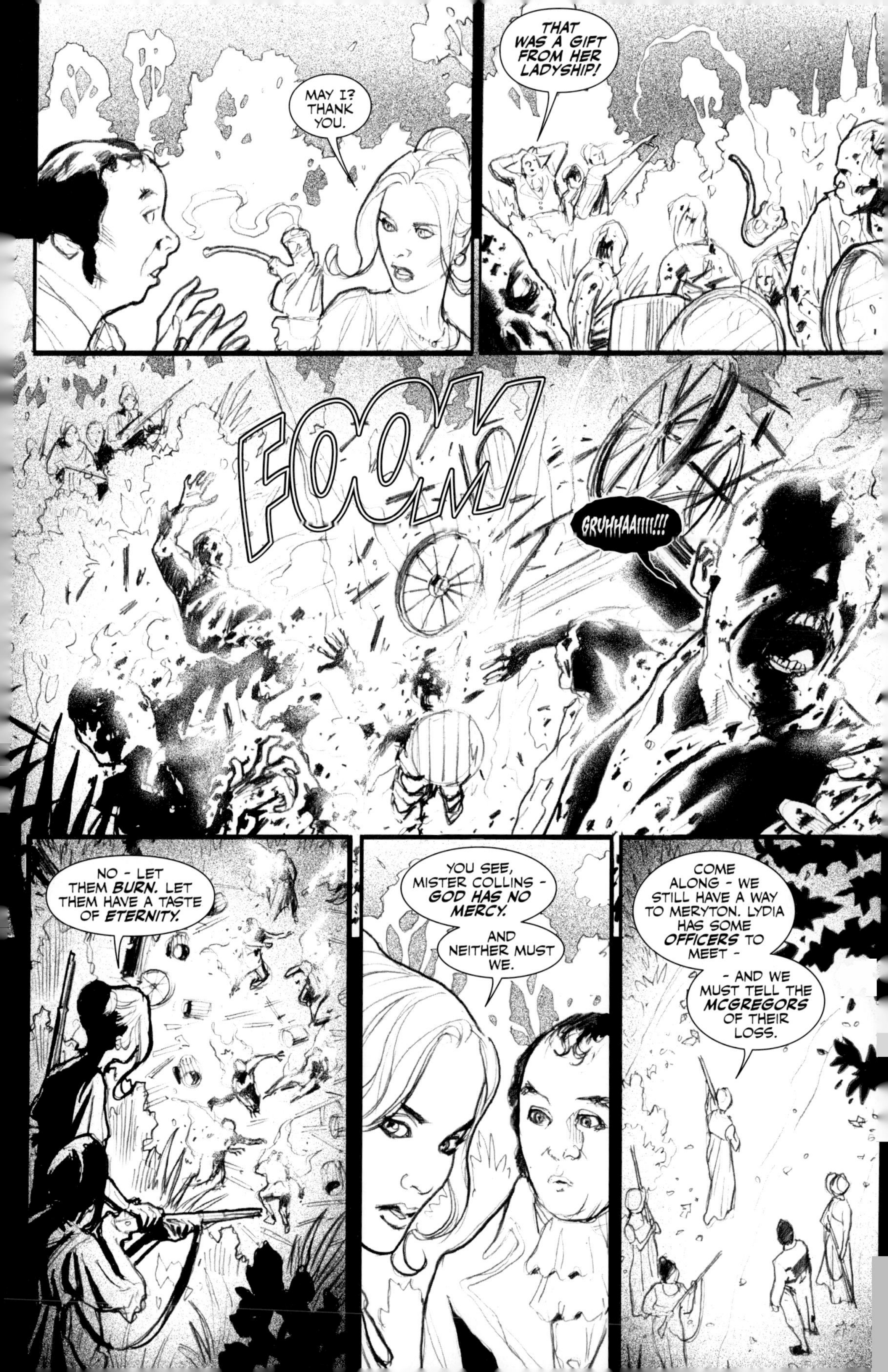
MAY I? THANK YOU.
THAT WAS A GIFT FROM HER LADYSHIP!
FOOM
GRUHHAA!!!!!!
NO - LET THEM BURN. LET THEM HAVE A TASTE OF ETERNITY.
YOU SEE, MISTER COLLINS - GOD HAS NO MERCY.
AND NEITHER MUST WE.
COME ALONG - WE STILL HAVE A WAY TO MERYTON. LYDIA HAS SOME OFFICERS TO MEET -
- AND WE MUST TELL THE MCGREGORS OF THEIR LOSS.

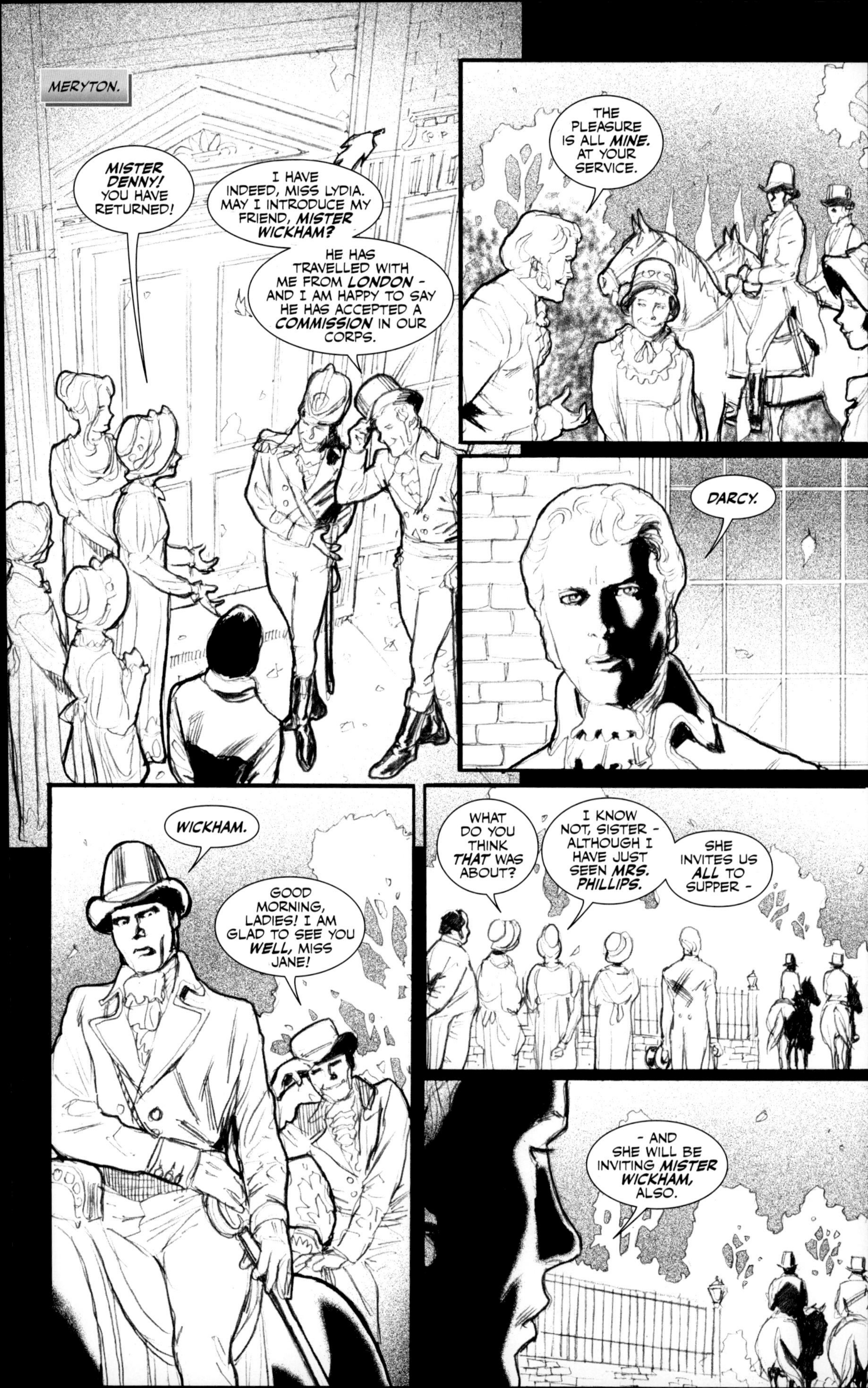
MERYTON.
MISTER DENNY! YOU HAVE RETURNED!
I HAVE INDEED, MISS LYDIA. MAY I INTRODUCE MY FRIEND, MISTER WICKHAM?
HE HAS TRAVELLED WITH ME FROM LONDON - AND I AM HAPPY TO SAY HE HAS ACCEPTED A COMMISSION IN OUR CORPS.
THE PLEASURE IS ALL MINE. AT YOUR SERVICE.
DARCY.
WICKHAM.
GOOD MORNING, LADIES! I AM GLAD TO SEE YOU WELL, MISS JANE!
WHAT DO YOU THINK THAT WAS ABOUT?
I KNOW NOT, SISTER - ALTHOUGH I HAVE JUST SEEN MRS. PHILLIPS.
SHE INVITES US ALL TO SUPPER -
- AND SHE WILL BE INVITING MISTER WICKHAM, ALSO.

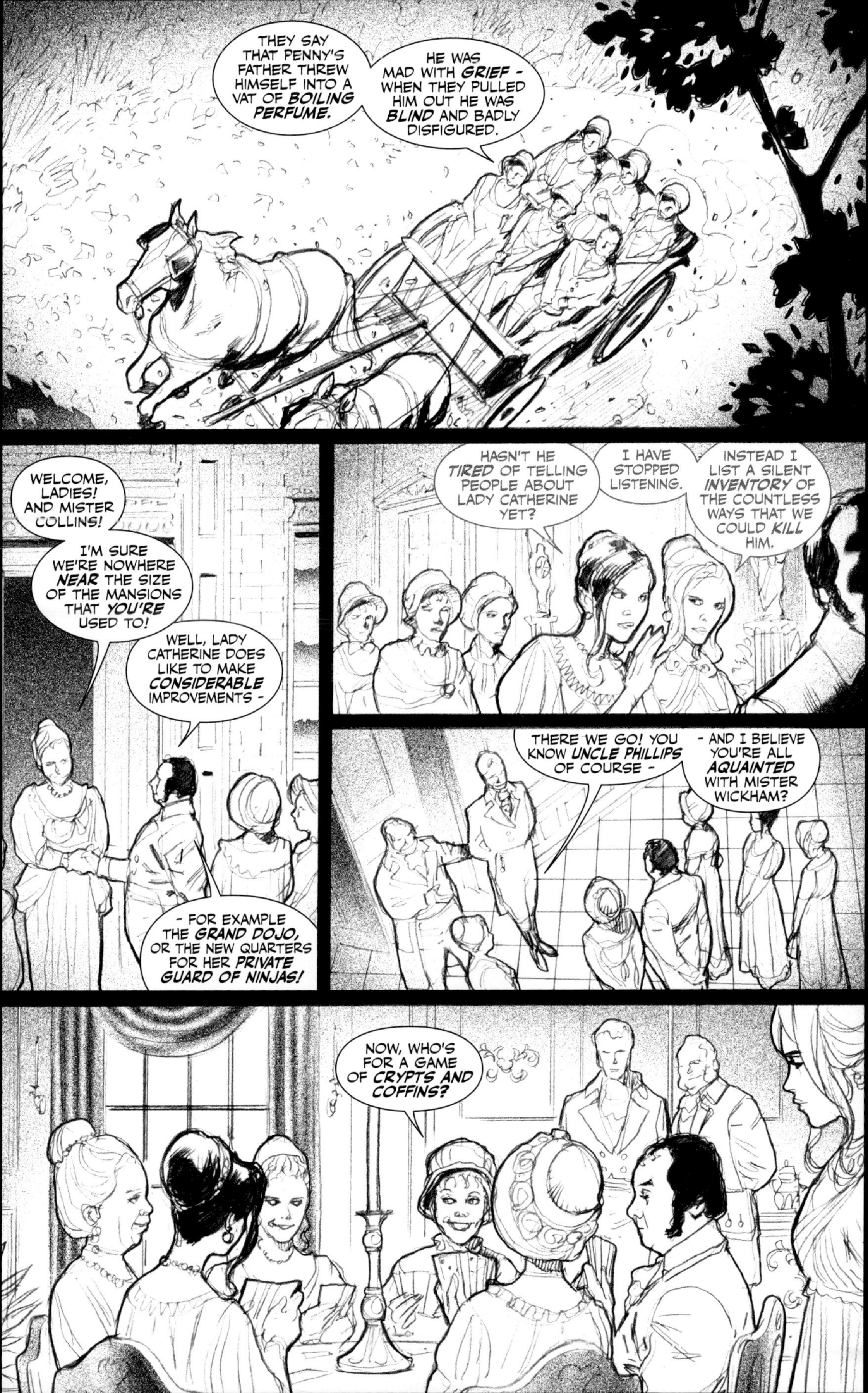
THEY SAY THAT PENNY'S FATHER THREW HIMSELF INTO A VAT OF BOILING PERFUME.
HE WAS MAD WITH GRIEF - WHEN THEY PULLED HIM OUT HE WAS BLIND AND BADLY DISFIGURED.
WELCOME, LADIES! AND MISTER COLLINS!
I'M SURE WE'RE NOWHERE NEAR THE SIZE OF THE MANSIONS THAT YOU'RE USED TO!
WELL, LADY CATHERINE DOES LIKE TO MAKE CONSIDERABLE IMPROVEMENTS -
- FOR EXAMPLE THE GRAND DOJO, OR THE NEW QUARTERS FOR HER PRIVATE GUARD OF NINJAS!
HASN'T HE TIRED OF TELLING PEOPLE ABOUT LADY CATHERINE YET?
I HAVE STOPPED LISTENING.
INSTEAD I LIST A SILENT INVENTORY OF THE COUNTLESS WAYS THAT WE COULD KILL HIM.
THERE WE GO! YOU KNOW UNCLE PHILLIPS OF COURSE -
- AND I BELIEVE YOU'RE ALL AQUAINTED WITH MISTER WICKHAM?
NOW, WHO'S FOR A GAME OF CRYPTS AND COFFINS?

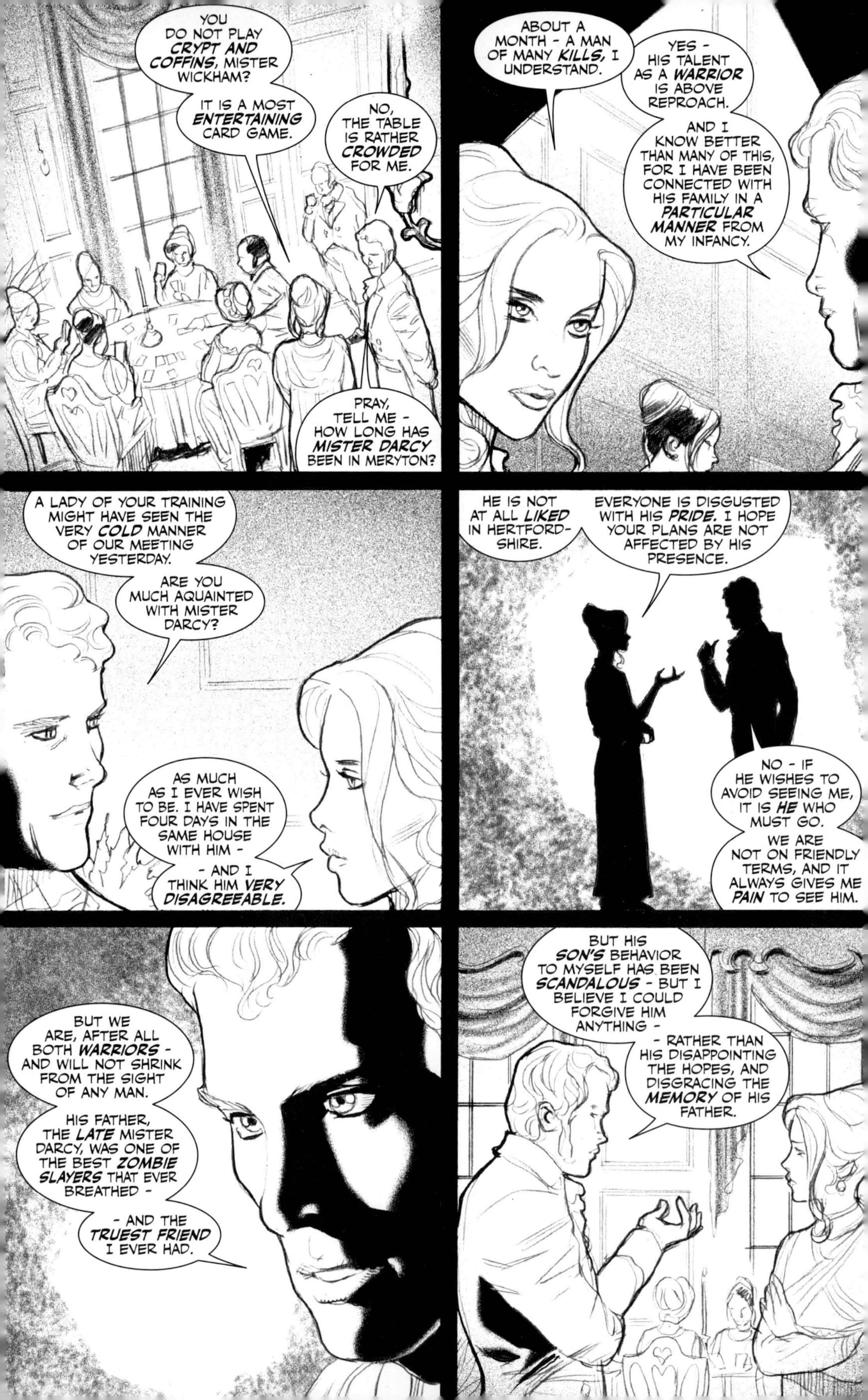

YOU DO NOT PLAY CRYPT AND COFFINS, MISTER WICKHAM?
IT IS A MOST ENTERTAINING CARD GAME.
NO, THE TABLE IS RATHER CROWDED FOR ME.
PRAY, TELL ME - HOW LONG HAS MISTER DARCY BEEN IN MERYTON?
ABOUT A MONTH - A MAN OF MANY KILLS, I UNDERSTAND.
YES - HIS TALENT AS A WARRIOR IS ABOVE REPROACH.
AND I KNOW BETTER THAN MANY OF THIS, FOR I HAVE BEEN CONNECTED WITH HIS FAMILY IN A PARTICULAR MANNER FROM MY INFANCY.
A LADY OF YOUR TRAINING MIGHT HAVE SEEN THE VERY COLD MANNER OF OUR MEETING YESTERDAY.
ARE YOU MUCH AQUAINTED WITH MISTER DARCY?
AS MUCH AS I EVER WISH TO BE. I HAVE SPENT FOUR DAYS IN THE SAME HOUSE WITH HIM -
- AND I THINK HIM VERY DISAGREEABLE.
HE IS NOT AT ALL LIKED IN HERTFORD-SHIRE.
EVERYONE IS DISGUSTED WITH HIS PRIDE. I HOPE YOUR PLANS ARE NOT AFFECTED BY HIS PRESENCE.
NO - IF HE WISHES TO AVOID SEEING ME, IT IS HE WHO MUST GO.
WE ARE NOT ON FRIENDLY TERMS, AND IT ALWAYS GIVES ME PAIN TO SEE HIM.
BUT WE ARE, AFTER ALL BOTH WARRIORS - AND WILL NOT SHRINK FROM THE SIGHT OF ANY MAN.
HIS FATHER, THE LATE MISTER DARCY, WAS ONE OF THE BEST ZOMBIE SLAYERS THAT EVER BREATHED -
- AND THE TRUEST FRIEND I EVER HAD.
BUT HIS SON'S BEHAVIOR TO MYSELF HAS BEEN SCANDALOUS - BUT I BELIEVE I COULD FORGIVE HIM ANYTHING -
- RATHER THAN HIS DISAPPOINTING THE HOPES, AND DISGRACING THE MEMORY OF HIS FATHER.

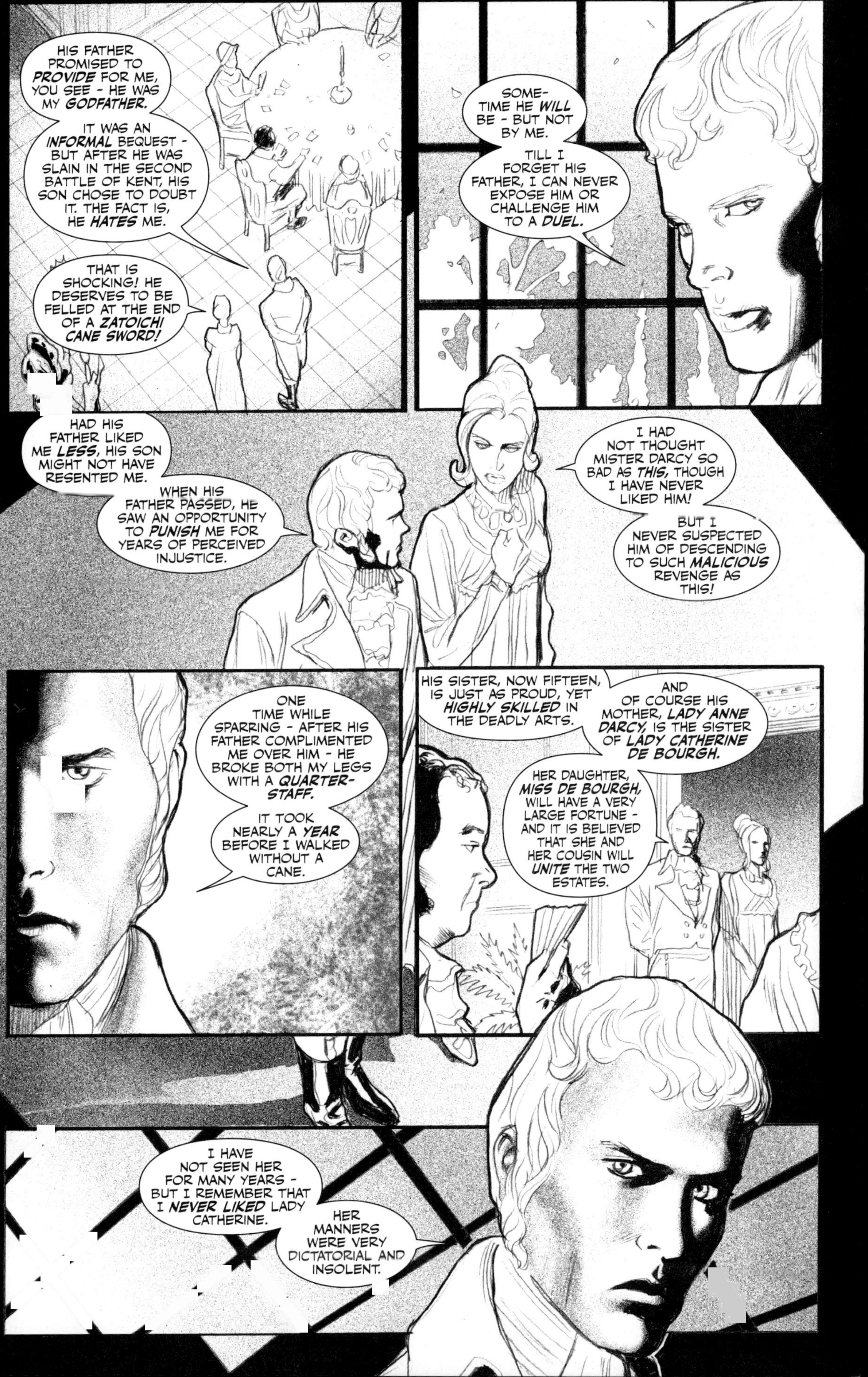
HIS FATHER PROMISED TO PROVIDE FOR ME, YOU SEE - HE WAS MY GODFATHER.
IT WAS AN INFORMAL BEQUEST - BUT AFTER HE WAS SLAIN IN THE SECOND BATTLE OF KENT, HIS SON CHOSE TO DOUBT IT. THE FACT IS, HE HATES ME.
THAT IS SHOCKING! HE DESERVES TO BE FELLED AT THE END OF A ZATOICHI CANE SWORD!
SOME-TIME HE WILL BE - BUT NOT BY ME.
TILL I FORGET HIS FATHER, I CAN NEVER EXPOSE HIM OR CHALLENGE HIM TO A DUEL.
HAD HIS FATHER LIKED ME LESS, HIS SON MIGHT NOT HAVE RESENTED ME.
WHEN HIS FATHER PASSED, HE SAW AN OPPORTUNITY TO PUNISH ME FOR YEARS OF PERCEIVED INJUSTICE.
I HAD NOT THOUGHT MISTER DARCY SO BAD AS THIS, THOUGH I HAVE NEVER LIKED HIM!
BUT I NEVER SUSPECTED HIM OF DESCENDING TO SUCH MALICIOUS REVENGE AS THIS!
ONE TIME WHILE SPARRING - AFTER HIS FATHER COMPLIMENTED ME OVER HIM - HE BROKE BOTH MY LEGS WITH A QUARTER-STAFF.
IT TOOK NEARLY A YEAR BEFORE I WALKED WITHOUT A CANE.
HIS SISTER, NOW FIFTEEN, IS JUST AS PROUD, YET HIGHLY SKILLED IN THE DEADLY ARTS.
AND OF COURSE HIS MOTHER, LADY ANNE DARCY, IS THE SISTER OF LADY CATHERINE DE BOURGH.
HER DAUGHTER, MISS DE BOURGH, WILL HAVE A VERY LARGE FORTUNE - AND IT IS BELIEVED THAT SHE AND HER COUSIN WILL UNITE THE TWO ESTATES.
I HAVE NOT SEEN HER FOR MANY YEARS - BUT I REMEMBER THAT I NEVER LIKED LADY CATHERINE.
HER MANNERS WERE VERY DICTATORIAL AND INSOLENT.

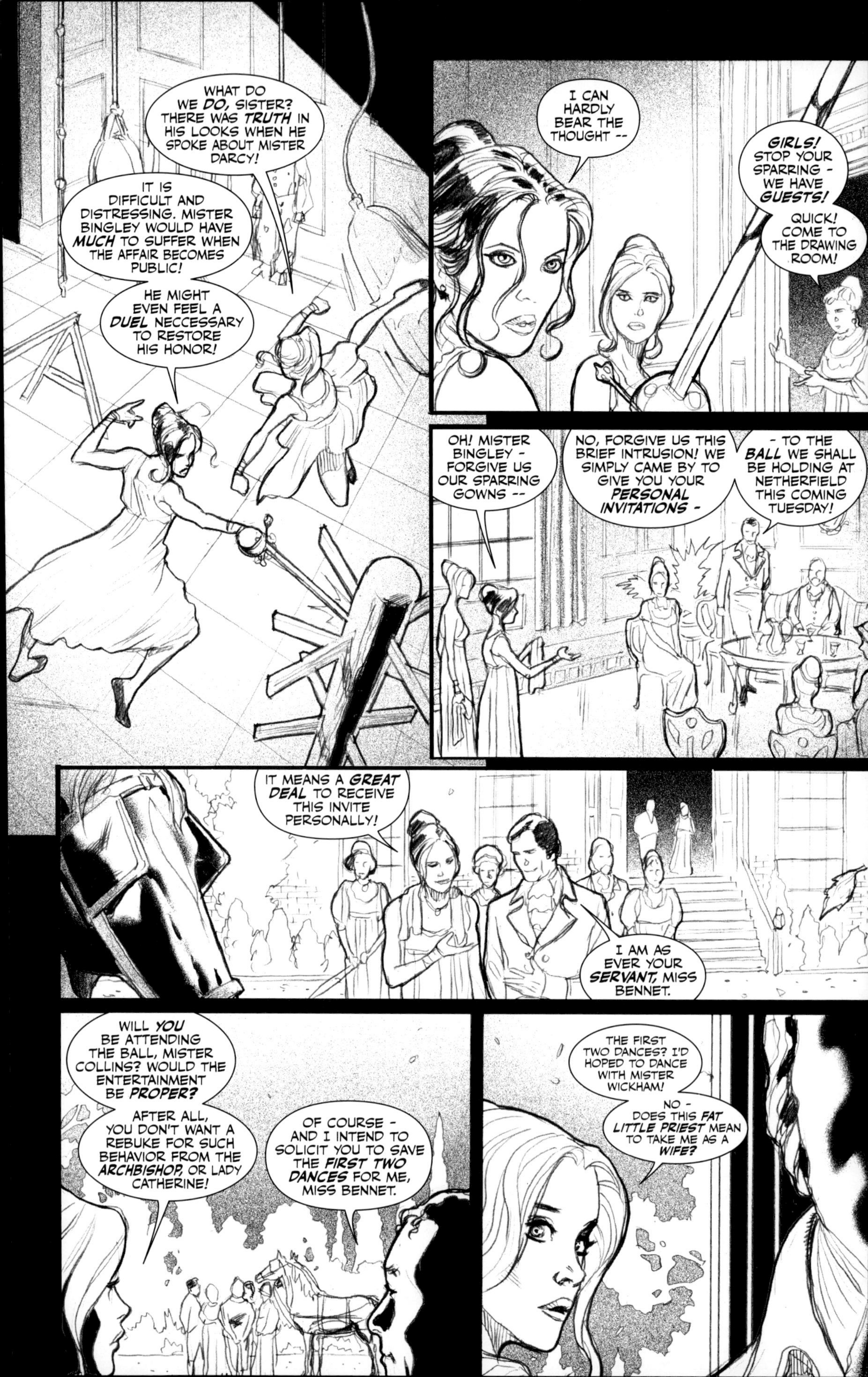

WHAT DO WE DO, SISTER? THERE WAS TRUTH IN HIS LOOKS WHEN HE SPOKE ABOUT MISTER DARCY!
IT IS DIFFICULT AND DISTRESSING. MISTER BINGLEY WOULD HAVE MUCH TO SUFFER WHEN THE AFFAIR BECOMES PUBLIC!
HE MIGHT EVEN FEEL A DUEL NECCESSARY TO RESTORE HIS HONOR!
I CAN HARDLY BEAR THE THOUGHT --
GIRLS! STOP YOUR SPARRING - WE HAVE GUESTS!
QUICK! COME TO THE DRAWING ROOM!
OH! MISTER BINGLEY - FORGIVE US OUR SPARRING GOWNS --
NO, FORGIVE US THIS BRIEF INTRUSION! WE SIMPLY CAME BY TO GIVE YOU YOUR PERSONAL INVITATIONS -
- TO THE BALL WE SHALL BE HOLDING AT NETHERFIELD THIS COMING TUESDAY!
IT MEANS A GREAT DEAL TO RECEIVE THIS INVITE PERSONALLY!
I AM AS EVER YOUR SERVANT, MISS BENNET.
WILL YOU BE ATTENDING THE BALL, MISTER COLLINS? WOULD THE ENTERTAINMENT BE PROPER?
AFTER ALL, YOU DON'T WANT A REBUKE FOR SUCH BEHAVIOR FROM THE ARCHBISHOP, OR LADY CATHERINE!
OF COURSE - AND I INTEND TO SOLICIT YOU TO SAVE THE FIRST TWO DANCES FOR ME, MISS BENNET.
THE FIRST TWO DANCES? I'D HOPED TO DANCE WITH MISTER WICKHAM!
NO - DOES THIS FAT LITTLE PRIEST MEAN TO TAKE ME AS A WIFE?

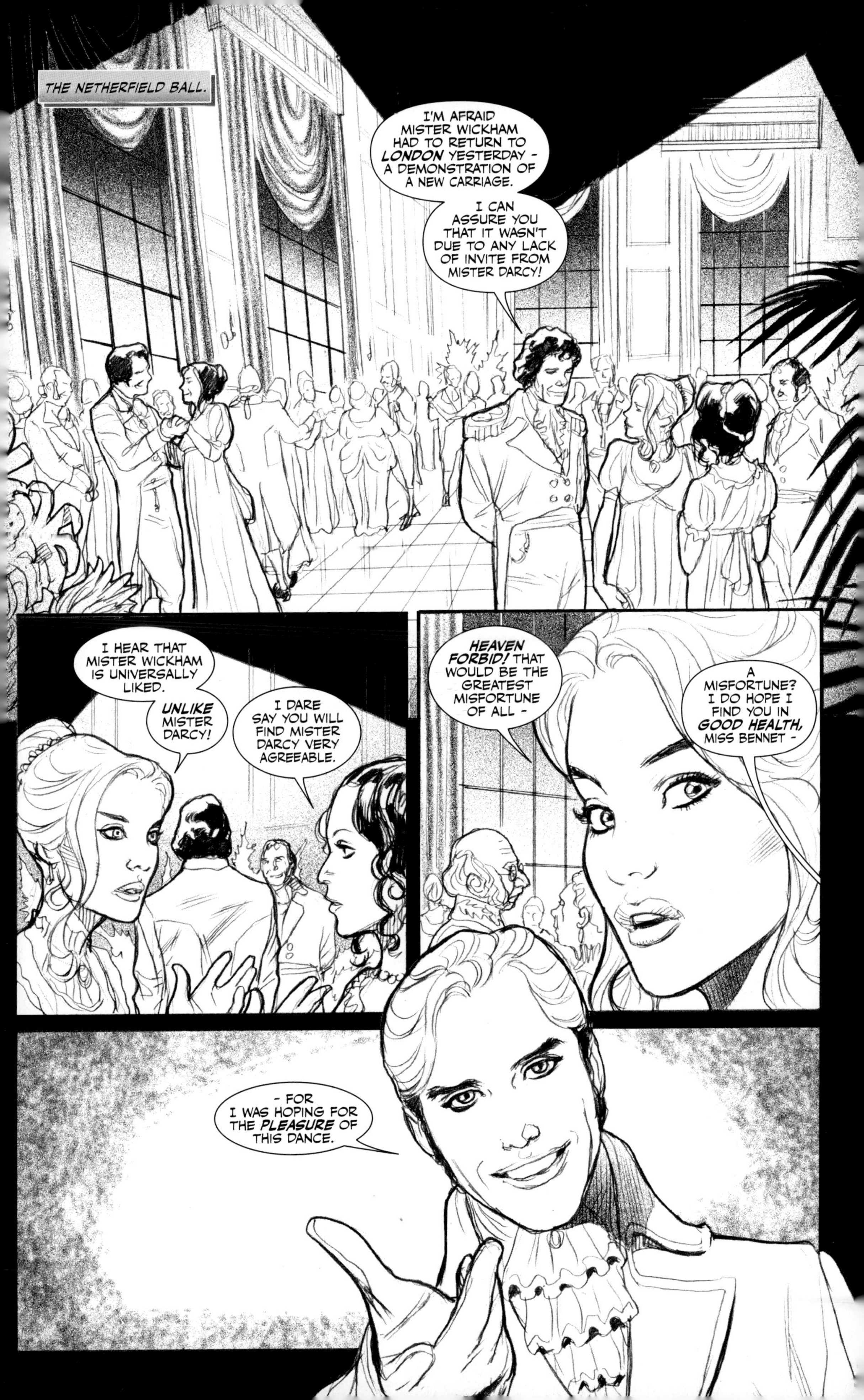
THE NETHERFIELD BALL.
I'M AFRAID MISTER WICKHAM HAD TO RETURN TO LONDON YESTERDAY - A DEMONSTRATION OF A NEW CARRIAGE.
I CAN ASSURE YOU THAT IT WASN'T DUE TO ANY LACK OF INVITE FROM MISTER DARCY!
I HEAR THAT MISTER WICKHAM IS UNIVERSALLY LIKED.
UNLIKE MISTER DARCY!
I DARE SAY YOU WILL FIND MISTER DARCY VERY AGREEABLE.
HEAVEN FORBID! THAT WOULD BE THE GREATEST MISFORTUNE OF ALL -
A MISFORTUNE? I DO HOPE I FIND YOU IN GOOD HEALTH, MISS BENNET -
- FOR I WAS HOPING FOR THE PLEASURE OF THIS DANCE.

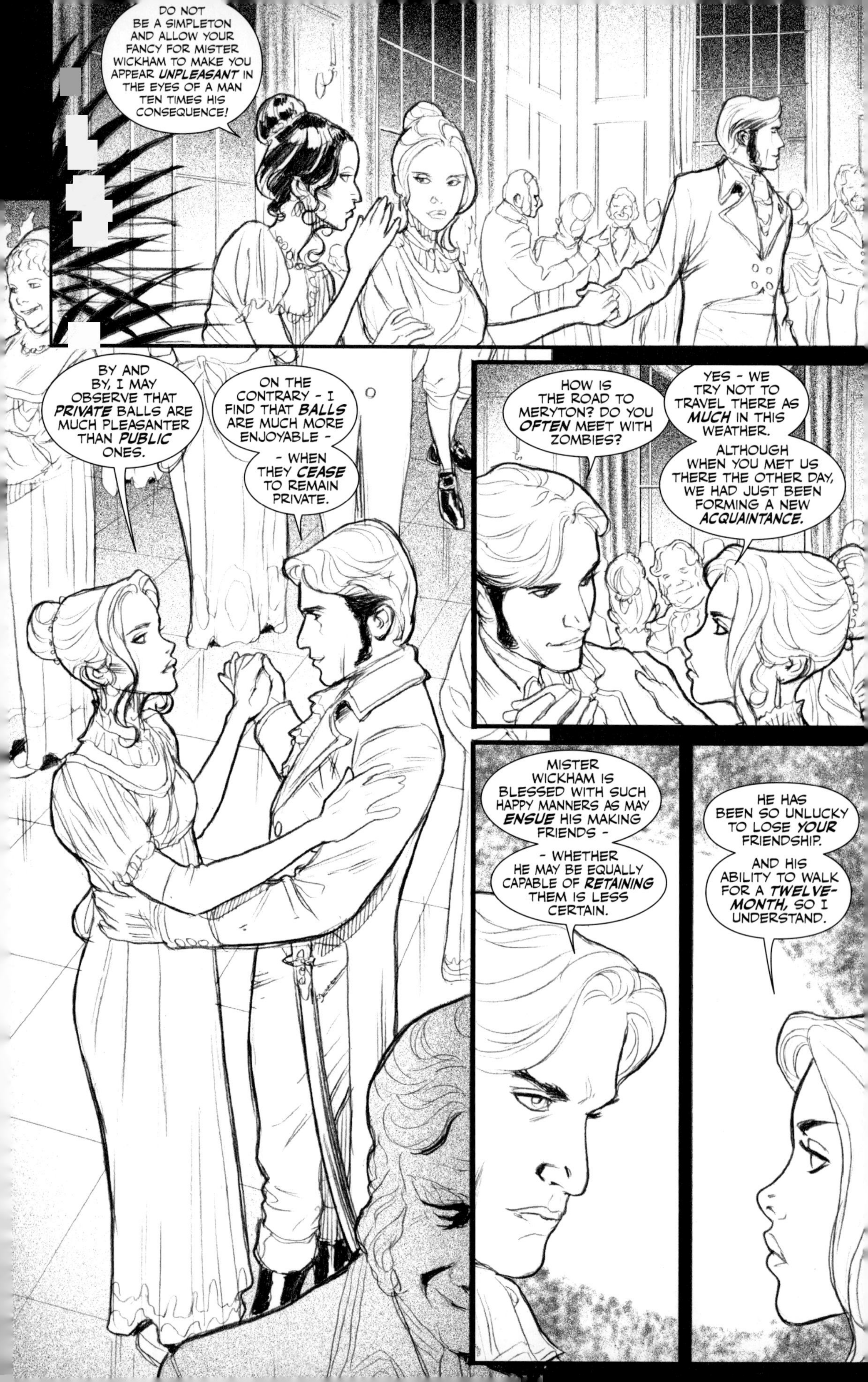
DO NOT BE A SIMPLETON AND ALLOW YOUR FANCY FOR MISTER WICKHAM TO MAKE YOU APPEAR UNPLEASANT IN THE EYES OF A MAN TEN TIMES HIS CONSEQUENCE!
BY AND BY, I MAY OBSERVE THAT PRIVATE BALLS ARE MUCH PLEASANTER THAN PUBLIC ONES.
ON THE CONTRARY - I FIND THAT BALLS ARE MUCH MORE ENJOYABLE -
- WHEN THEY CEASE TO REMAIN PRIVATE.
HOW IS THE ROAD TO MERYTON? DO YOU OFTEN MEET WITH ZOMBIES?
YES - WE TRY NOT TO TRAVEL THERE AS MUCH IN THIS WEATHER.
ALTHOUGH WHEN YOU MET US THERE THE OTHER DAY, WE HAD JUST BEEN FORMING A NEW ACQUAINTANCE.
MISTER WICKHAM IS BLESSED WITH SUCH HAPPY MANNERS AS MAY ENSUE HIS MAKING FRIENDS -
- WHETHER HE MAY BE EQUALLY CAPABLE OF RETAINING THEM IS LESS CERTAIN.
HE HAS BEEN SO UNLUCKY TO LOSE YOUR FRIENDSHIP.
AND HIS ABILITY TO WALK FOR A TWELVE-MONTH, SO I UNDERSTAND.

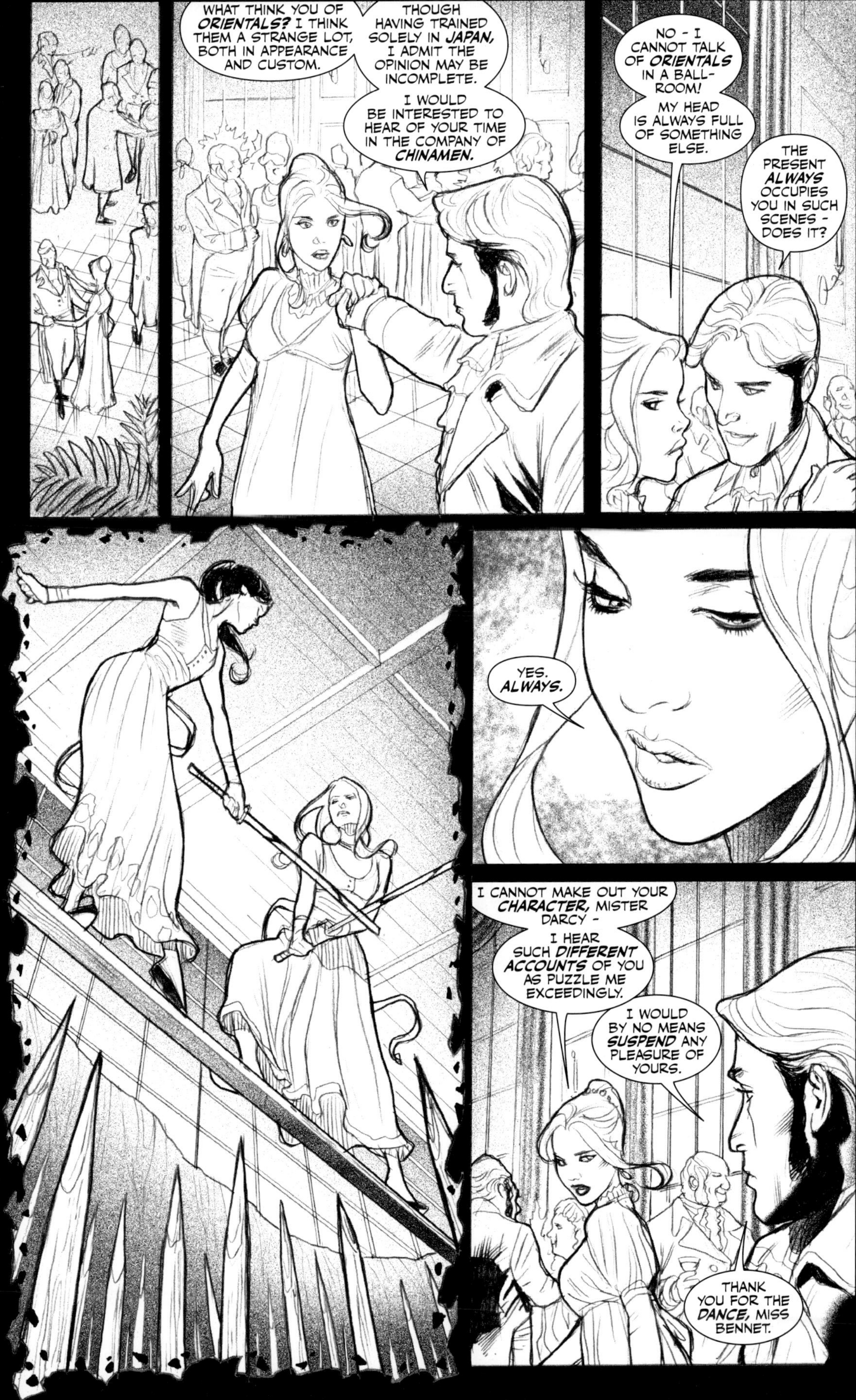
WHAT THINK YOU OF ORIENTALS? I THINK THEM A STRANGE LOT, BOTH IN APPEARANCE AND CUSTOM.
THOUGH HAVING TRAINED SOLELY IN JAPAN, I ADMIT THE OPINION MAY BE INCOMPLETE.
I WOULD BE INTERESTED TO HEAR OF YOUR TIME IN THE COMPANY OF CHINAMEN.
NO - I CANNOT TALK OF ORIENTALS IN A BALL-ROOM!
MY HEAD IS ALWAYS FULL OF SOMETHING ELSE.
THE PRESENT ALWAYS OCCUPIES YOU IN SUCH SCENES - DOES IT?
YES. ALWAYS.
I CANNOT MAKE OUT YOUR CHARACTER, MISTER DARCY -
I HEAR SUCH DIFFERENT ACCOUNTS OF YOU AS PUZZLE ME EXCEEDINGLY.
I WOULD BY NO MEANS SUSPEND ANY PLEASURE OF YOURS.
THANK YOU FOR THE DANCE, MISS BENNET.

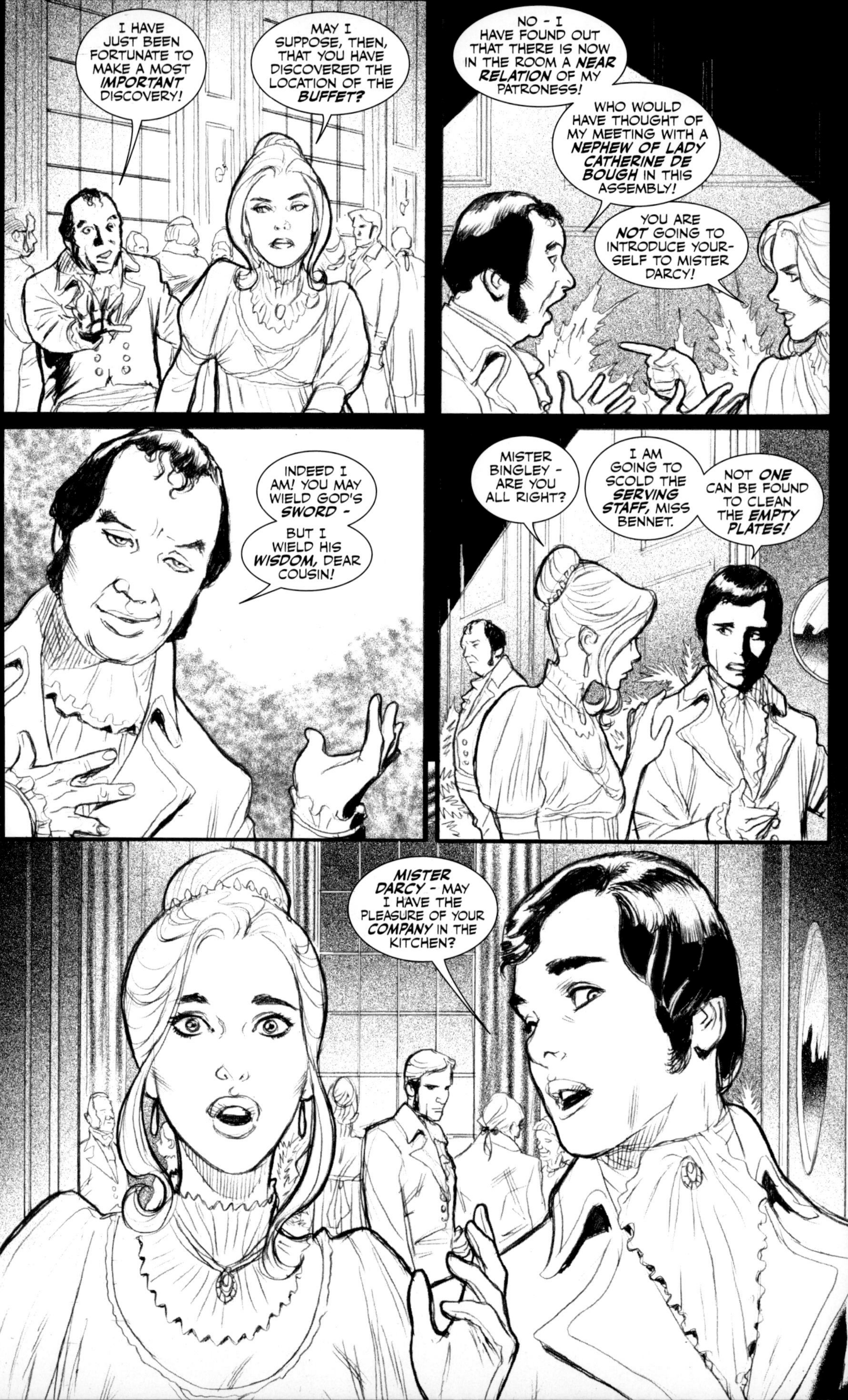
I HAVE JUST BEEN FORTUNATE TO MAKE A MOST IMPORTANT DISCOVERY!
MAY I SUPPOSE, THEN, THAT YOU HAVE DISCOVERED THE LOCATION OF THE BUFFET?
NO - I HAVE FOUND OUT THAT THERE IS NOW IN THE ROOM A NEAR RELATION OF MY PATRONESS!
WHO WOULD HAVE THOUGHT OF MY MEETING WITH A NEPHEW OF LADY CATHERINE DE BOUGH IN THIS ASSEMBLY!
YOU ARE NOT GOING TO INTRODUCE YOURSELF TO MISTER DARCY!
INDEED I AM! YOU MAY WIELD GOD'S SWORD -
BUT I WIELD HIS WISDOM, DEAR COUSIN!
MISTER BINGLEY - ARE YOU ALL RIGHT?
I AM GOING TO SCOLD THE SERVING STAFF, MISS BENNET.
NOT ONE CAN BE FOUND TO CLEAN THE EMPTY PLATES!
MISTER DARCY - MAY I HAVE THE PLEASURE OF YOUR COMPANY IN THE KITCHEN?

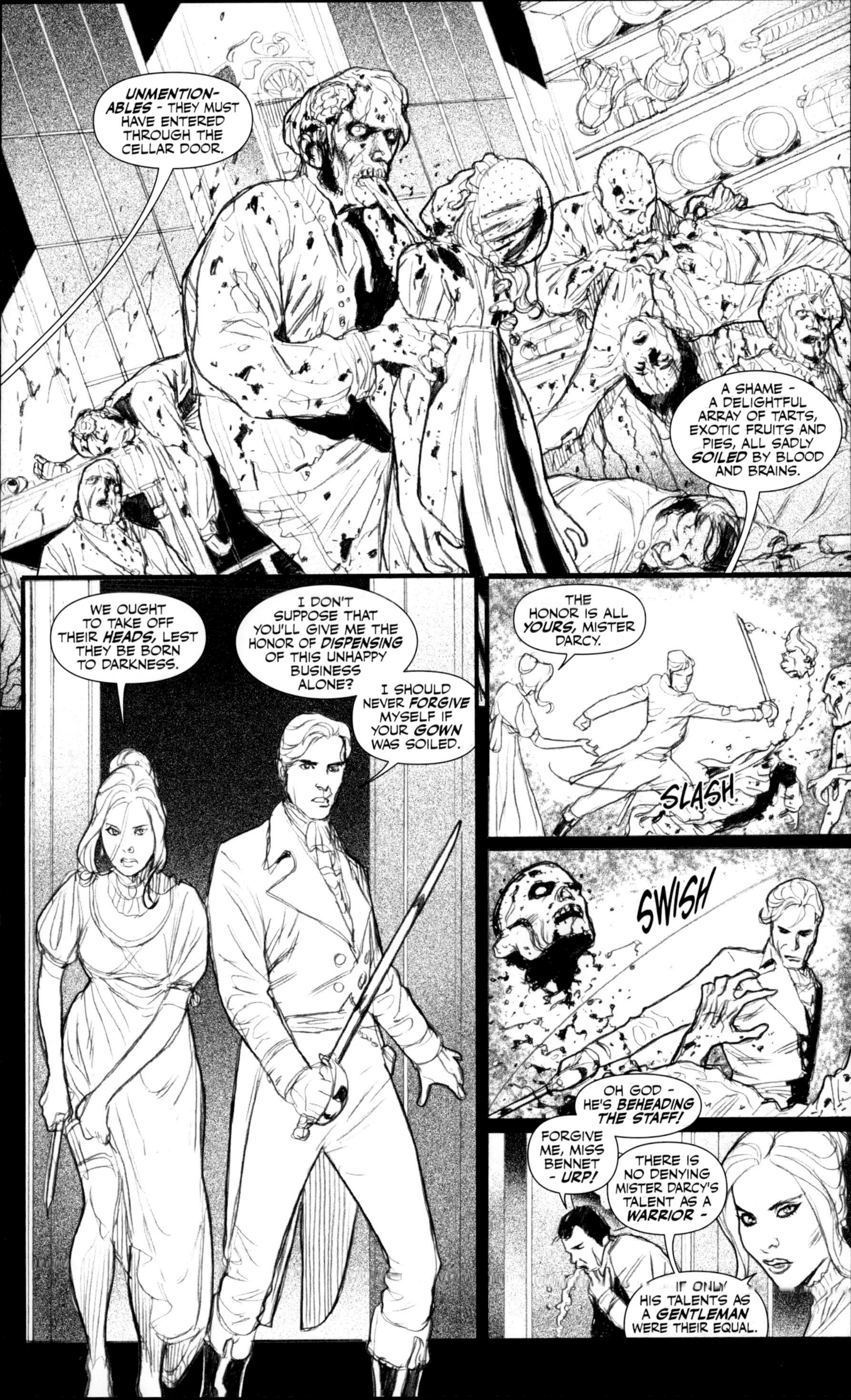
UNMENTIONABLES - THEY MUST HAVE ENTERED THROUGH THE CELLAR DOOR.
A SHAME - A DELIGHTFUL ARRAY OF TARTS, EXOTIC FRUITS AND PIES, ALL SADLY SOILED BY BLOOD AND BRAINS.
WE OUGHT TO TAKE OFF THEIR HEADS, LEST THEY BE BORN TO DARKNESS.
I DON'T SUPPOSE THAT YOU'LL GIVE ME THE HONOR OF DISPENSING OF THIS UNHAPPY BUSINESS ALONE?
I SHOULD NEVER FORGIVE MYSELF IF YOUR GOWN WAS SOILED.
THE HONOR IS ALL YOURS, MISTER DARCY.
SLASH
SWISH
OH GOD - HE'S BEHEADING THE STAFF!
FORGIVE ME, MISS BENNET - URP!
THERE IS NO DENYING MISTER DARCY'S TALENT AS A WARRIOR -
IF ONLY HIS TALENTS AS A GENTLEMAN WERE THEIR EQUAL.

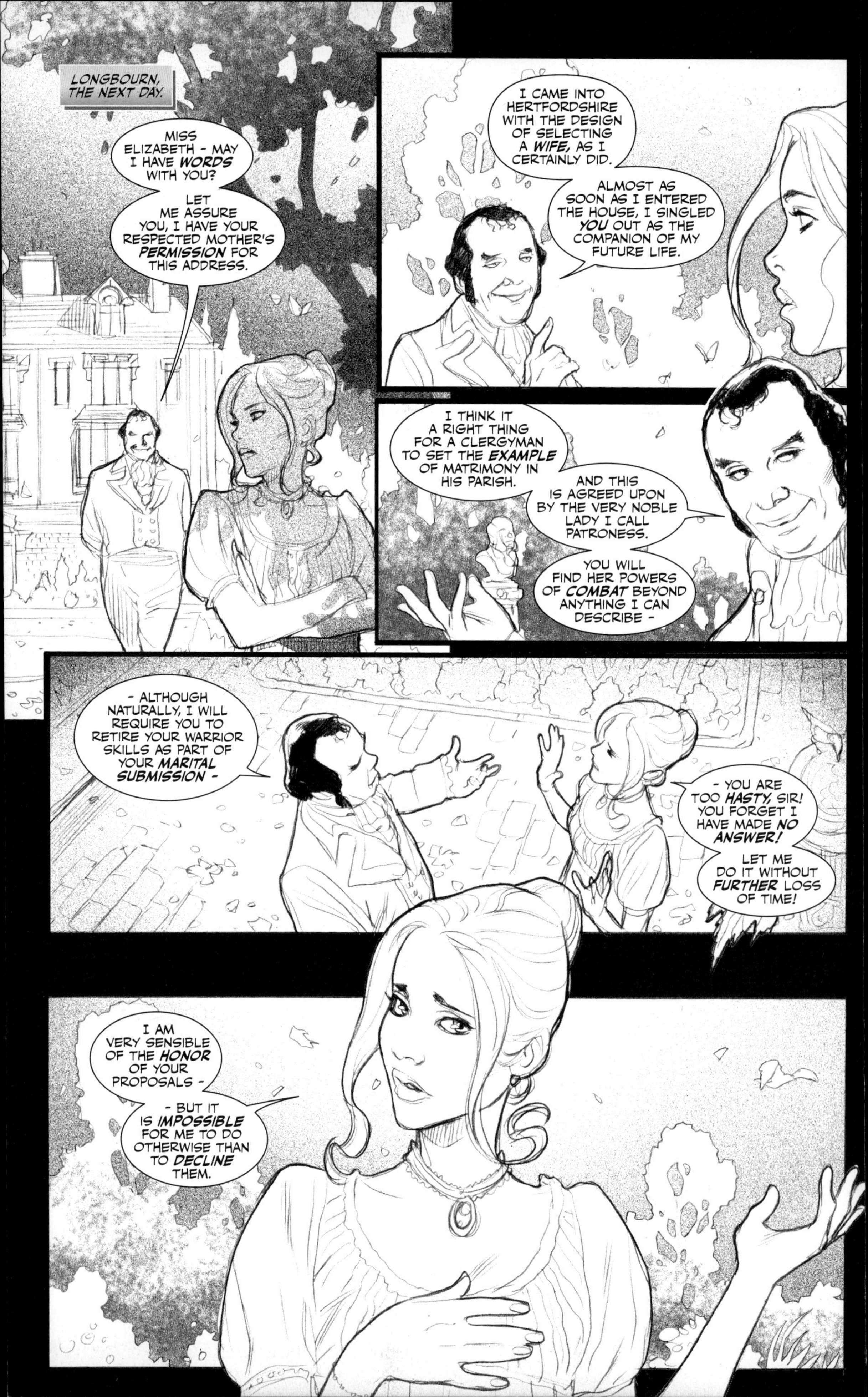
LONGBOURN, THE NEXT DAY.
MISS ELIZABETH - MAY I HAVE WORDS WITH YOU?
LET ME ASSURE YOU, I HAVE YOUR RESPECTED MOTHER'S PERMISSION FOR THIS ADDRESS.
I CAME INTO HERTFORDSHIRE WITH THE DESIGN OF SELECTING A WIFE, AS I CERTAINLY DID.
ALMOST AS SOON AS I ENTERED THE HOUSE, I SINGLED YOU OUT AS THE COMPANION OF MY FUTURE LIFE.
I THINK IT A RIGHT THING FOR A CLERGYMAN TO SET THE EXAMPLE OF MATRIMONY IN HIS PARISH.
AND THIS IS AGREED UPON BY THE VERY NOBLE LADY I CALL PATRONESS.
YOU WILL FIND HER POWERS OF COMBAT BEYOND ANYTHING I CAN DESCRIBE -
- ALTHOUGH NATURALLY, I WILL REQUIRE YOU TO RETIRE YOUR WARRIOR SKILLS AS PART OF YOUR MARITAL SUBMISSION -
- YOU ARE TOO HASTY, SIR! YOU FORGET I HAVE MADE NO ANSWER!
LET ME DO IT WITHOUT FURTHER LOSS OF TIME!
I AM VERY SENSIBLE OF THE HONOR OF YOUR PROPOSALS -
- BUT IT IS IMPOSSIBLE FOR ME TO DO OTHERWISE THAN TO DECLINE THEM.

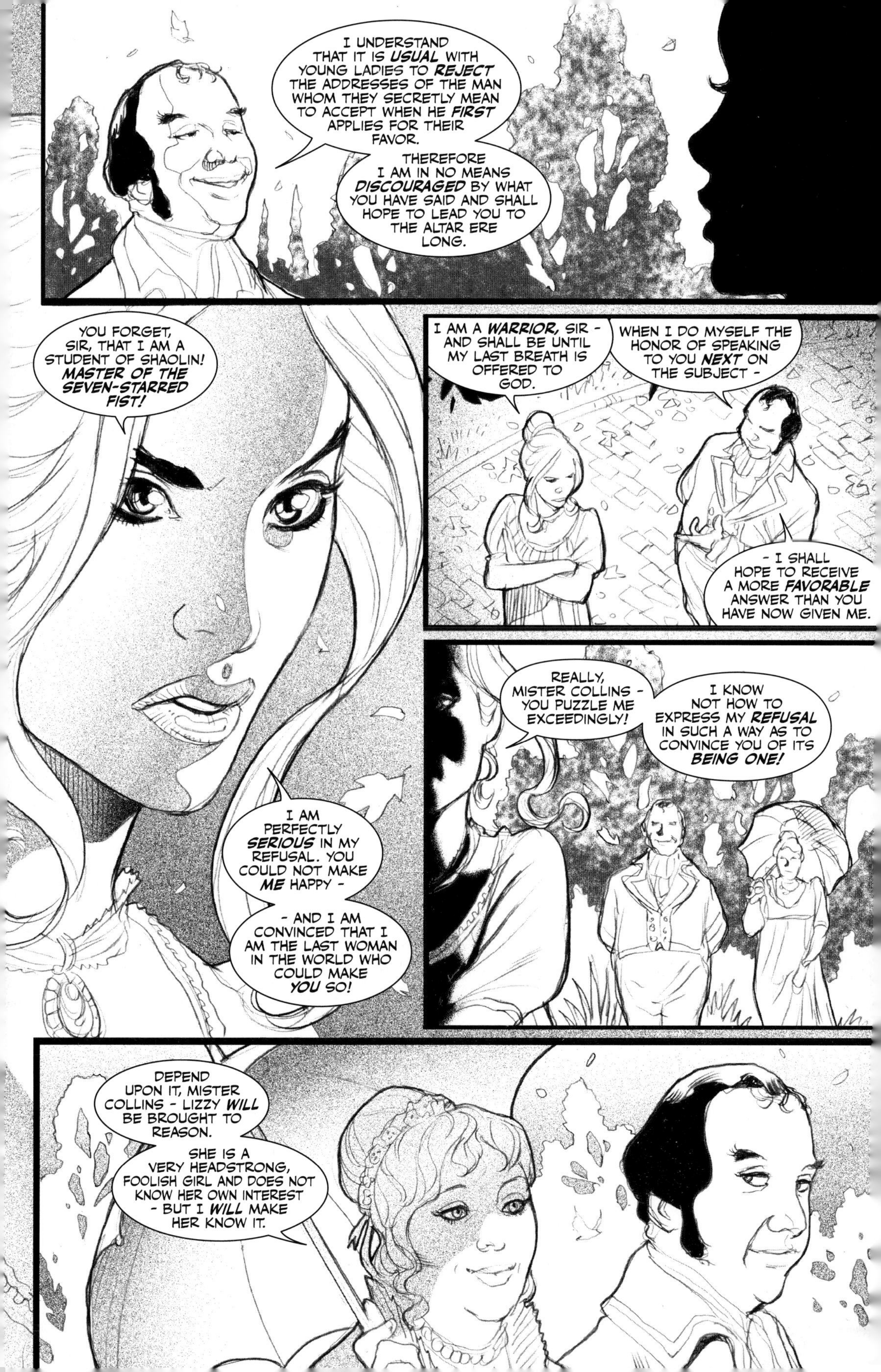
I UNDERSTAND THAT IT IS USUAL WITH YOUNG LADIES TO REJECT THE ADDRESSES OF THE MAN WHOM THEY SECRETLY MEAN TO ACCEPT WHEN HE FIRST APPLIES FOR THEIR FAVOR.
THEREFORE I AM IN NO MEANS DISCOURAGED BY WHAT YOU HAVE SAID AND SHALL HOPE TO LEAD YOU TO THE ALTAR ERE LONG.
YOU FORGET, SIR, THAT I AM A STUDENT OF SHAOLIN! MASTER OF THE SEVEN-STARRED FIST!
I AM A WARRIOR, SIR - AND SHALL BE UNTIL MY LAST BREATH IS OFFERED TO GOD.
WHEN I DO MYSELF THE HONOR OF SPEAKING TO YOU NEXT ON THE SUBJECT -
- I SHALL HOPE TO RECEIVE A MORE FAVORABLE ANSWER THAN YOU HAVE NOW GIVEN ME.
I AM PERFECTLY SERIOUS IN MY REFUSAL. YOU COULD NOT MAKE ME HAPPY -
- AND I AM CONVINCED THAT I AM THE LAST WOMAN IN THE WORLD WHO COULD MAKE YOU SO!
REALLY, MISTER COLLINS - YOU PUZZLE ME EXCEEDINGLY!
I KNOW NOT HOW TO EXPRESS MY REFUSAL IN SUCH A WAY AS TO CONVINCE YOU OF ITS BEING ONE!
DEPEND UPON IT, MISTER COLLINS - LIZZY WILL BE BROUGHT TO REASON.
SHE IS A VERY HEADSTRONG, FOOLISH GIRL AND DOES NOT KNOW HER OWN INTEREST - BUT I WILL MAKE HER KNOW IT.

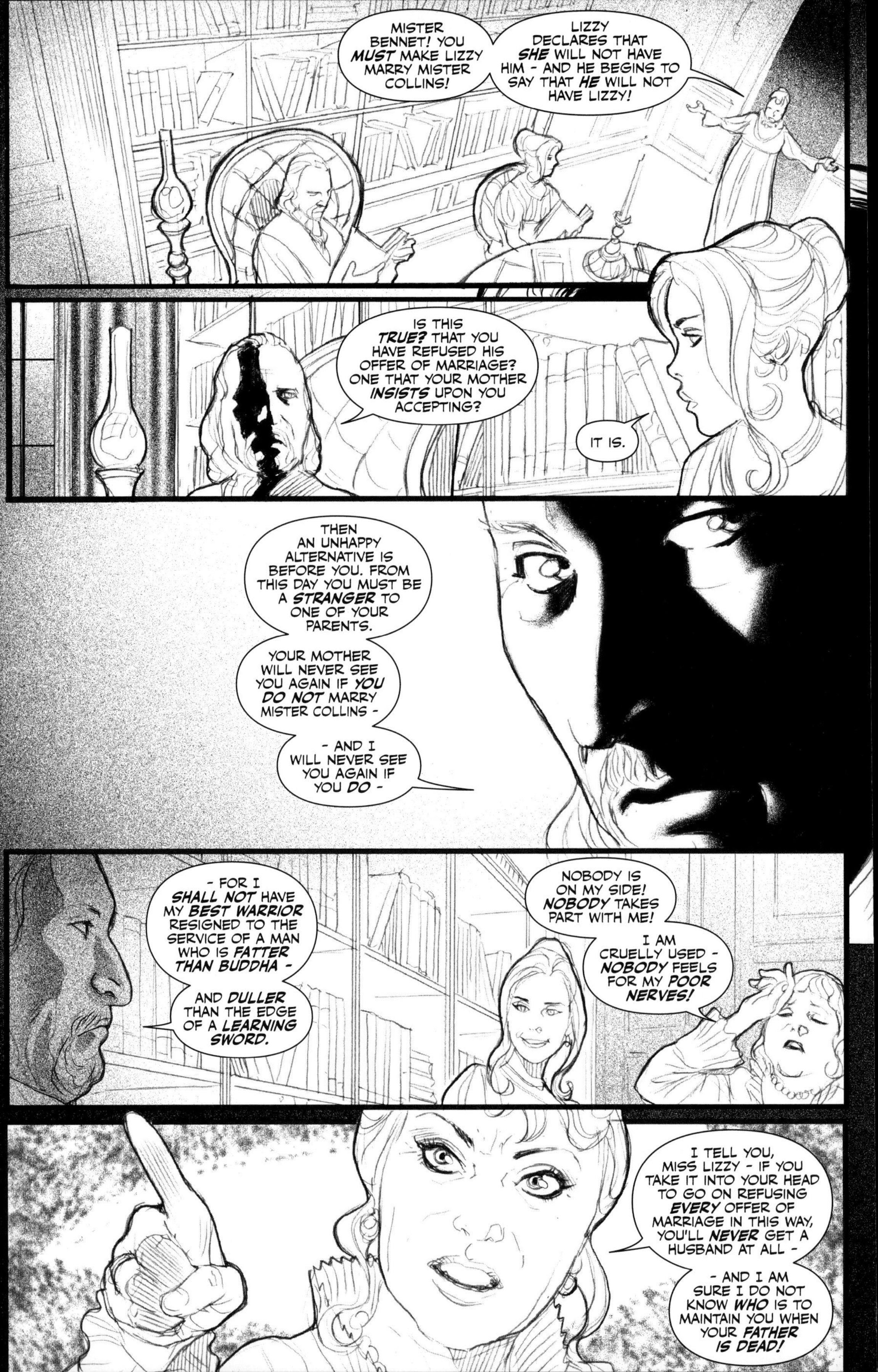
MISTER BENNET! YOU MUST MAKE LIZZY MARRY MISTER COLLINS!
LIZZY DECLARES THAT SHE WILL NOT HAVE HIM - AND HE BEGINS TO SAY THAT HE WILL NOT HAVE LIZZY!
IS THIS TRUE? THAT YOU HAVE REFUSED HIS OFFER OF MARRIAGE? ONE THAT YOUR MOTHER INSISTS UPON YOU ACCEPTING?
IT IS.
THEN AN UNHAPPY ALTERNATIVE IS BEFORE YOU. FROM THIS DAY YOU MUST BE A STRANGER TO ONE OF YOUR PARENTS.
YOUR MOTHER WILL NEVER SEE YOU AGAIN IF YOU DO NOT MARRY MISTER COLLINS -
- AND I WILL NEVER SEE YOU AGAIN IF YOU DO -
- FOR I SHALL NOT HAVE MY BEST WARRIOR RESIGNED TO THE SERVICE OF A MAN WHO IS FATTER THAN BUDDHA -
AND DULLER THAN THE EDGE OF A LEARNING SWORD.
NOBODY IS ON MY SIDE! NOBODY TAKES PART WITH ME!
I AM CRUELLY USED - NOBODY FEELS FOR MY POOR NERVES!
I TELL YOU, MISS LIZZY - IF YOU TAKE IT INTO YOUR HEAD TO GO ON REFUSING EVERY OFFER OF MARRIAGE IN THIS WAY, YOU'LL NEVER GET A HUSBAND AT ALL -
- AND I AM SURE I DO NOT KNOW WHO IS TO MAINTAIN YOU WHEN YOUR FATHER IS DEAD!

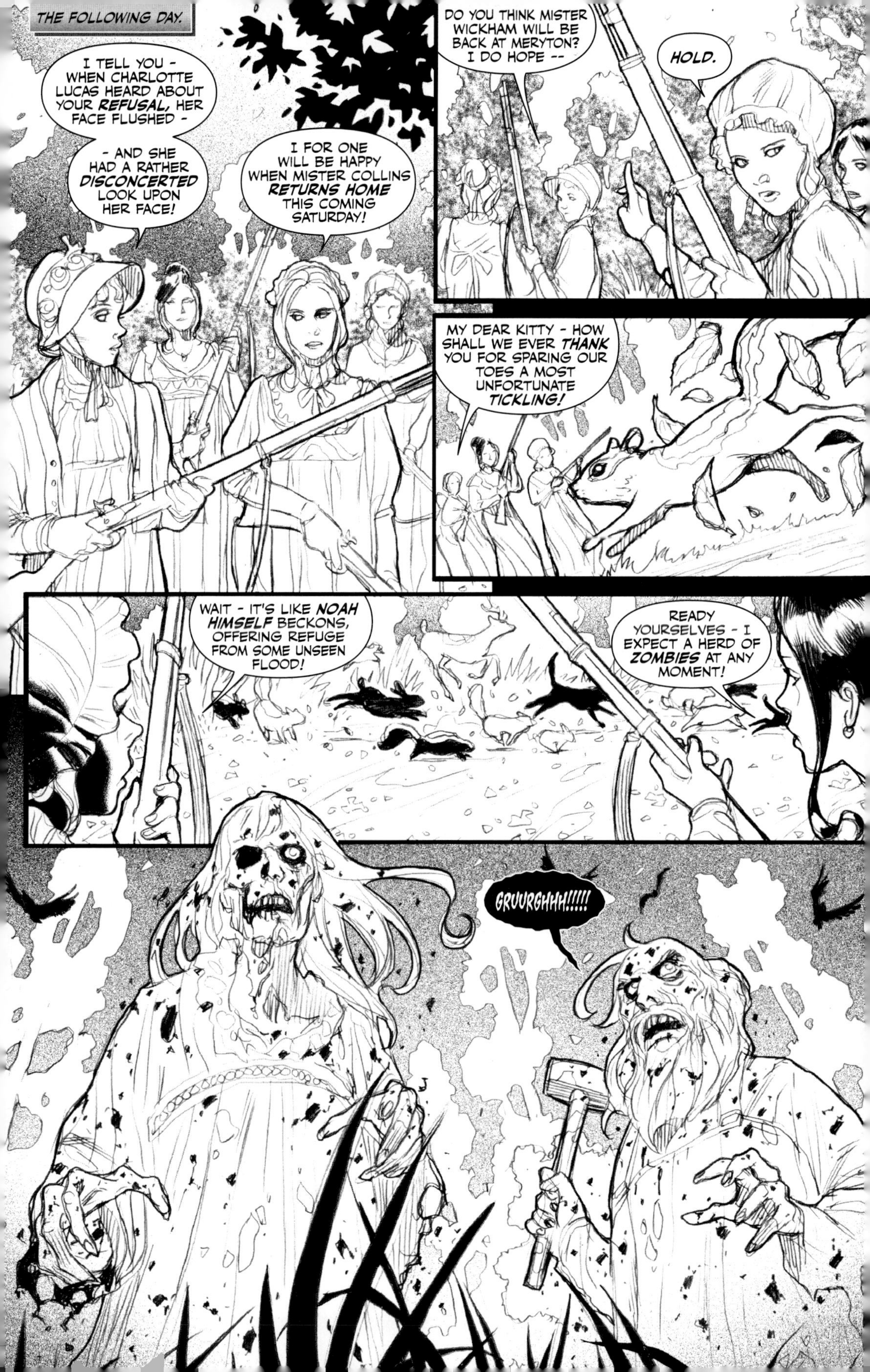
THE FOLLOWING DAY.
I TELL YOU - WHEN CHARLOTTE LUCAS HEARD ABOUT YOUR REFUSAL, HER FACE FLUSHED -
- AND SHE HAD A RATHER DISCONCERTED LOOK UPON HER FACE!
I FOR ONE WILL BE HAPPY WHEN MISTER COLLINS RETURNS HOME THIS COMING SATURDAY!
DO YOU THINK MISTER WICKHAM WILL BE BACK AT MERYTON? I DO HOPE --
HOLD.
MY DEAR KITTY - HOW SHALL WE EVER THANK YOU FOR SPARING OUR TOES A MOST UNFORTUNATE TICKLING!
WAIT - IT'S LIKE NOAH HIMSELF BECKONS, OFFERING REFUGE FROM SOME UNSEEN FLOOD!
READY YOURSELVES - I EXPECT A HERD OF ZOMBIES AT ANY MOMENT!
GRUURGHHH!!!!!

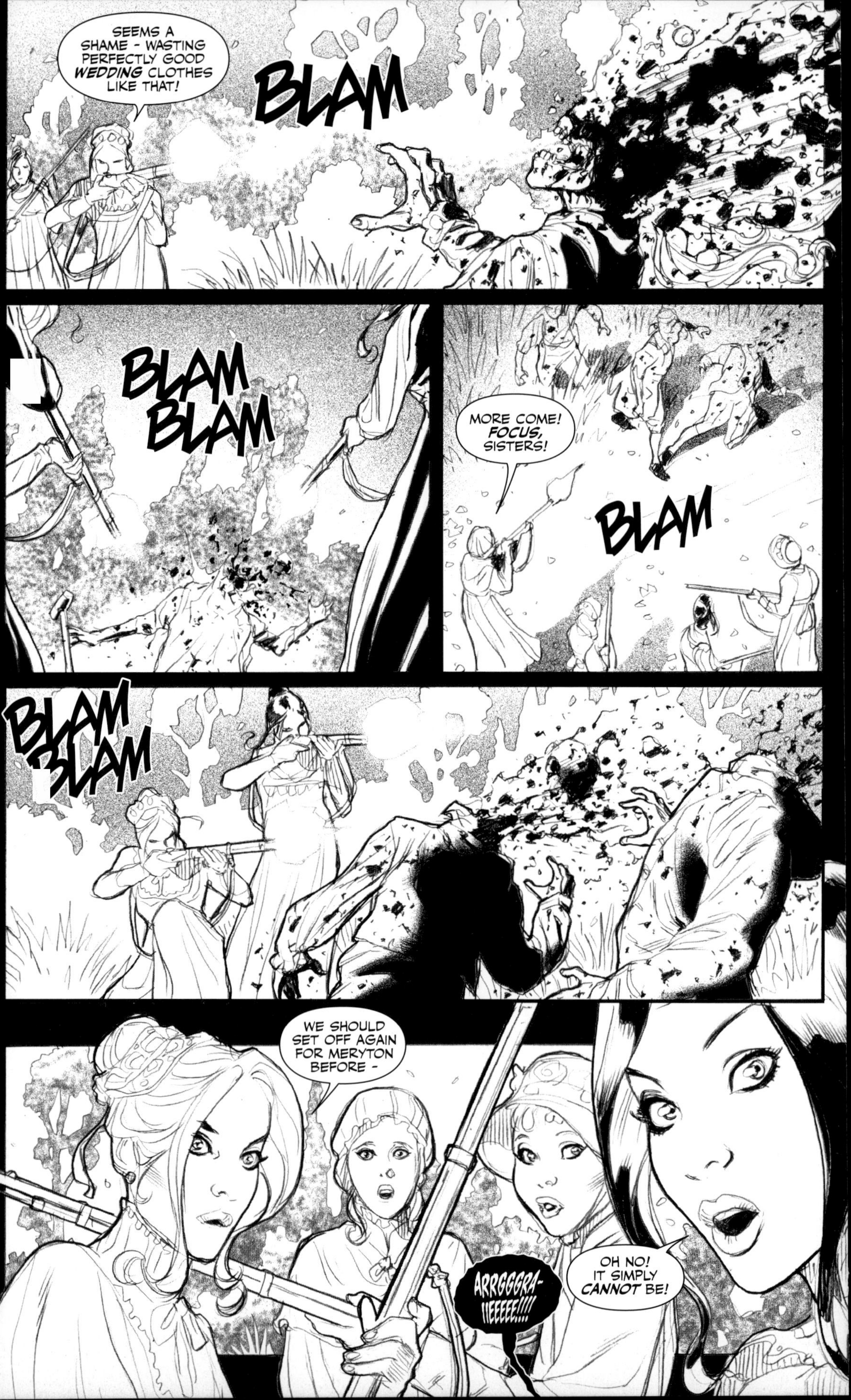
SEEMS A SHAME - WASTING PERFECTLY GOOD WEDDING CLOTHES LIKE THAT!
BLAM
BLAM BLAM
MORE COME! FOCUS, SISTERS!
BLAM
BLAM BLAM
WE SHOULD SET OFF AGAIN FOR MERYTON BEFORE -
ARRGGGRA-IIEEEEE!!!!
OH NO! IT SIMPLY CANNOT BE!

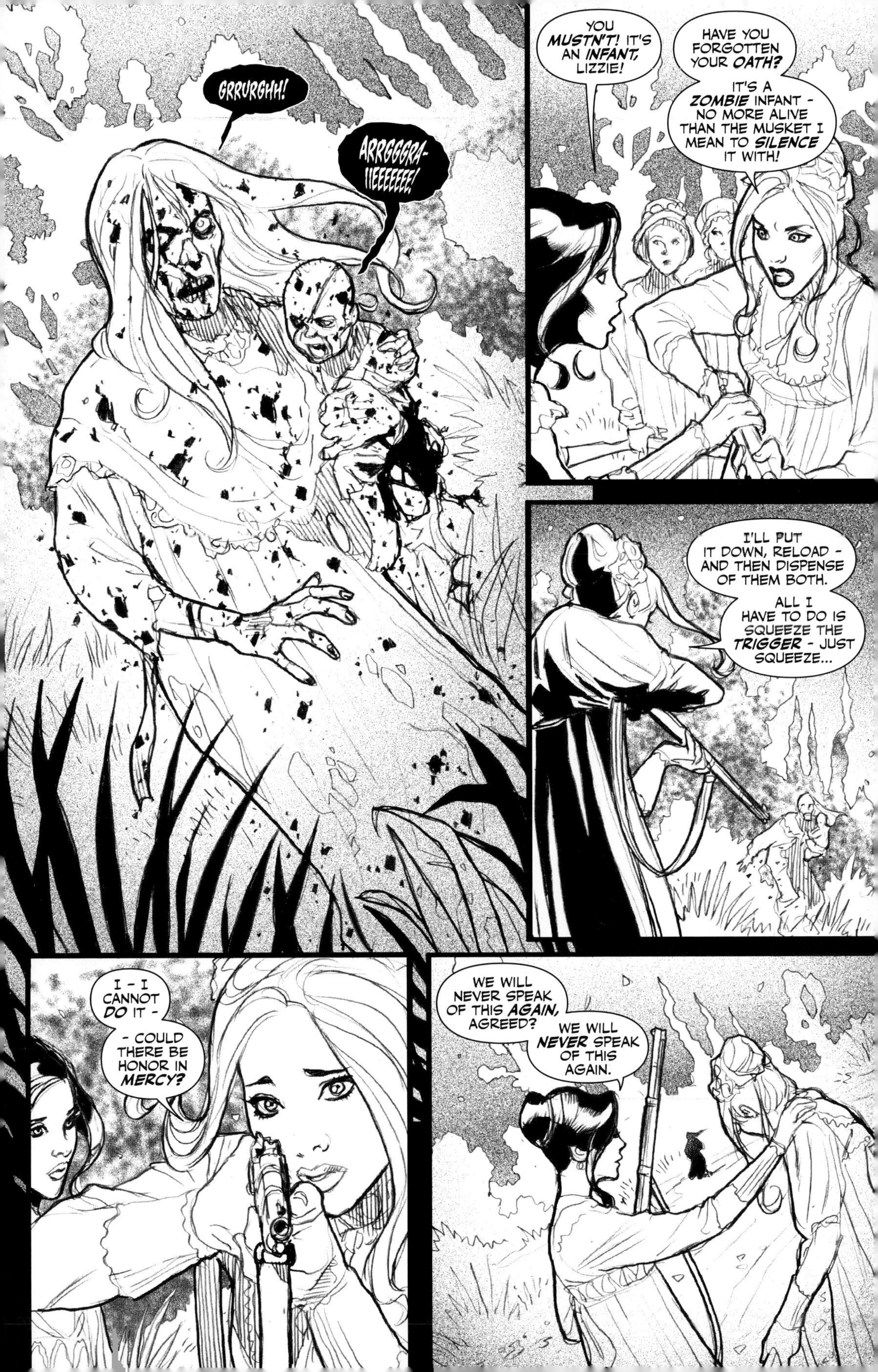
GRRURGHH!
ARRGGGRA-IIEEEEEEE!
YOU MUSTN'T! IT'S AN INFANT, LIZZIE!
HAVE YOU FORGOTTEN YOUR OATH?
IT'S A ZOMBIE INFANT - NO MORE ALIVE THAN THE MUSKET I MEAN TO SILENCE IT WITH!
I'LL PUT IT DOWN, RELOAD - AND THEN DISPENSE OF THEM BOTH.
ALL I HAVE TO DO IS SQUEEZE THE TRIGGER - JUST SQUEEZE...
I - I CANNOT DO IT -
- COULD THERE BE HONOR IN MERCY?
WE WILL NEVER SPEAK OF THIS AGAIN, AGREED?
WE WILL NEVER SPEAK OF THIS AGAIN.

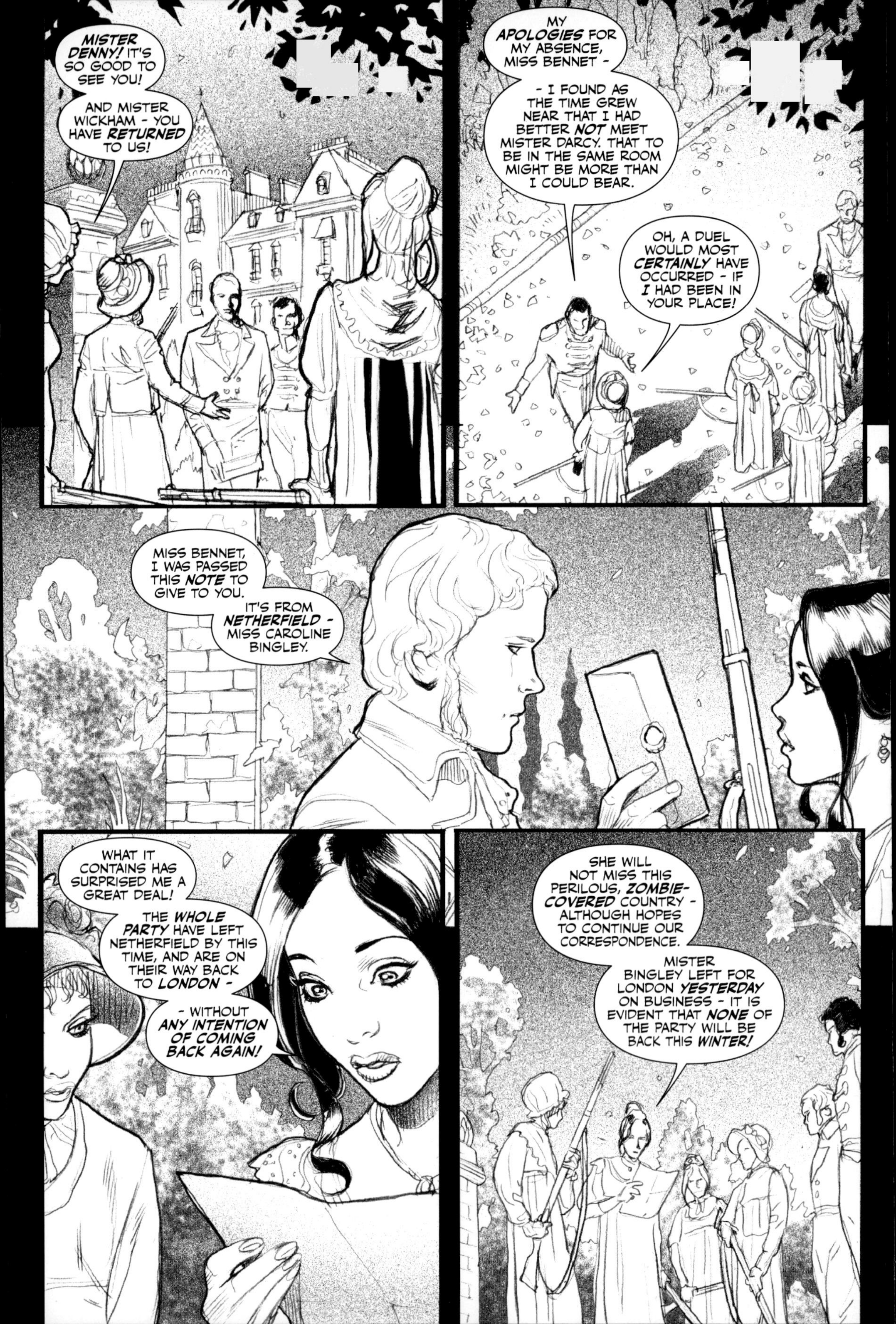
MISTER DENNY! IT'S SO GOOD TO SEE YOU!
AND MISTER WICKHAM - YOU HAVE RETURNED TO US!
MY APOLOGIES FOR MY ABSENCE, MISS BENNET -
- I FOUND AS THE TIME GREW NEAR THAT I HAD BETTER NOT MEET MISTER DARCY. THAT TO BE IN THE SAME ROOM MIGHT BE MORE THAN I COULD BEAR.
OH, A DUEL WOULD MOST CERTAINLY HAVE OCCURRED - IF I HAD BEEN IN YOUR PLACE!
MISS BENNET, I WAS PASSED THIS NOTE TO GIVE TO YOU.
IT'S FROM NETHERFIELD - MISS CAROLINE BINGLEY.
WHAT IT CONTAINS HAS SURPRISED ME A GREAT DEAL!
THE WHOLE PARTY HAVE LEFT NETHERFIELD BY THIS TIME, AND ARE ON THEIR WAY BACK TO LONDON -
- WITHOUT ANY INTENTION OF COMING BACK AGAIN!
SHE WILL NOT MISS THIS PERILOUS, ZOMBIE-COVERED COUNTRY - ALTHOUGH HOPES TO CONTINUE OUR CORRESPONDENCE.
MISTER BINGLEY LEFT FOR LONDON YESTERDAY ON BUSINESS - IT IS EVIDENT THAT NONE OF THE PARTY WILL BE BACK THIS WINTER!

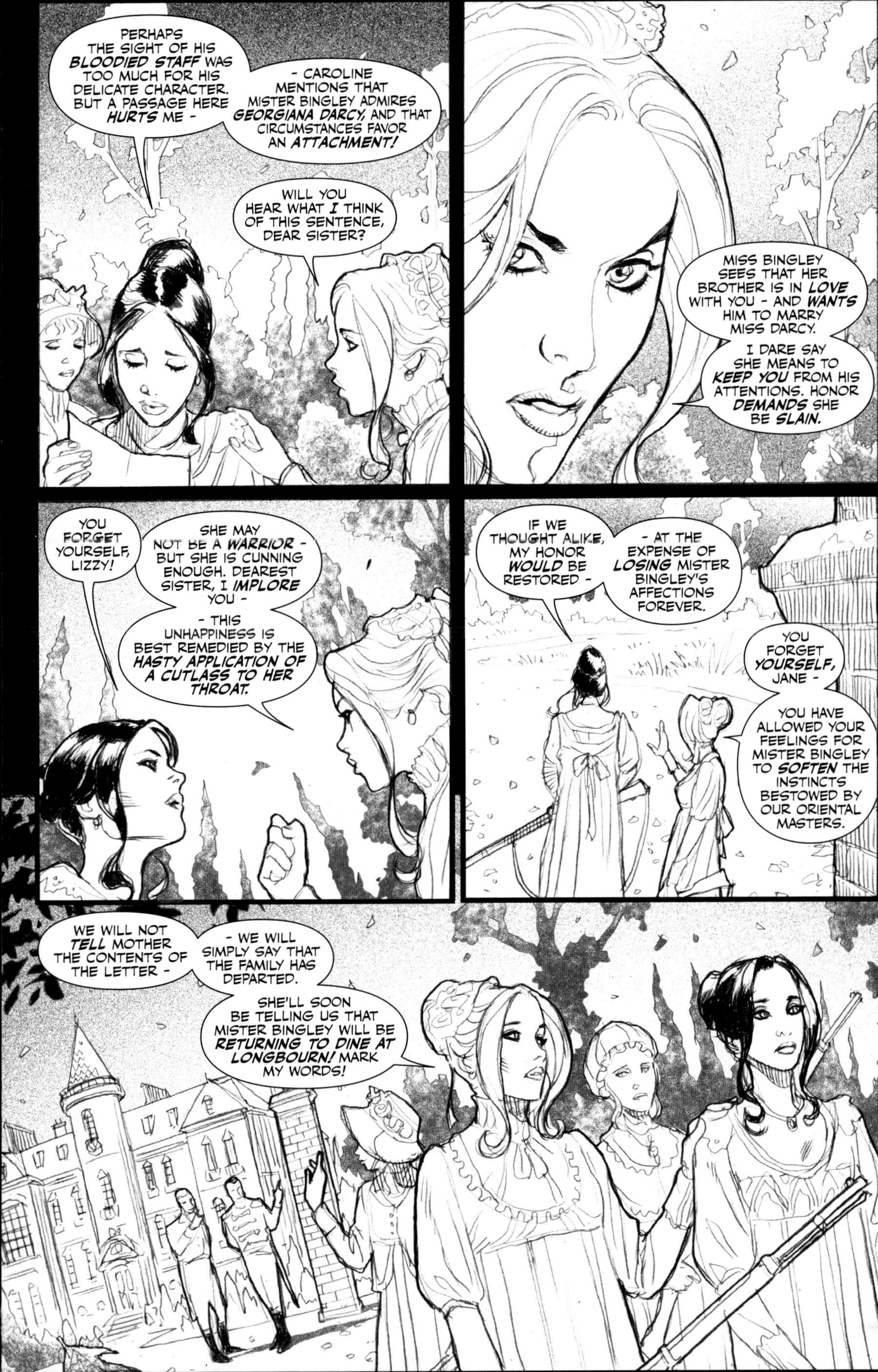
PERHAPS THE SIGHT OF HIS BLOODIED STAFF WAS TOO MUCH FOR HIS DELICATE CHARACTER. BUT A PASSAGE HERE HURTS ME -
- CAROLINE MENTIONS THAT MISTER BINGLEY ADMIRES GEORGIANA DARCY, AND THAT CIRCUMSTANCES FAVOR AN ATTACHMENT!
WILL YOU HEAR WHAT I THINK OF THIS SENTENCE, DEAR SISTER?
MISS BINGLEY SEES THAT HER BROTHER IS IN LOVE WITH YOU - AND WANTS HIM TO MARRY MISS DARCY.
I DARE SAY SHE MEANS TO KEEP YOU FROM HIS ATTENTIONS. HONOR DEMANDS SHE BE SLAIN.
YOU FORGET YOURSELF, LIZZY!
SHE MAY NOT BE A WARRIOR - BUT SHE IS CUNNING ENOUGH. DEAREST SISTER, I IMPLORE YOU -
- THIS UNHAPPINESS IS BEST REMEDIED BY THE HASTY APPLICATION OF A CUTLASS TO HER THROAT.
IF WE THOUGHT ALIKE, MY HONOR WOULD BE RESTORED -
- AT THE EXPENSE OF LOSING MISTER BINGLEY'S AFFECTIONS FOREVER.
YOU FORGET YOURSELF, JANE -
YOU HAVE ALLOWED YOUR FEELINGS FOR MISTER BINGLEY TO SOFTEN THE INSTINCTS BESTOWED BY OUR ORIENTAL MASTERS.
WE WILL NOT TELL MOTHER THE CONTENTS OF THE LETTER -
- WE WILL SIMPLY SAY THAT THE FAMILY HAS DEPARTED.
SHE'LL SOON BE TELLING US THAT MISTER BINGLEY WILL BE RETURNING TO DINE AT LONGBOURN! MARK MY WORDS!

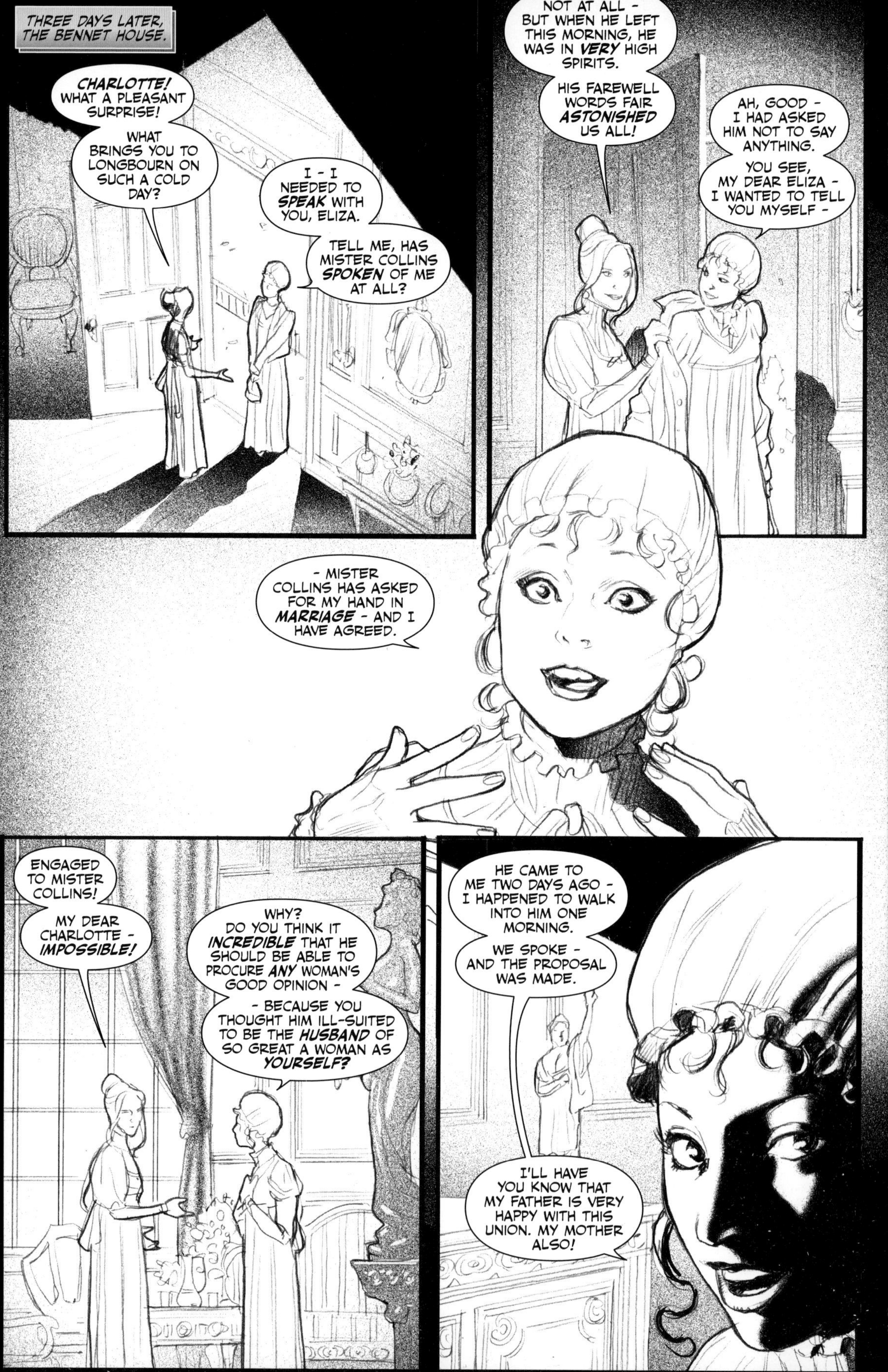
THREE DAYS LATER, THE BENNET HOUSE.
CHARLOTTE! WHAT A PLEASANT SURPRISE!
WHAT BRINGS YOU TO LONGBOURN ON SUCH A COLD DAY?
I - I NEEDED TO SPEAK WITH YOU, ELIZA.
TELL ME, HAS MISTER COLLINS SPOKEN OF ME AT ALL?
NOT AT ALL - BUT WHEN HE LEFT THIS MORNING, HE WAS IN VERY HIGH SPIRITS.
HIS FAREWELL WORDS FAIR ASTONISHED US ALL!
AH, GOOD - I HAD ASKED HIM NOT TO SAY ANYTHING.
YOU SEE, MY DEAR ELIZA - I WANTED TO TELL YOU MYSELF -
- MISTER COLLINS HAS ASKED FOR MY HAND IN MARRIAGE - AND I HAVE AGREED.
ENGAGED TO MISTER COLLINS!
MY DEAR CHARLOTTE - IMPOSSIBLE!
WHY? DO YOU THINK IT INCREDIBLE THAT HE SHOULD BE ABLE TO PROCURE ANY WOMAN'S GOOD OPINION -
- BECAUSE YOU THOUGHT HIM ILL-SUITED TO BE THE HUSBAND OF SO GREAT A WOMAN AS YOURSELF?
HE CAME TO ME TWO DAYS AGO - I HAPPENED TO WALK INTO HIM ONE MORNING.
WE SPOKE - AND THE PROPOSAL WAS MADE.
I'LL HAVE YOU KNOW THAT MY FATHER IS VERY HAPPY WITH THIS UNION. MY MOTHER ALSO!

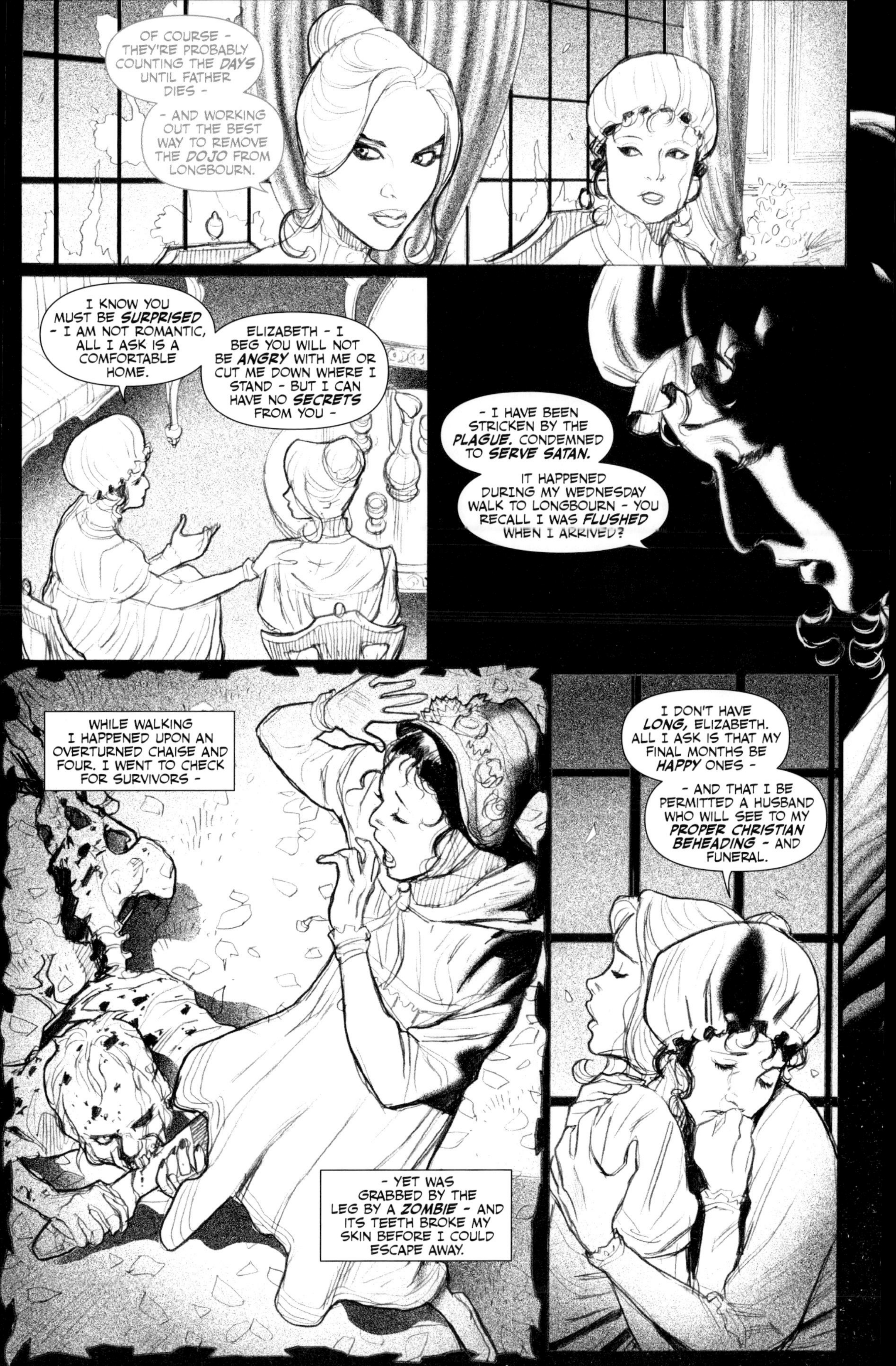
OF COURSE - THEY'RE PROBABLY COUNTING THE DAYS UNTIL FATHER DIES -
- AND WORKING OUT THE BEST WAY TO REMOVE THE DOJO FROM LONGBOURN.
I KNOW YOU MUST BE SURPRISED - I AM NOT ROMANTIC, ALL I ASK IS A COMFORTABLE HOME.
ELIZABETH - I BEG YOU WILL NOT BE ANGRY WITH ME OR CUT ME DOWN WHERE I STAND - BUT I CAN HAVE NO SECRETS FROM YOU -
- I HAVE BEEN STRICKEN BY THE PLAGUE. CONDEMNED TO SERVE SATAN.
IT HAPPENED DURING MY WEDNESDAY WALK TO LONGBOURN - YOU RECALL I WAS FLUSHED WHEN I ARRIVED?
WHILE WALKING I HAPPENED UPON AN OVERTURNED CHAISE AND FOUR. I WENT TO CHECK FOR SURVIVORS -
- YET WAS GRABBED BY THE LEG BY A ZOMBIE - AND ITS TEETH BROKE MY SKIN BEFORE I COULD ESCAPE AWAY.
I DON'T HAVE LONG, ELIZABETH. ALL I ASK IS THAT MY FINAL MONTHS BE HAPPY ONES -
- AND THAT I BE PERMITTED A HUSBAND WHO WILL SEE TO MY PROPER CHRISTIAN BEHEADING - AND FUNERAL.

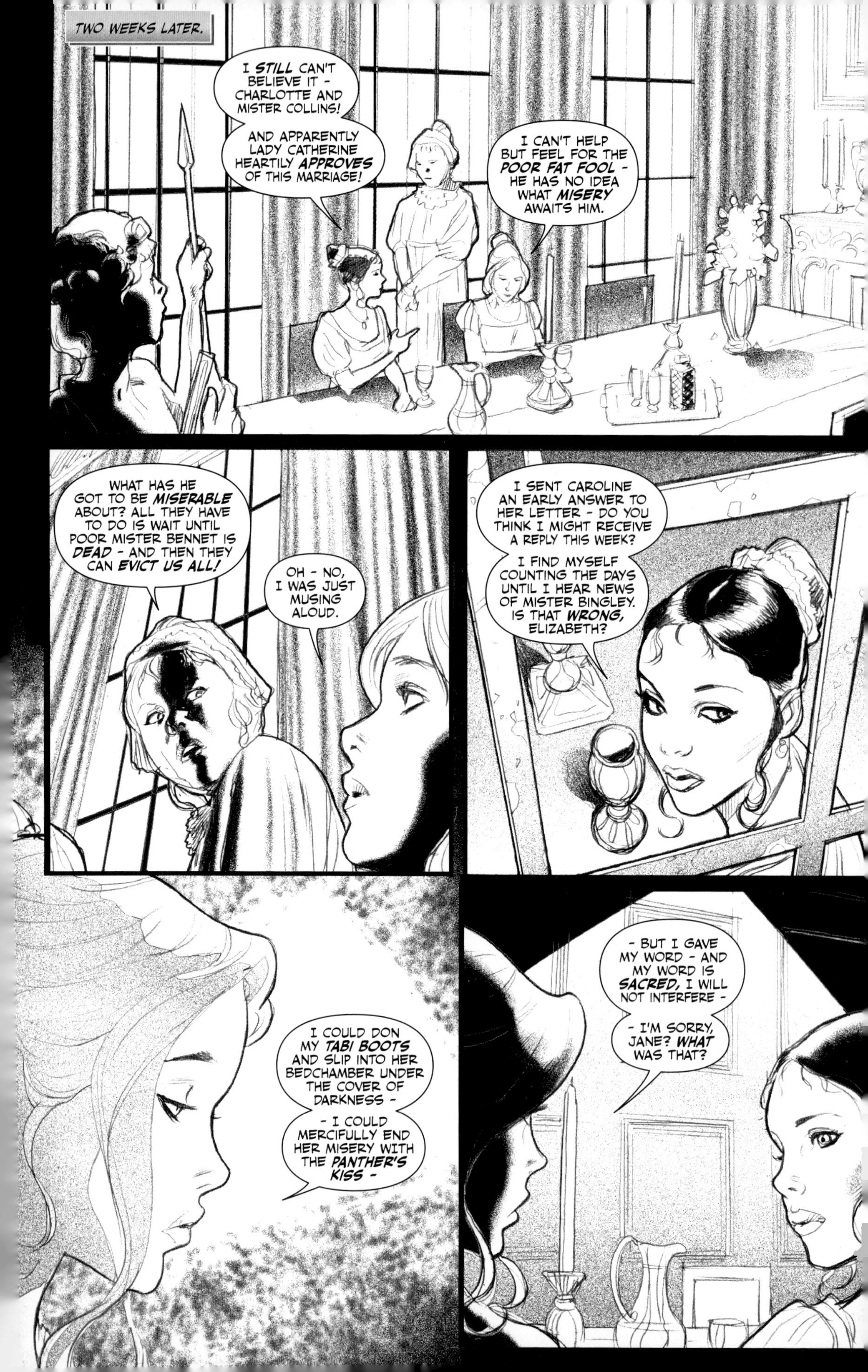
TWO WEEKS LATER.
I STILL CAN'T BELIEVE IT - CHARLOTTE AND MISTER COLLINS!
AND APPARENTLY LADY CATHERINE HEARTILY APPROVES OF THIS MARRIAGE!
I CAN'T HELP BUT FEEL FOR THE POOR FAT FOOL - HE HAS NO IDEA WHAT MISERY AWAITS HIM.
WHAT HAS HE GOT TO BE MISERABLE ABOUT? ALL THEY HAVE TO DO IS WAIT UNTIL POOR MISTER BENNET IS DEAD - AND THEN THEY CAN EVICT US ALL!
OH - NO, I WAS JUST MUSING ALOUD.
I SENT CAROLINE AN EARLY ANSWER TO HER LETTER - DO YOU THINK I MIGHT RECEIVE A REPLY THIS WEEK?
I FIND MYSELF COUNTING THE DAYS UNTIL I HEAR NEWS OF MISTER BINGLEY. IS THAT WRONG, ELIZABETH?
I COULD DON MY TABI BOOTS AND SLIP INTO HER BEDCHAMBER UNDER THE COVER OF DARKNESS -
- I COULD MERCIFULLY END HER MISERY WITH THE PANTHER'S KISS -
- BUT I GAVE MY WORD - AND MY WORD IS SACRED, I WILL NOT INTERFERE -
- I'M SORRY, JANE? WHAT WAS THAT?

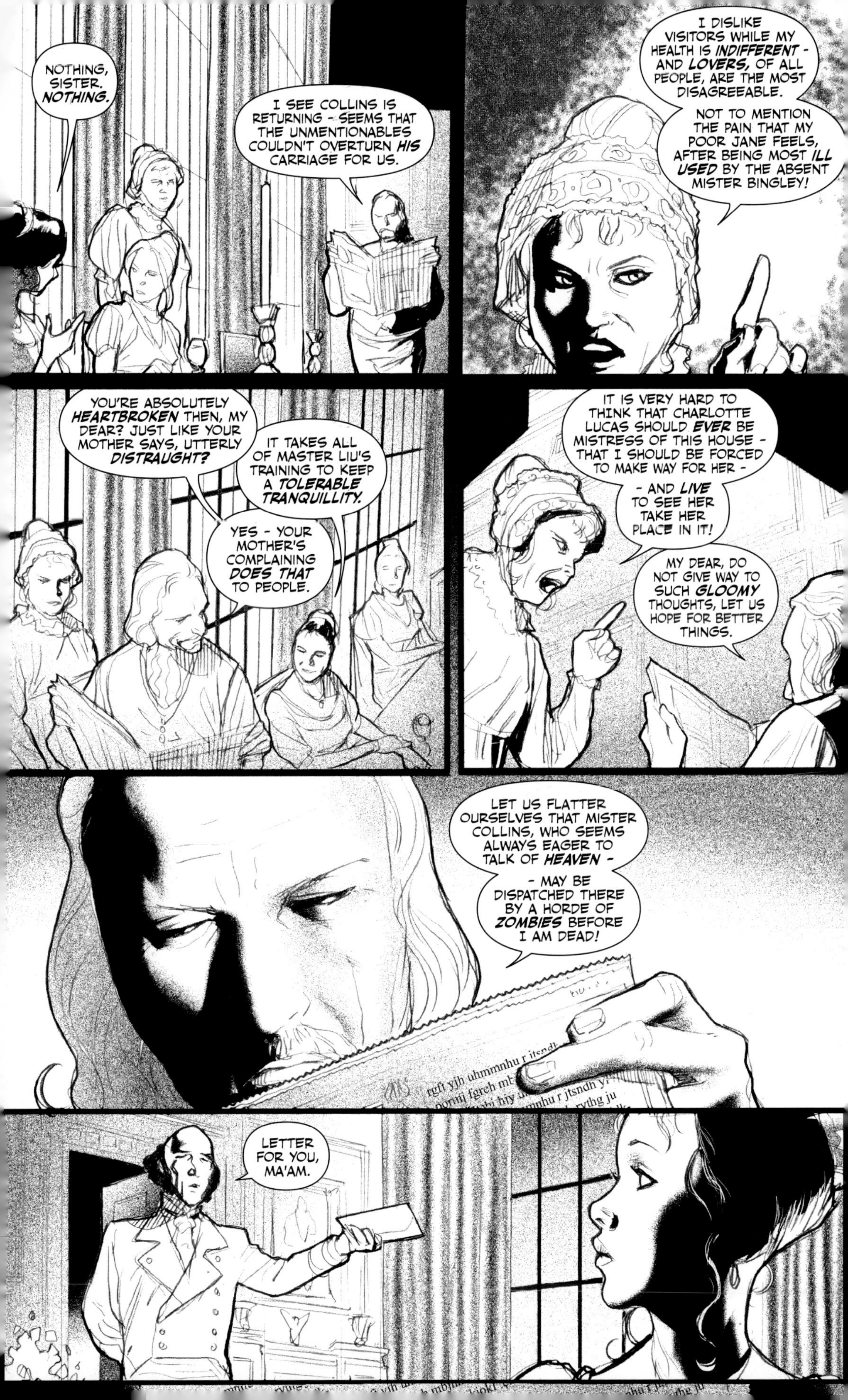
NOTHING, SISTER. NOTHING.
I SEE COLLINS IS RETURNING - SEEMS THAT THE UNMENTIONABLES COULDN'T OVERTURN HIS CARRIAGE FOR US.
I DISLIKE VISITORS WHILE MY HEALTH IS INDIFFERENT - AND LOVERS, OF ALL PEOPLE, ARE THE MOST DISAGREEABLE.
NOT TO MENTION THE PAIN THAT MY POOR JANE FEELS, AFTER BEING MOST ILL USED BY THE ABSENT MISTER BINGLEY!
YOU'RE ABSOLUTELY HEARTBROKEN THEN, MY DEAR? JUST LIKE YOUR MOTHER SAYS, UTTERLY DISTRAUGHT?
IT TAKES ALL OF MASTER LIU'S TRAINING TO KEEP A TOLERABLE TRANQUILLITY.
YES - YOUR MOTHER'S COMPLAINING DOES THAT TO PEOPLE.
IT IS VERY HARD TO THINK THAT CHARLOTTE LUCAS SHOULD EVER BE MISTRESS OF THIS HOUSE - THAT I SHOULD BE FORCED TO MAKE WAY FOR HER -
- AND LIVE TO SEE HER TAKE HER PLACE IN IT!
MY DEAR, DO NOT GIVE WAY TO SUCH GLOOMY THOUGHTS, LET US HOPE FOR BETTER THINGS.
LET US FLATTER OURSELVES THAT MISTER COLLINS, WHO SEEMS ALWAYS EAGER TO TALK OF HEAVEN -
- MAY BE DISPATCHED THERE BY A HORDE OF ZOMBIES BEFORE I AM DEAD!
LETTER FOR YOU, MA'AM.

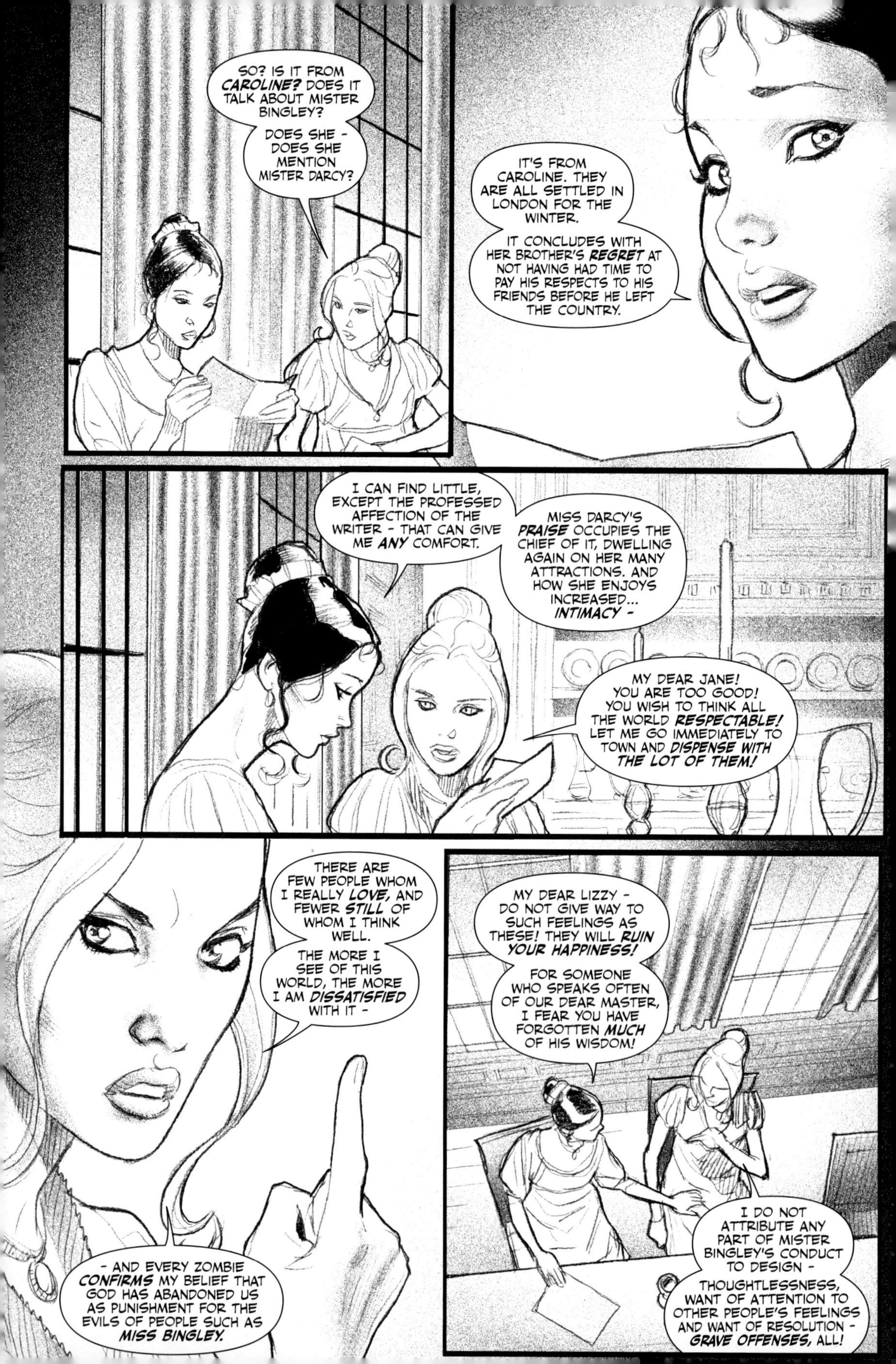
SO? IS IT FROM CAROLINE? DOES IT TALK ABOUT MISTER BINGLEY?
DOES SHE - DOES SHE MENTION MISTER DARCY?
IT'S FROM CAROLINE. THEY ARE ALL SETTLED IN LONDON FOR THE WINTER.
IT CONCLUDES WITH HER BROTHER'S REGRET AT NOT HAVING HAD TIME TO PAY HIS RESPECTS TO HIS FRIENDS BEFORE HE LEFT THE COUNTRY.
I CAN FIND LITTLE, EXCEPT THE PROFESSED AFFECTION OF THE WRITER - THAT CAN GIVE ME ANY COMFORT.
MISS DARCY'S PRAISE OCCUPIES THE CHIEF OF IT, DWELLING AGAIN ON HER MANY ATTRACTIONS. AND HOW SHE ENJOYS INCREASED... INTIMACY -
MY DEAR JANE! YOU ARE TOO GOOD! YOU WISH TO THINK ALL THE WORLD RESPECTABLE! LET ME GO IMMEDIATELY TO TOWN AND DISPENSE WITH THE LOT OF THEM!
THERE ARE FEW PEOPLE WHOM I REALLY LOVE, AND FEWER STILL OF WHOM I THINK WELL.
THE MORE I SEE OF THIS WORLD, THE MORE I AM DISSATISFIED WITH IT -
- AND EVERY ZOMBIE CONFIRMS MY BELIEF THAT GOD HAS ABANDONED US AS PUNISHMENT FOR THE EVILS OF PEOPLE SUCH AS MISS BINGLEY.
MY DEAR LIZZY - DO NOT GIVE WAY TO SUCH FEELINGS AS THESE! THEY WILL RUIN YOUR HAPPINESS!
FOR SOMEONE WHO SPEAKS OFTEN OF OUR DEAR MASTER, I FEAR YOU HAVE FORGOTTEN MUCH OF HIS WISDOM!
I DO NOT ATTRIBUTE ANY PART OF MISTER BINGLEY'S CONDUCT TO DESIGN -
THOUGHTLESSNESS, WANT OF ATTENTION TO OTHER PEOPLE'S FEELINGS AND WANT OF RESOLUTION - GRAVE OFFENSES, ALL!

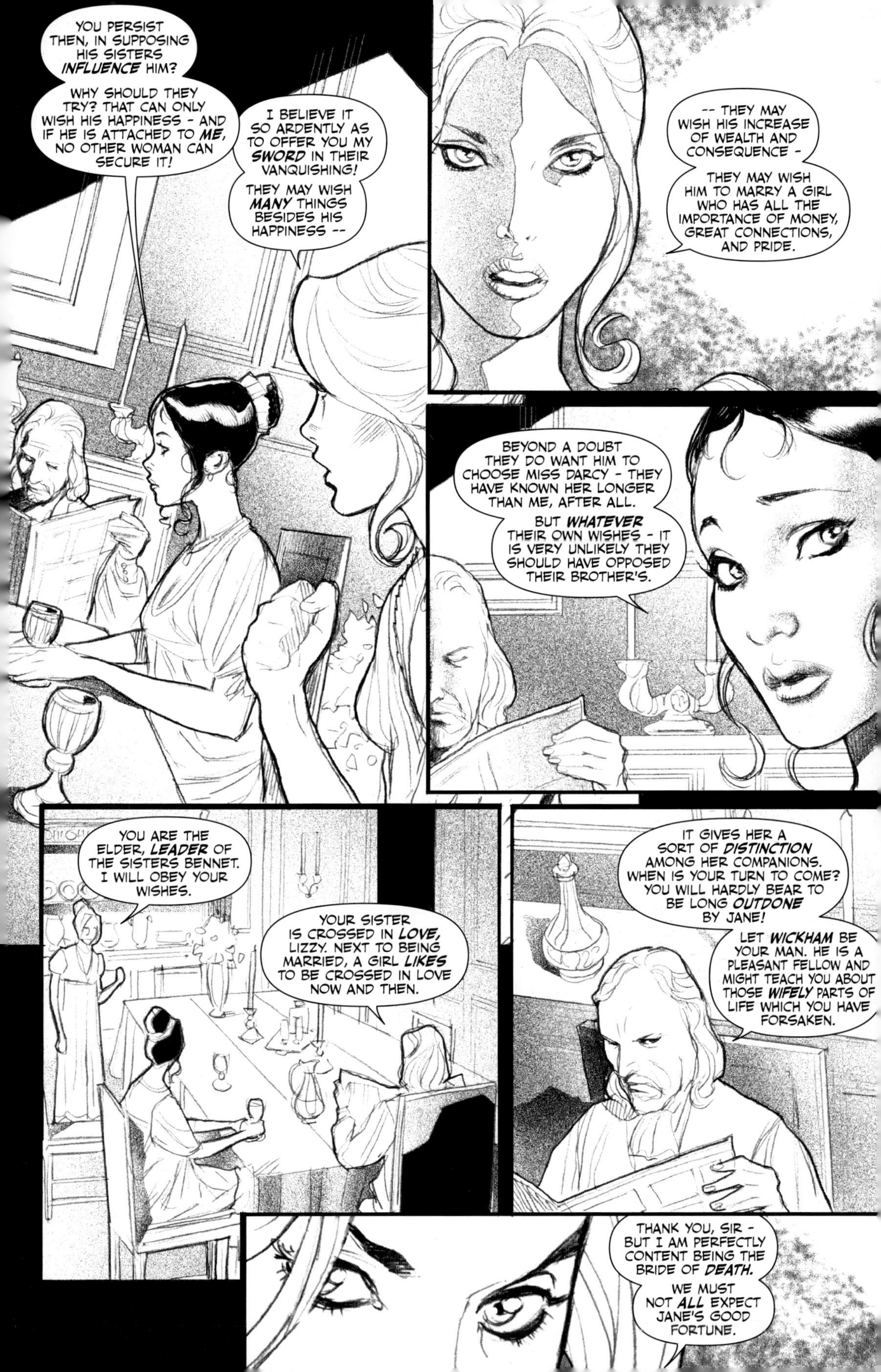
YOU PERSIST THEN, IN SUPPOSING HIS SISTERS *INFLUENCE* HIM?
WHY SHOULD THEY TRY? THAT CAN ONLY WISH HIS HAPPINESS - AND IF HE IS ATTACHED TO *ME*, NO OTHER WOMAN CAN SECURE IT!
I BELIEVE IT SO ARDENTLY AS TO OFFER YOU MY *SWORD* IN THEIR VANQUISHING!
THEY MAY WISH *MANY* THINGS BESIDES HIS HAPPINESS --
-- THEY MAY WISH HIS INCREASE OF WEALTH AND CONSEQUENCE -
THEY MAY WISH HIM TO MARRY A GIRL WHO HAS ALL THE IMPORTANCE OF MONEY, GREAT CONNECTIONS, AND PRIDE.
BEYOND A DOUBT THEY DO WANT HIM TO CHOOSE MISS DARCY - THEY HAVE KNOWN HER LONGER THAN ME, AFTER ALL.
BUT *WHATEVER* THEIR OWN WISHES - IT IS VERY UNLIKELY THEY SHOULD HAVE OPPOSED THEIR BROTHER'S.
YOU ARE THE ELDER, *LEADER* OF THE SISTERS BENNET. I WILL OBEY YOUR WISHES.
YOUR SISTER IS CROSSED IN *LOVE,* LIZZY. NEXT TO BEING MARRIED, A GIRL *LIKES* TO BE CROSSED IN LOVE NOW AND THEN.
IT GIVES HER A SORT OF *DISTINCTION* AMONG HER COMPANIONS. WHEN IS YOUR TURN TO COME? YOU WILL HARDLY BEAR TO BE LONG *OUTDONE* BY JANE!
LET *WICKHAM* BE YOUR MAN. HE IS A PLEASANT FELLOW AND MIGHT TEACH YOU ABOUT THOSE *WIFELY* PARTS OF LIFE WHICH YOU HAVE FORSAKEN.
THANK YOU, SIR - BUT I AM PERFECTLY CONTENT BEING THE BRIDE OF *DEATH.*
WE MUST NOT *ALL* EXPECT JANE'S GOOD FORTUNE.

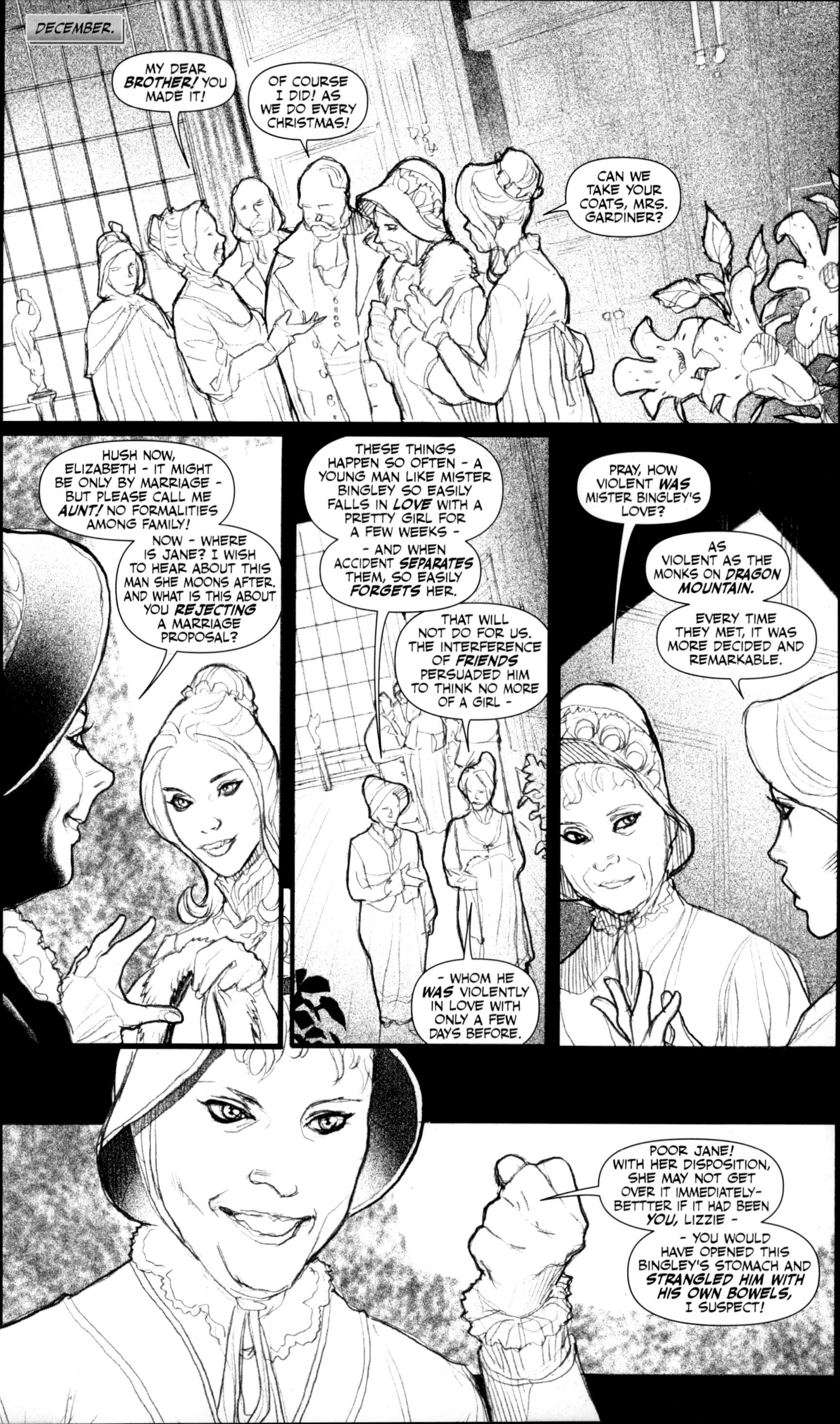

DECEMBER.
MY DEAR BROTHER! YOU MADE IT!
OF COURSE I DID! AS WE DO EVERY CHRISTMAS!
CAN WE TAKE YOUR COATS, MRS. GARDINER?
HUSH NOW, ELIZABETH - IT MIGHT BE ONLY BY MARRIAGE - BUT PLEASE CALL ME AUNT! NO FORMALITIES AMONG FAMILY!
NOW - WHERE IS JANE? I WISH TO HEAR ABOUT THIS MAN SHE MOONS AFTER. AND WHAT IS THIS ABOUT YOU REJECTING A MARRIAGE PROPOSAL?
THESE THINGS HAPPEN SO OFTEN - A YOUNG MAN LIKE MISTER BINGLEY SO EASILY FALLS IN LOVE WITH A PRETTY GIRL FOR A FEW WEEKS -
- AND WHEN ACCIDENT SEPARATES THEM, SO EASILY FORGETS HER.
THAT WILL NOT DO FOR US. THE INTERFERENCE OF FRIENDS PERSUADED HIM TO THINK NO MORE OF A GIRL -
- WHOM HE WAS VIOLENTLY IN LOVE WITH ONLY A FEW DAYS BEFORE.
PRAY, HOW VIOLENT WAS MISTER BINGLEY'S LOVE?
AS VIOLENT AS THE MONKS ON DRAGON MOUNTAIN.
EVERY TIME THEY MET, IT WAS MORE DECIDED AND REMARKABLE.
POOR JANE! WITH HER DISPOSITION, SHE MAY NOT GET OVER IT IMMEDIATELY- BETTTER IF IT HAD BEEN YOU, LIZZIE -
- YOU WOULD HAVE OPENED THIS BINGLEY'S STOMACH AND STRANGLED HIM WITH HIS OWN BOWELS, I SUSPECT!

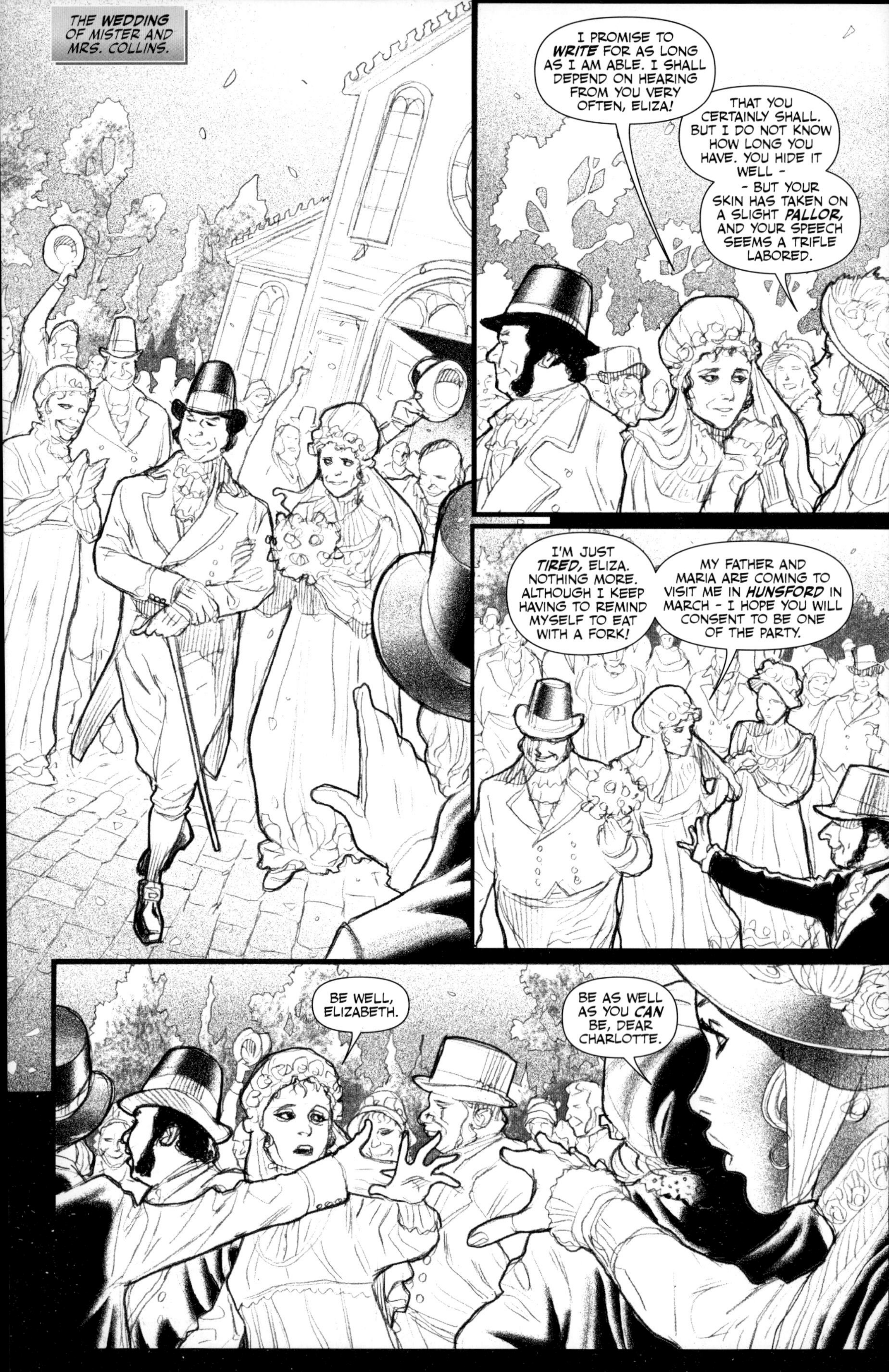
THE WEDDING OF MISTER AND MRS. COLLINS.
I PROMISE TO WRITE FOR AS LONG AS I AM ABLE. I SHALL DEPEND ON HEARING FROM YOU VERY OFTEN, ELIZA!
THAT YOU CERTAINLY SHALL. BUT I DO NOT KNOW HOW LONG YOU HAVE. YOU HIDE IT WELL -
- BUT YOUR SKIN HAS TAKEN ON A SLIGHT PALLOR, AND YOUR SPEECH SEEMS A TRIFLE LABORED.
I'M JUST TIRED, ELIZA. NOTHING MORE. ALTHOUGH I KEEP HAVING TO REMIND MYSELF TO EAT WITH A FORK!
MY FATHER AND MARIA ARE COMING TO VISIT ME IN HUNSFORD IN MARCH - I HOPE YOU WILL CONSENT TO BE ONE OF THE PARTY.
BE WELL, ELIZABETH.
BE AS WELL AS YOU CAN BE, DEAR CHARLOTTE.

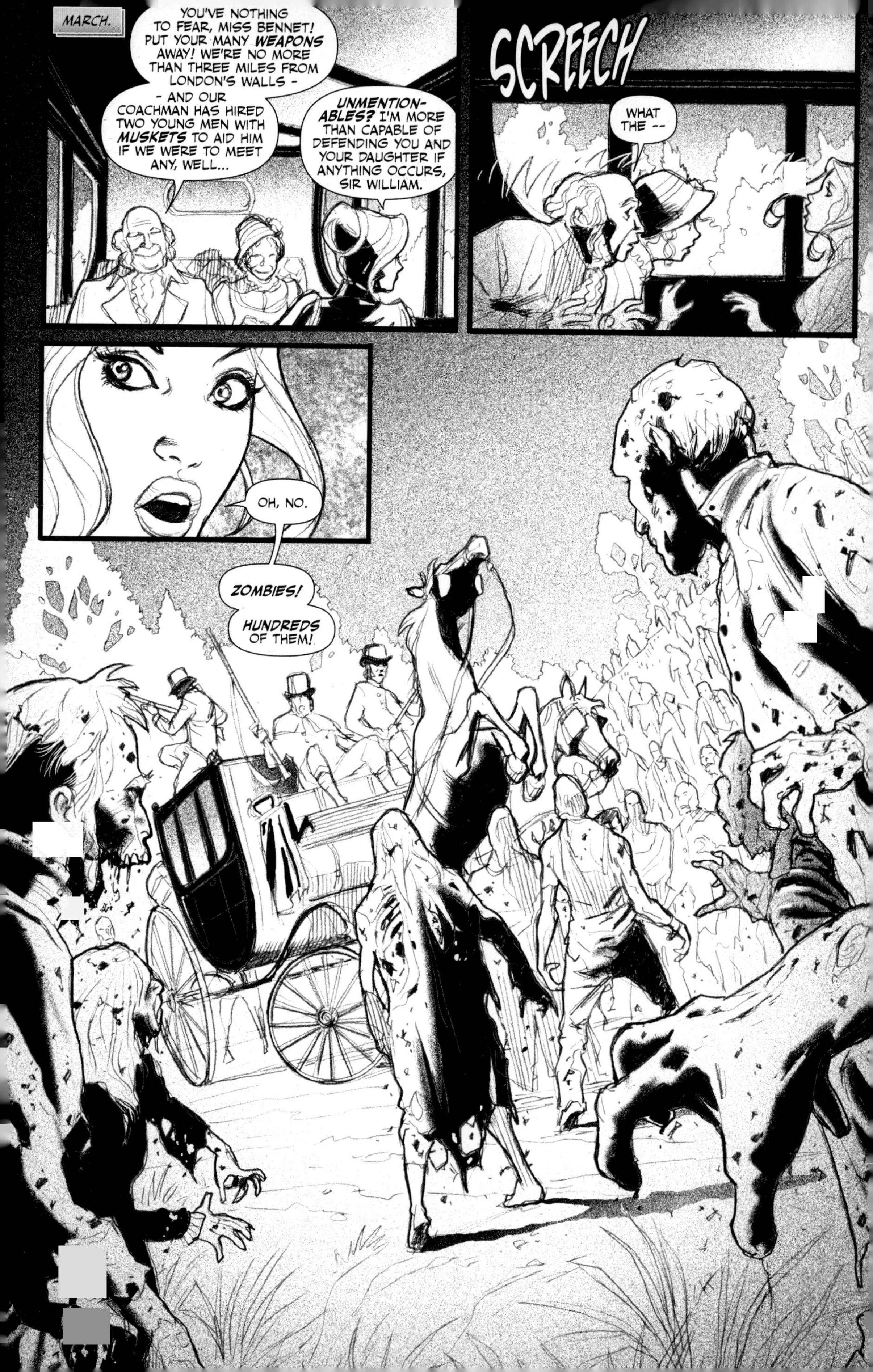
MARCH.
YOU'VE NOTHING TO FEAR, MISS BENNET! PUT YOUR MANY WEAPONS AWAY! WE'RE NO MORE THAN THREE MILES FROM LONDON'S WALLS -
- AND OUR COACHMAN HAS HIRED TWO YOUNG MEN WITH MUSKETS TO AID HIM IF WE WERE TO MEET ANY, WELL...
UNMENTION-ABLES? I'M MORE THAN CAPABLE OF DEFENDING YOU AND YOUR DAUGHTER IF ANYTHING OCCURS, SIR WILLIAM.
SCREECH
WHAT THE --
OH, NO.
ZOMBIES!
HUNDREDS OF THEM!

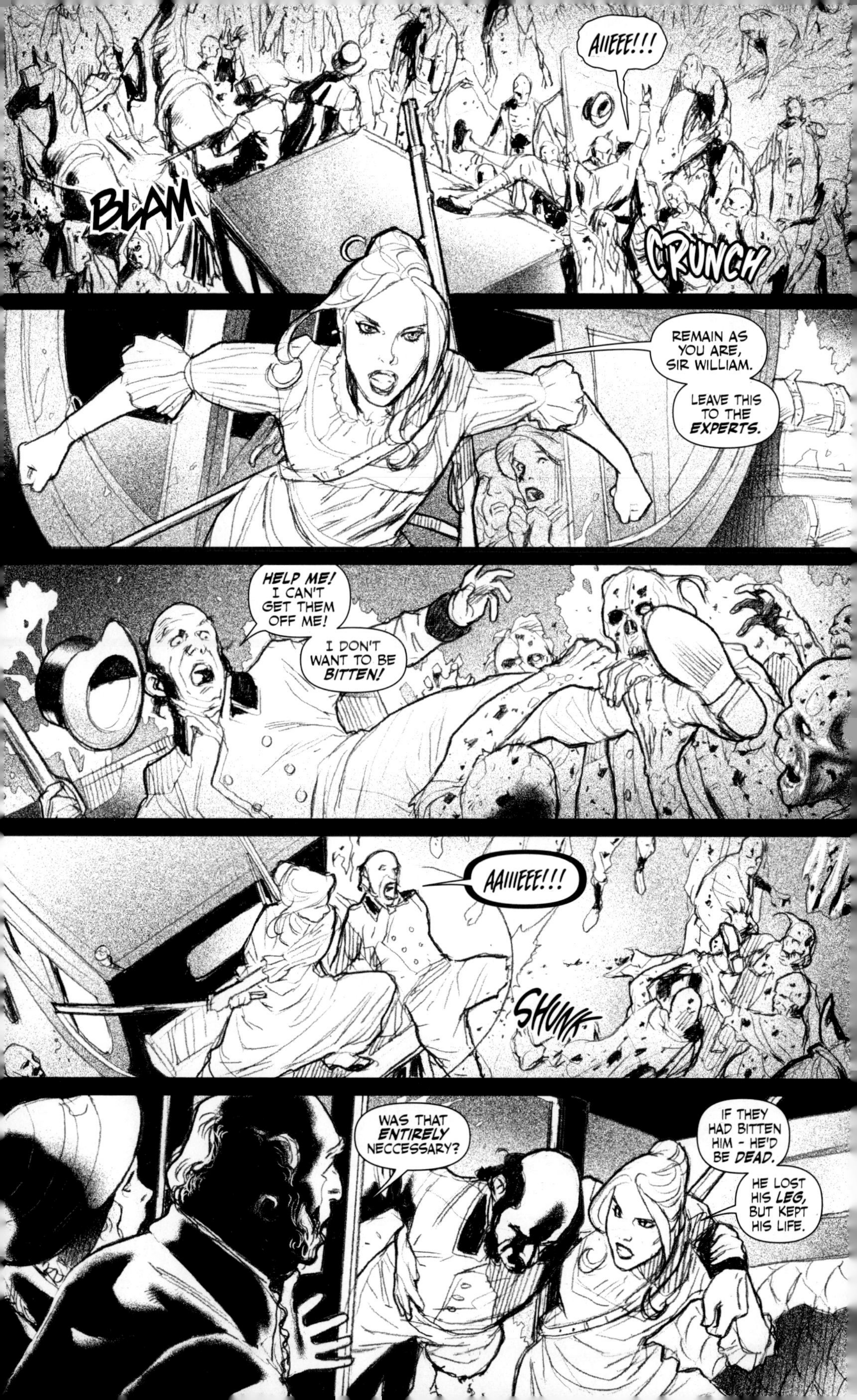
AIIEEE!!!
BLAM
CRUNCH
REMAIN AS YOU ARE, SIR WILLIAM.
LEAVE THIS TO THE *EXPERTS.*
HELP ME! I CAN'T GET THEM OFF ME!
I DON'T WANT TO BE *BITTEN!*
AAIIIEEE!!!
SHUNK
WAS THAT *ENTIRELY* NECCESSARY?
IF THEY HAD BITTEN HIM - HE'D BE *DEAD.*
HE LOST HIS *LEG,* BUT KEPT HIS LIFE.

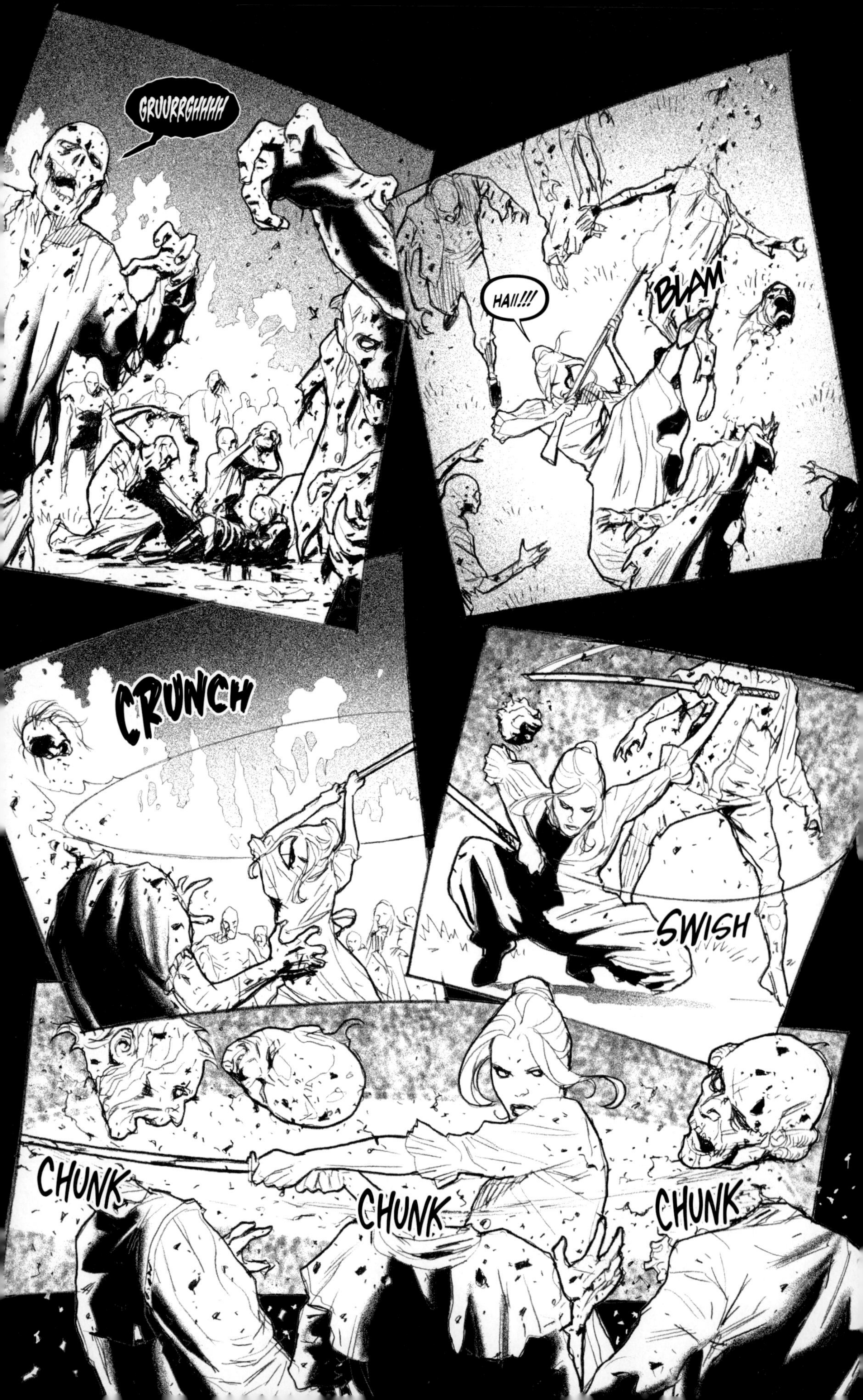
GRUURRGHHHH
HAI!!!
BLAM
CRUNCH
SWISH
CHUNK
CHUNK
CHUNK

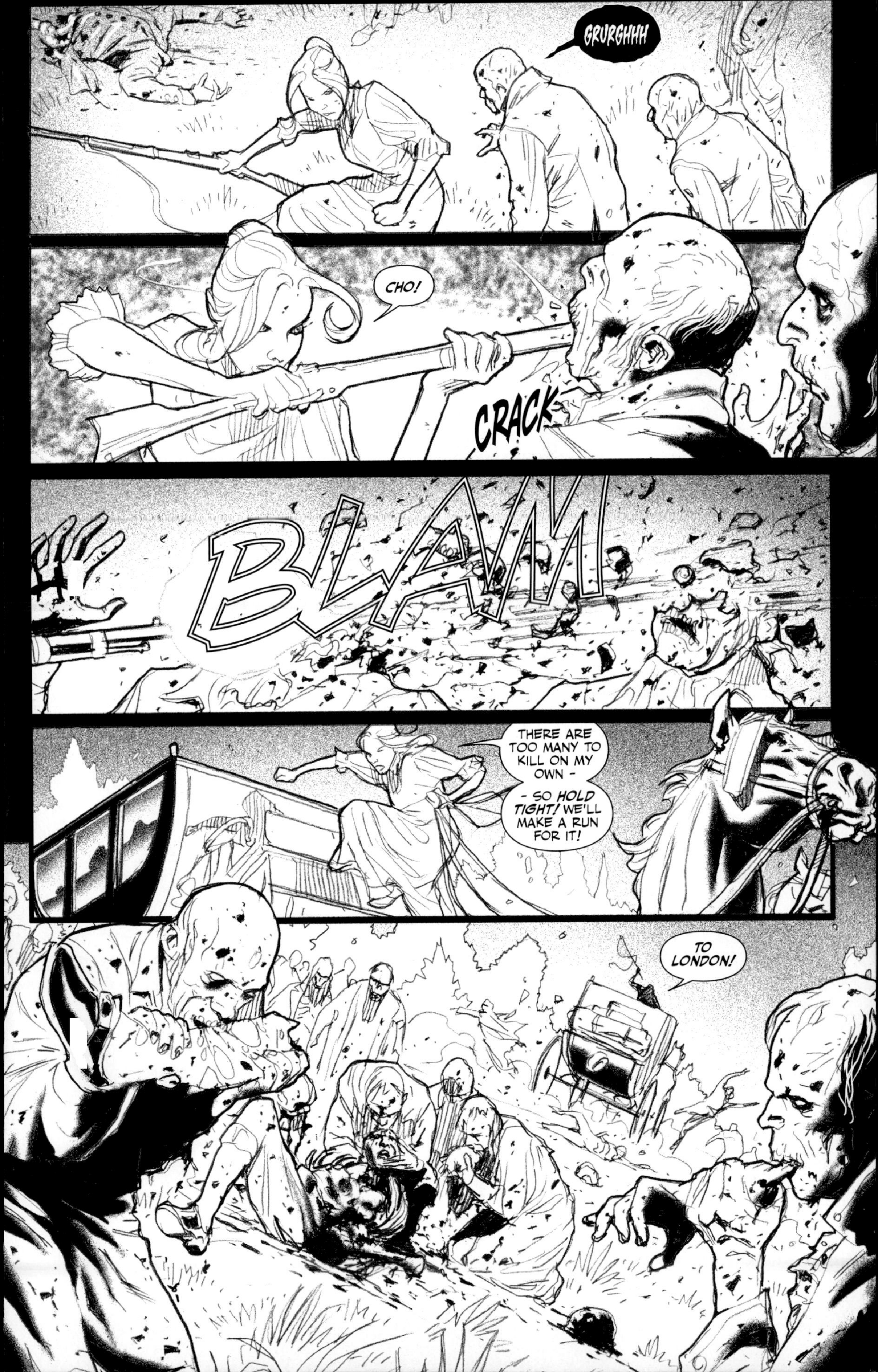
GRURGHHH
CHO!
CRACK
BLAM
THERE ARE TOO MANY TO KILL ON MY OWN –
– SO HOLD TIGHT! WE'LL MAKE A RUN FOR IT!
TO LONDON!

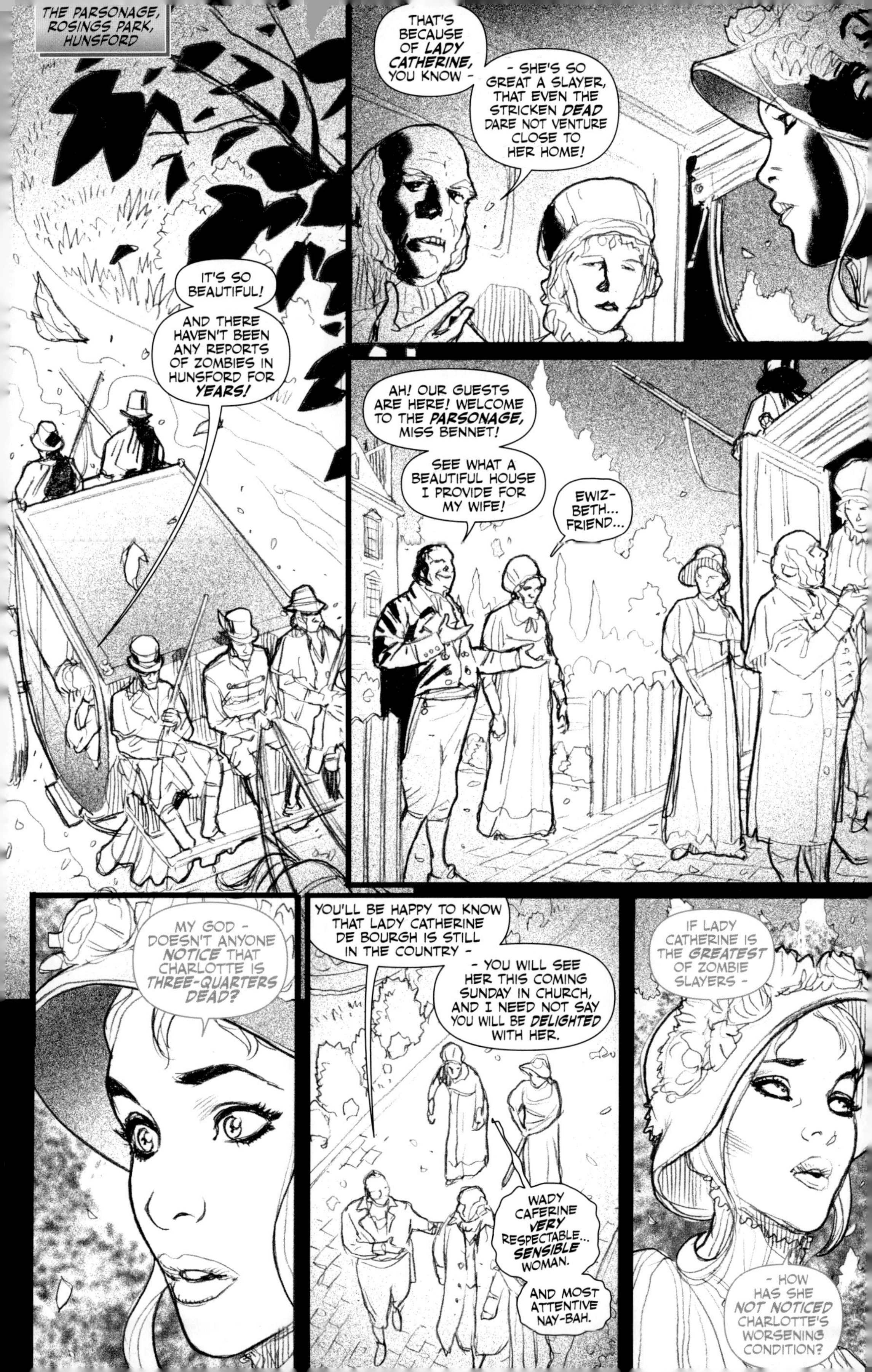
THE PARSONAGE, ROSINGS PARK, HUNSFORD
IT'S SO BEAUTIFUL!
AND THERE HAVEN'T BEEN ANY REPORTS OF ZOMBIES IN HUNSFORD FOR *YEARS!*
THAT'S BECAUSE OF *LADY CATHERINE,* YOU KNOW -
- SHE'S SO GREAT A SLAYER, THAT EVEN THE STRICKEN *DEAD* DARE NOT VENTURE CLOSE TO HER HOME!
AH! OUR GUESTS ARE HERE! WELCOME TO THE *PARSONAGE,* MISS BENNET!
SEE WHAT A BEAUTIFUL HOUSE I PROVIDE FOR MY WIFE!
EWIZ-BETH... FRIEND...
MY GOD - DOESN'T ANYONE *NOTICE* THAT CHARLOTTE IS *THREE-QUARTERS DEAD?*
YOU'LL BE HAPPY TO KNOW THAT LADY CATHERINE DE BOURGH IS STILL IN THE COUNTRY -
- YOU WILL SEE HER THIS COMING SUNDAY IN CHURCH, AND I NEED NOT SAY YOU WILL BE *DELIGHTED* WITH HER.
WADY CAFERINE *VERY* RESPECTABLE... *SENSIBLE* WOMAN.
AND MOST ATTENTIVE NAY-BAH.
IF LADY CATHERINE IS THE *GREATEST* OF ZOMBIE SLAYERS -
- HOW HAS SHE *NOT NOTICED* CHARLOTTE'S WORSENING CONDITION?

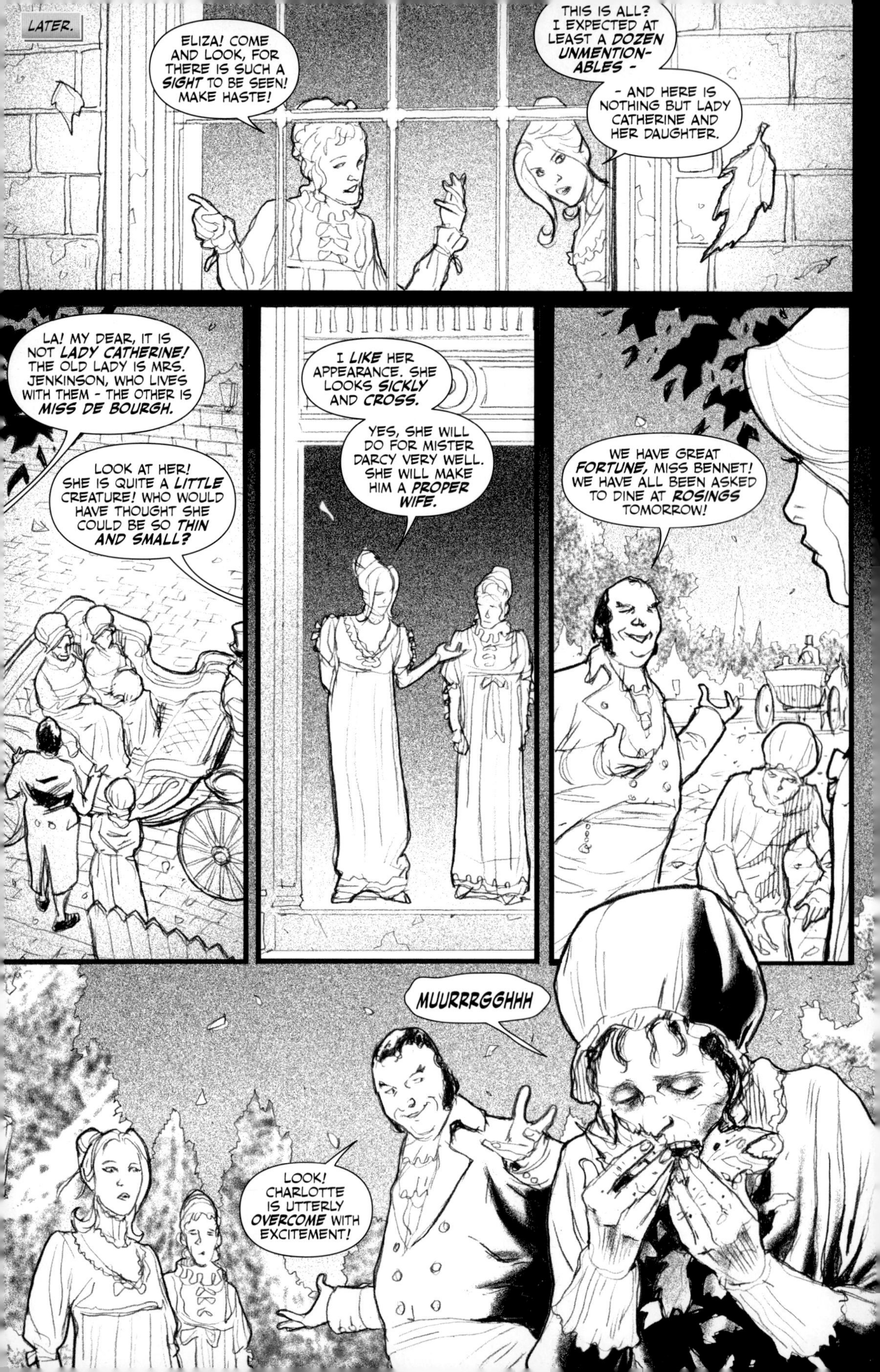
LATER.
ELIZA! COME AND LOOK, FOR THERE IS SUCH A SIGHT TO BE SEEN! MAKE HASTE!
THIS IS ALL? I EXPECTED AT LEAST A DOZEN UNMENTION-ABLES -
- AND HERE IS NOTHING BUT LADY CATHERINE AND HER DAUGHTER.
LA! MY DEAR, IT IS NOT LADY CATHERINE! THE OLD LADY IS MRS. JENKINSON, WHO LIVES WITH THEM - THE OTHER IS MISS DE BOURGH.
LOOK AT HER! SHE IS QUITE A LITTLE CREATURE! WHO WOULD HAVE THOUGHT SHE COULD BE SO THIN AND SMALL?
I LIKE HER APPEARANCE. SHE LOOKS SICKLY AND CROSS.
YES, SHE WILL DO FOR MISTER DARCY VERY WELL. SHE WILL MAKE HIM A PROPER WIFE.
WE HAVE GREAT FORTUNE, MISS BENNET! WE HAVE ALL BEEN ASKED TO DINE AT ROSINGS TOMORROW!
MUURRRGGHHH
LOOK! CHARLOTTE IS UTTERLY OVERCOME WITH EXCITEMENT!

MISTER COLLINS TELLS ME THAT YOU ARE SCHOOLED IN THE *DEADLY ARTS*, MISS BENNET.

SOME TIME OR ANOTHER I SHALL BE HAPPY TO SEE YOU SPAR WITH ONE OF MY *NINJAS*. ARE YOUR SISTERS LIKELY TRAINED?

ARE THOSE SHAOLIN MONKS *STILL* SELLING THEIR CLUMSY *KUNG FU* TO THE ENGLISH?

HAD YOUR FATHER MORE MEANS, HE SHOULD HAVE TAKEN YOU TO *JAPAN* - TO KYOTO.

HERE, USE THE *SPOON*, CHARLOTTE.

UNFORTUNATELY, MY FATHER *HATES* JAPAN. AS SUCH WE HAVE NO *NINJAS* EITHER.

WE ARE - THOUGH NOT TO *HALF* THE PROFICIENCY YOUR LADYSHIP HAS ATTAINED.

WE WERE SCHOOLED IN *CHINA*, UNDER MASTER LIU.

NO NINJAS? HOW IS THAT *POSSIBLE?* THEN WHO PROTECTED YOU WHEN YOU SAW YOUR FIRST COMBAT?

WITHOUT NINJAS, YOU MUST HAVE BEEN A *SORRY SPECTACLE INDEED!*

NOT AT ALL, LADY CATHERINE - WE ARE A *FAMILY*. AND WHEN YOU HAVE FAMILY FIGHTING WITH YOU -

- YOU DON'T NEED TO RELY ON THE "HIRED HELP," LEST YOU BECOME *COMPLACENT*, WOULDN'T YOU SAY?

I BEG YA-OAR PAHDUN, YA-OAR *WADYSHIP* -

COME, CHARLOTTE, LET ME HELP YOU.

IF I HAVE YOUR LADY-SHIP'S LEAVE, THAT IS?

OF COURSE. PERHAPS YOU WOULD ENTERTAIN US AFTER DINNER WITH A DEMON-STRATION?

A SPARRING SESSION WITH MY NINJAS?

I WOULD BE *DELIGHTED* TO, LADY CATHERINE.

"CATHERINE THE GREAT" INDEED. I SHOULD HAVE SLIT HER *THROAT* FOR THE SLUR TO YOU, MASTER LIU.

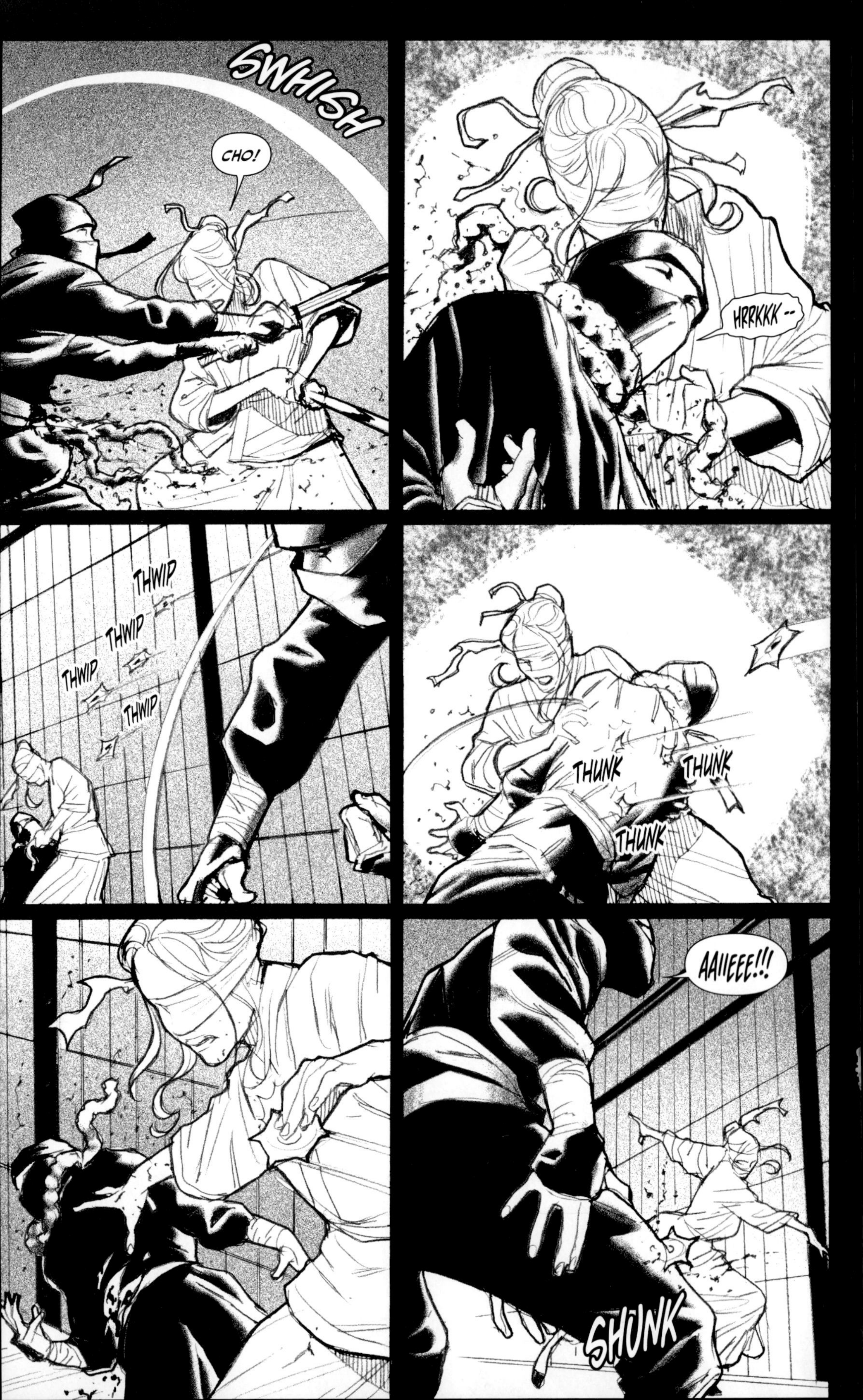
SWHISH
CHO!
HRRKKK --
THWIP
THWIP
THWIP
THWIP
THUNK
THUNK
THUNK
AAIIEEE!!!
SHUNK

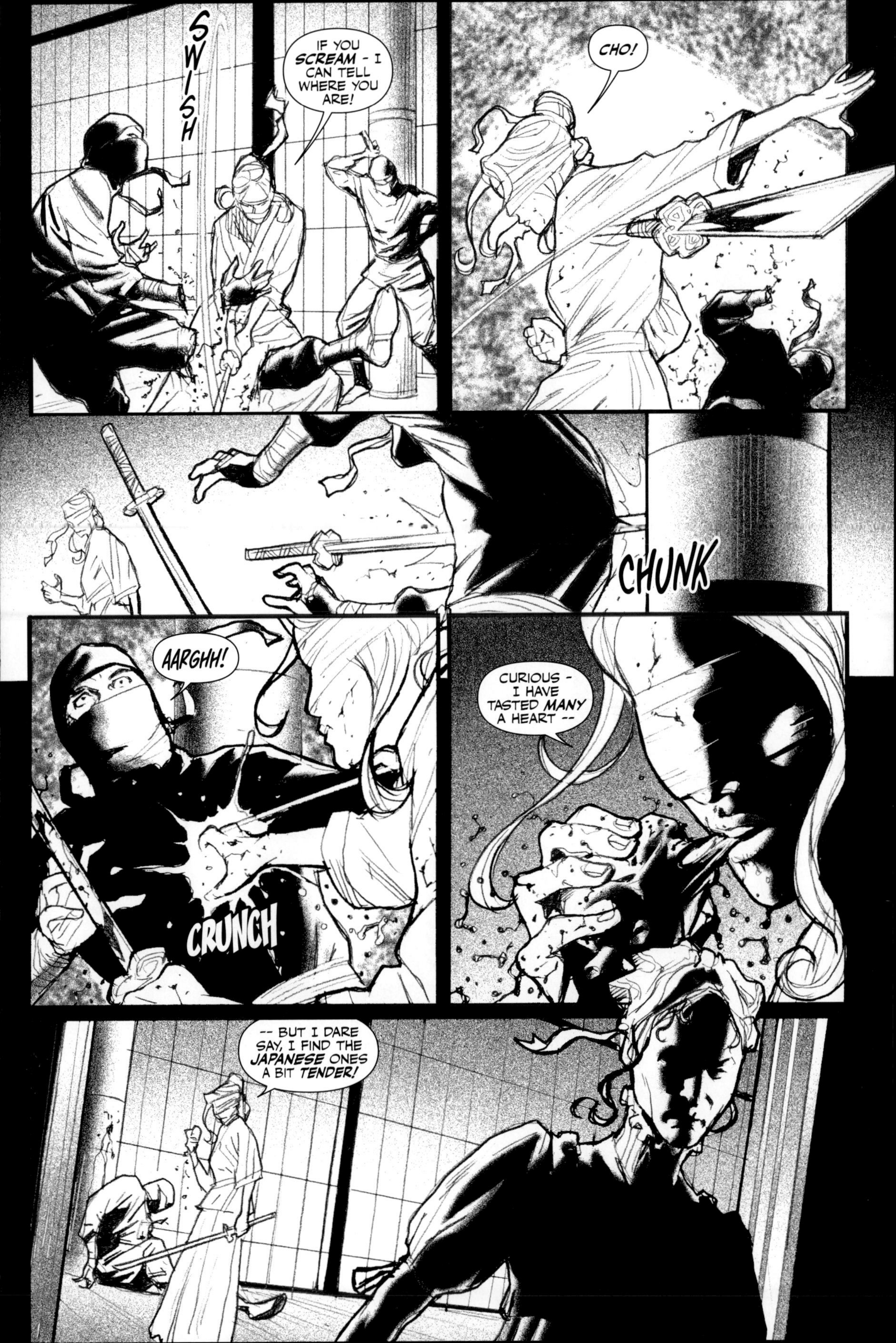
SWISH
IF YOU SCREAM - I CAN TELL WHERE YOU ARE!
CHO!
CHUNK
AARGHH!
CRUNCH
CURIOUS - I HAVE TASTED MANY A HEART --
-- BUT I DARE SAY, I FIND THE JAPANESE ONES A BIT TENDER!

TWO WEEKS LATER.

HEW-WO MIS-TAH DAH-CEY.

MAY I INTRODUCE MY FRIEND, *COLONEL FITZWILLIAM.* HE IS VISITING WITH ME.

AND GOOD MORNING TO YOU TOO, MRS COLLINS. THE AIR - UM, DOES YOU *WELL* HERE.

MISTER *DARCY!* HOW UTTERLY WONDERFUL TO SEE YOU AGAIN!

I KNOW THAT YOUR AUNT HAS BEEN LOOKING FORWARD TO YOUR VISIT WITH *MUCH* EXPECTATION!

THANK YOU, MISTER - *COLLINS,* WASN'T IT?

AND MISS *BENNET* - LONDON HAS BEEN QUITE *DULL* WITHOUT YOU OR YOUR FAMILY THERE.

MY ELDEST SISTER HAS BEEN IN TOWN THESE THREE MONTHS.

HAVE YOU NEVER HAPPENED TO *SEE* HER THERE?

UH - NO, MISS BENNET - I HAVE NEVER BEEN SO FORTUNATE TO. *MEET* MISS BENNET WHILE IN THE CITY.

IT SEEMS THAT MY SISTER'S TRAINING IN THE ARTS OF STEALTH IS SO COMPLETE THAT SHE IS LIKE A *GHOST* IN LONDON -

- IGNORED BY MANY PEOPLE SHE ONCE CALLED FRIENDS, WHO OBVIOUSLY DO NOT *SEE* HER THERE.

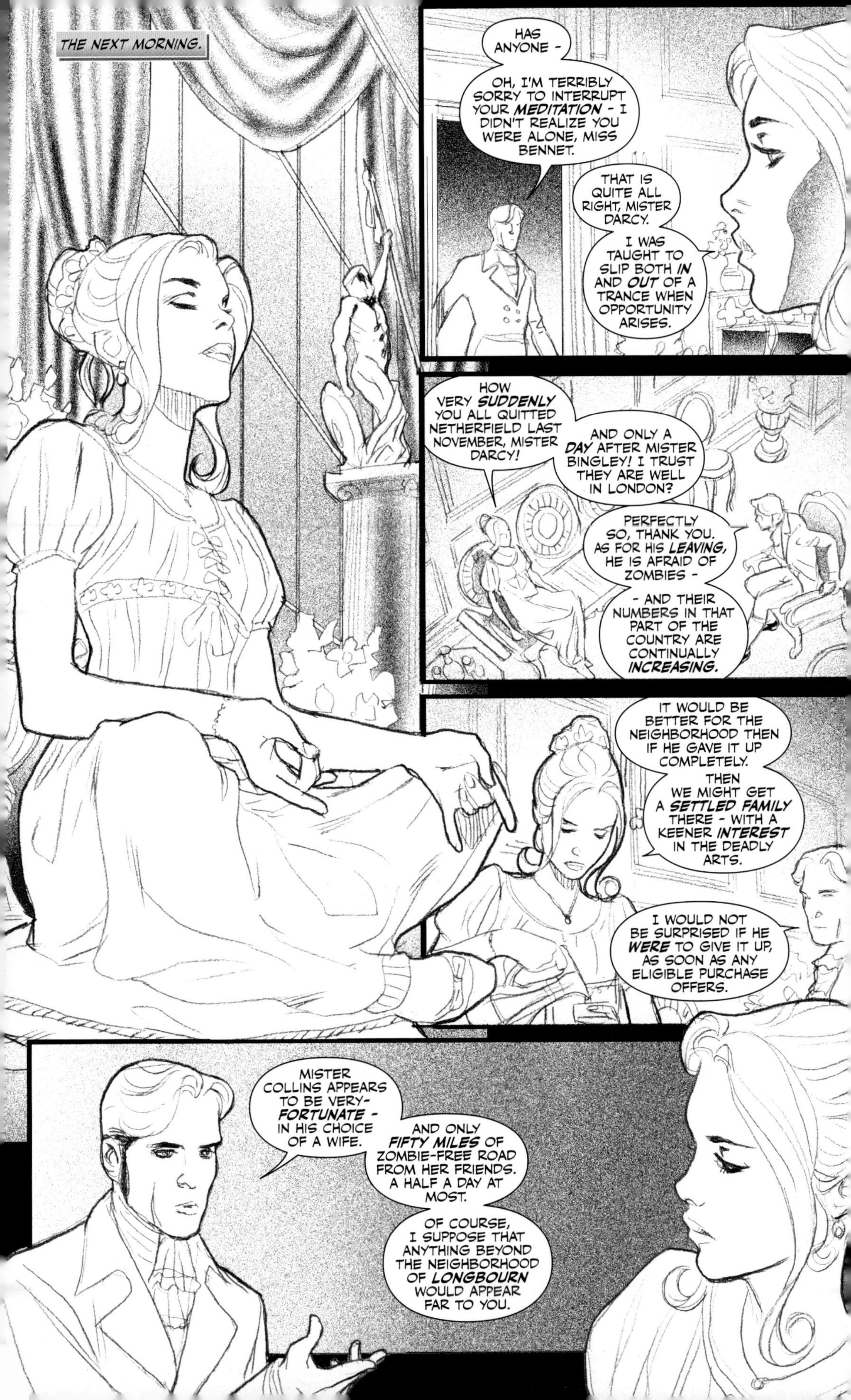
THE NEXT MORNING.
HAS ANYONE -
OH, I'M TERRIBLY SORRY TO INTERRUPT YOUR MEDITATION - I DIDN'T REALIZE YOU WERE ALONE, MISS BENNET.
THAT IS QUITE ALL RIGHT, MISTER DARCY.
I WAS TAUGHT TO SLIP BOTH IN AND OUT OF A TRANCE WHEN OPPORTUNITY ARISES.
HOW VERY SUDDENLY YOU ALL QUITTED NETHERFIELD LAST NOVEMBER, MISTER DARCY!
AND ONLY A DAY AFTER MISTER BINGLEY! I TRUST THEY ARE WELL IN LONDON?
PERFECTLY SO, THANK YOU. AS FOR HIS LEAVING, HE IS AFRAID OF ZOMBIES -
- AND THEIR NUMBERS IN THAT PART OF THE COUNTRY ARE CONTINUALLY INCREASING.
IT WOULD BE BETTER FOR THE NEIGHBORHOOD THEN IF HE GAVE IT UP COMPLETELY.
THEN WE MIGHT GET A SETTLED FAMILY THERE - WITH A KEENER INTEREST IN THE DEADLY ARTS.
I WOULD NOT BE SURPRISED IF HE WERE TO GIVE IT UP, AS SOON AS ANY ELIGIBLE PURCHASE OFFERS.
MISTER COLLINS APPEARS TO BE VERY- FORTUNATE - IN HIS CHOICE OF A WIFE.
AND ONLY FIFTY MILES OF ZOMBIE-FREE ROAD FROM HER FRIENDS. A HALF A DAY AT MOST.
OF COURSE, I SUPPOSE THAT ANYTHING BEYOND THE NEIGHBORHOOD OF LONGBOURN WOULD APPEAR FAR TO YOU.

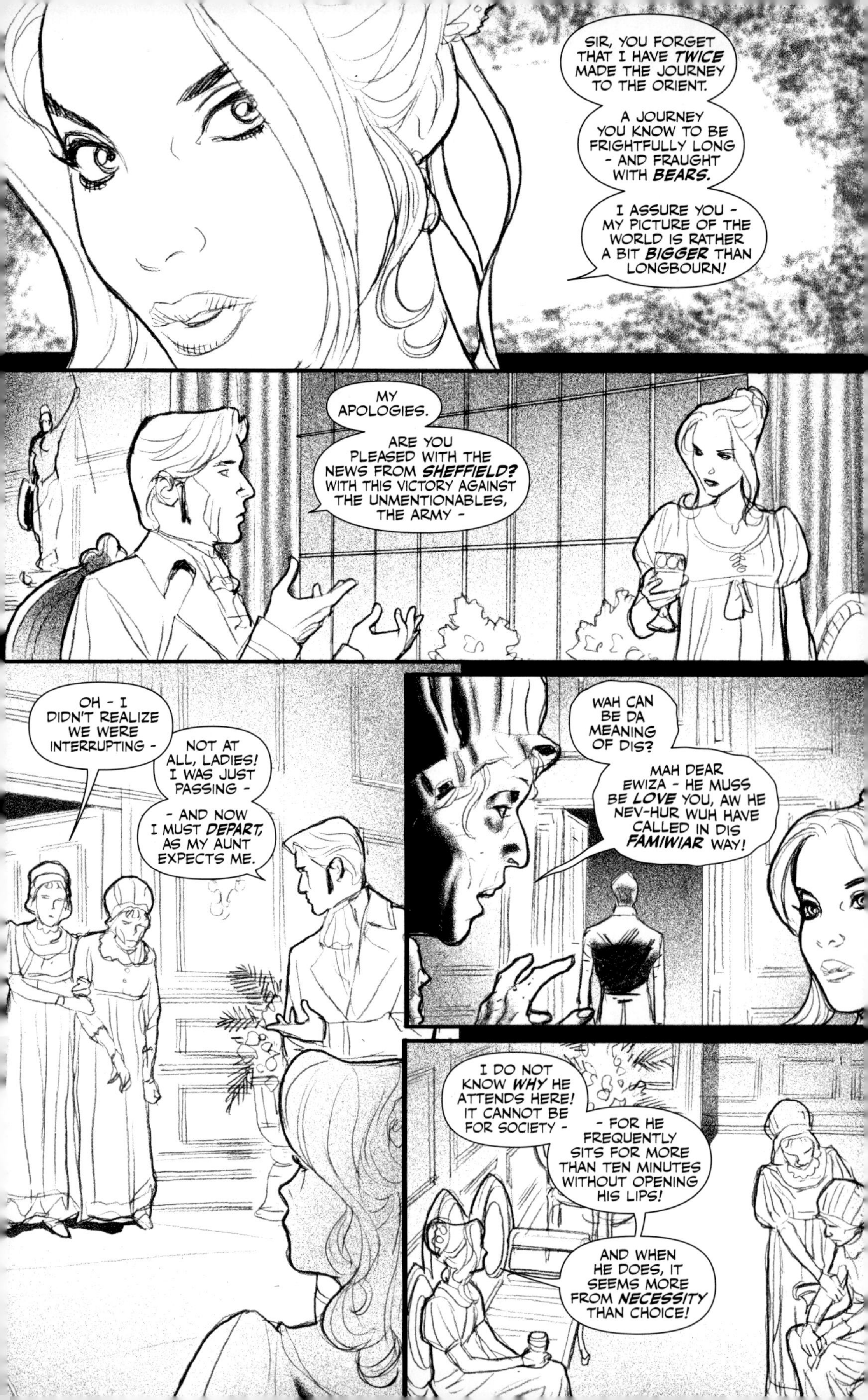
SIR, YOU FORGET THAT I HAVE TWICE MADE THE JOURNEY TO THE ORIENT.
A JOURNEY YOU KNOW TO BE FRIGHTFULLY LONG - AND FRAUGHT WITH BEARS.
I ASSURE YOU - MY PICTURE OF THE WORLD IS RATHER A BIT BIGGER THAN LONGBOURN!
MY APOLOGIES.
ARE YOU PLEASED WITH THE NEWS FROM SHEFFIELD? WITH THIS VICTORY AGAINST THE UNMENTIONABLES, THE ARMY -
OH - I DIDN'T REALIZE WE WERE INTERRUPTING -
NOT AT ALL, LADIES! I WAS JUST PASSING -
- AND NOW I MUST DEPART, AS MY AUNT EXPECTS ME.
WAH CAN BE DA MEANING OF DIS?
MAH DEAR EWIZA - HE MUSS BE LOVE YOU, AW HE NEV-HUR WUH HAVE CALLED IN DIS FAMIWIAR WAY!
I DO NOT KNOW WHY HE ATTENDS HERE! IT CANNOT BE FOR SOCIETY -
- FOR HE FREQUENTLY SITS FOR MORE THAN TEN MINUTES WITHOUT OPENING HIS LIPS!
AND WHEN HE DOES, IT SEEMS MORE FROM NECESSITY THAN CHOICE!

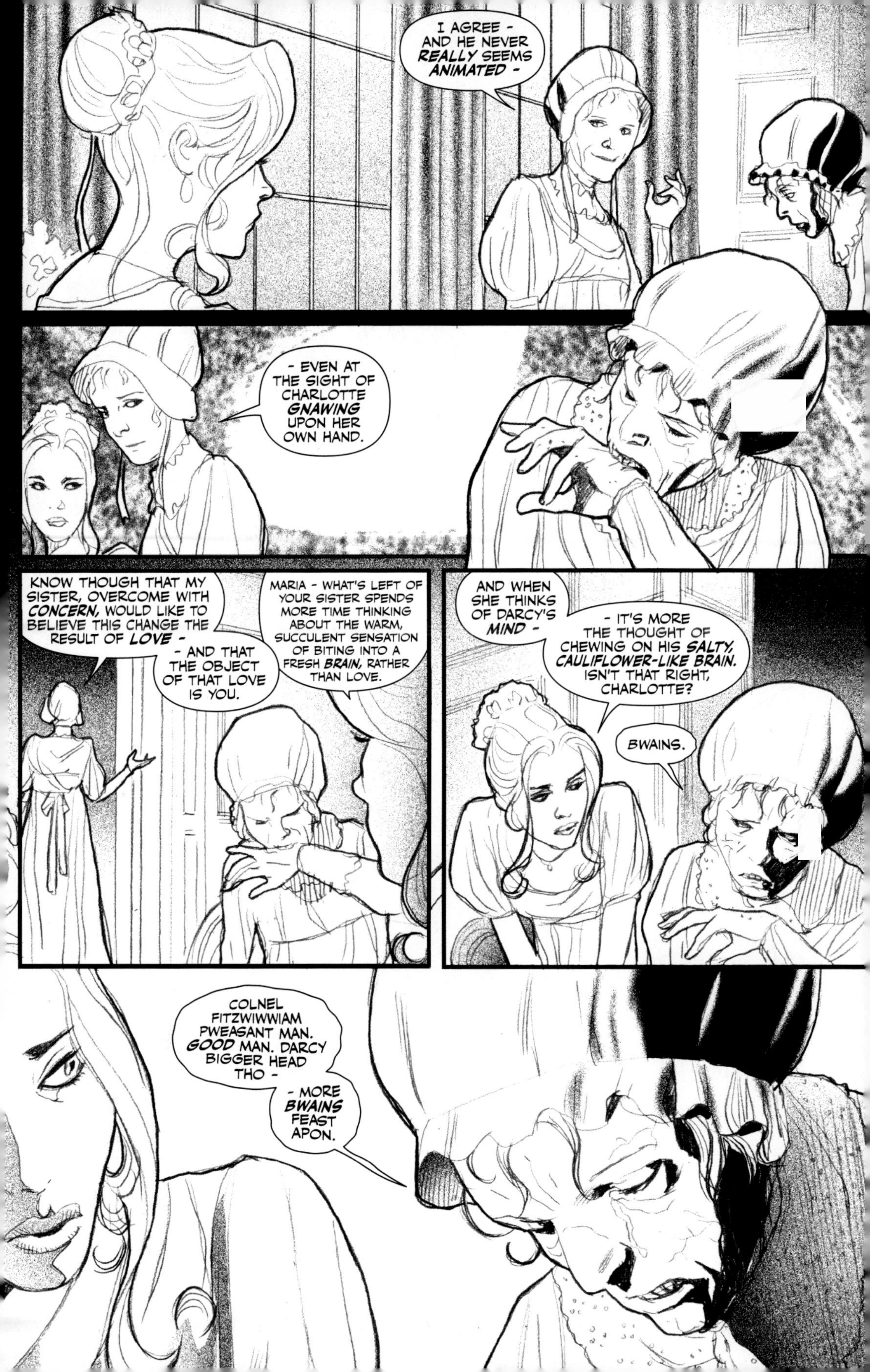
I AGREE - AND HE NEVER REALLY SEEMS ANIMATED -
- EVEN AT THE SIGHT OF CHARLOTTE GNAWING UPON HER OWN HAND.
KNOW THOUGH THAT MY SISTER, OVERCOME WITH CONCERN, WOULD LIKE TO BELIEVE THIS CHANGE THE RESULT OF LOVE -
- AND THAT THE OBJECT OF THAT LOVE IS YOU.
MARIA - WHAT'S LEFT OF YOUR SISTER SPENDS MORE TIME THINKING ABOUT THE WARM, SUCCULENT SENSATION OF BITING INTO A FRESH BRAIN, RATHER THAN LOVE.
AND WHEN SHE THINKS OF DARCY'S MIND -
- IT'S MORE THE THOUGHT OF CHEWING ON HIS SALTY, CAULIFLOWER-LIKE BRAIN. ISN'T THAT RIGHT, CHARLOTTE?
BWAINS.
COLNEL FITZWIWWIAM PWEASANT MAN. GOOD MAN. DARCY BIGGER HEAD THO -
- MORE BWAINS FEAST APON.

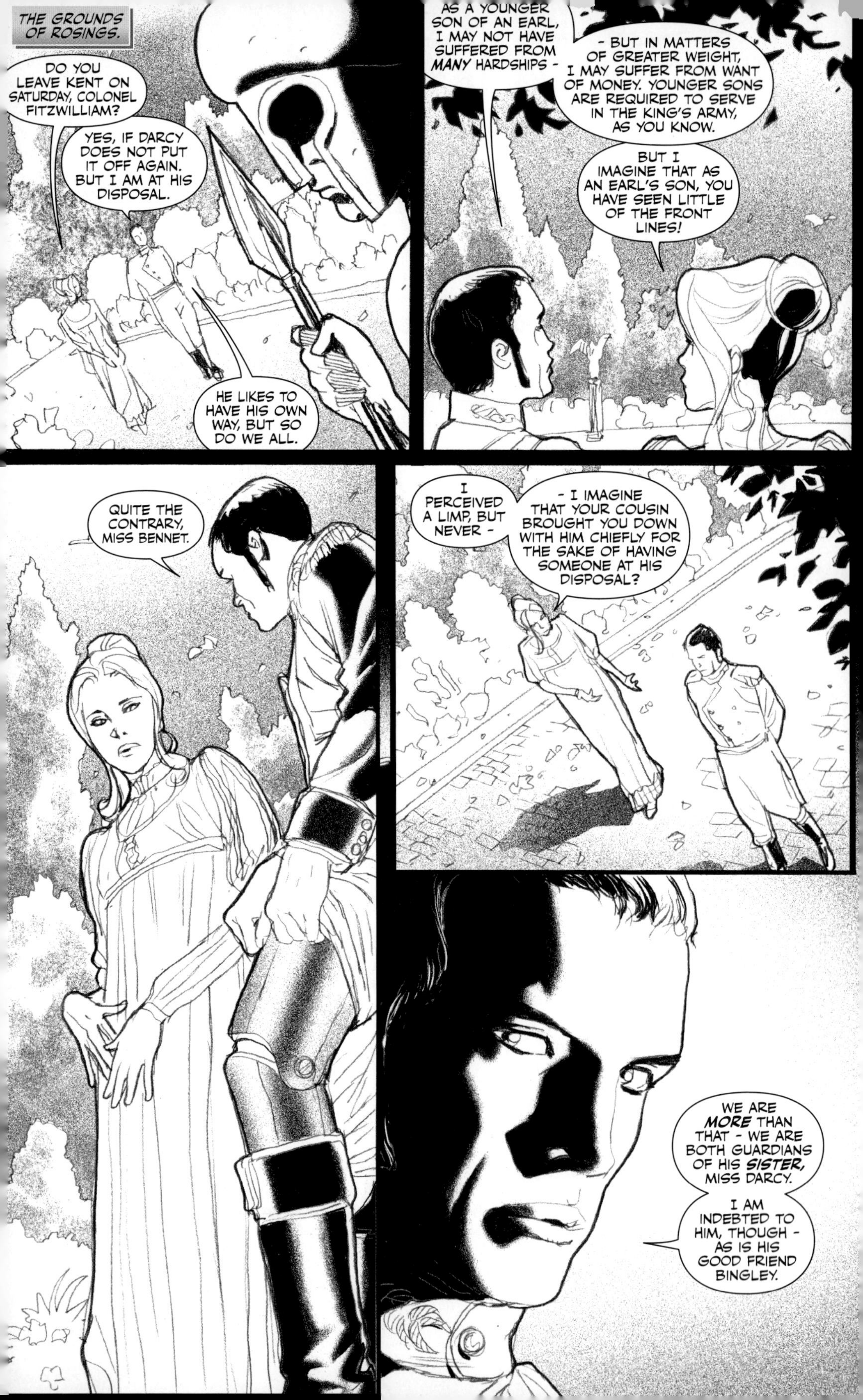
THE GROUNDS OF ROSINGS.
DO YOU LEAVE KENT ON SATURDAY, COLONEL FITZWILLIAM?
YES, IF DARCY DOES NOT PUT IT OFF AGAIN. BUT I AM AT HIS DISPOSAL.
HE LIKES TO HAVE HIS OWN WAY, BUT SO DO WE ALL.
AS A YOUNGER SON OF AN EARL, I MAY NOT HAVE SUFFERED FROM *MANY* HARDSHIPS -
- BUT IN MATTERS OF GREATER WEIGHT, I MAY SUFFER FROM WANT OF MONEY. YOUNGER SONS ARE REQUIRED TO SERVE IN THE KING'S ARMY, AS YOU KNOW.
BUT I IMAGINE THAT AS AN EARL'S SON, YOU HAVE SEEN LITTLE OF THE FRONT LINES!
QUITE THE CONTRARY, MISS BENNET.
I PERCEIVED A LIMP, BUT NEVER -
- I IMAGINE THAT YOUR COUSIN BROUGHT YOU DOWN WITH HIM CHIEFLY FOR THE SAKE OF HAVING SOMEONE AT HIS DISPOSAL?
WE ARE *MORE* THAN THAT - WE ARE BOTH GUARDIANS OF HIS *SISTER,* MISS DARCY.
I AM INDEBTED TO HIM, THOUGH - AS IS HIS GOOD FRIEND BINGLEY.

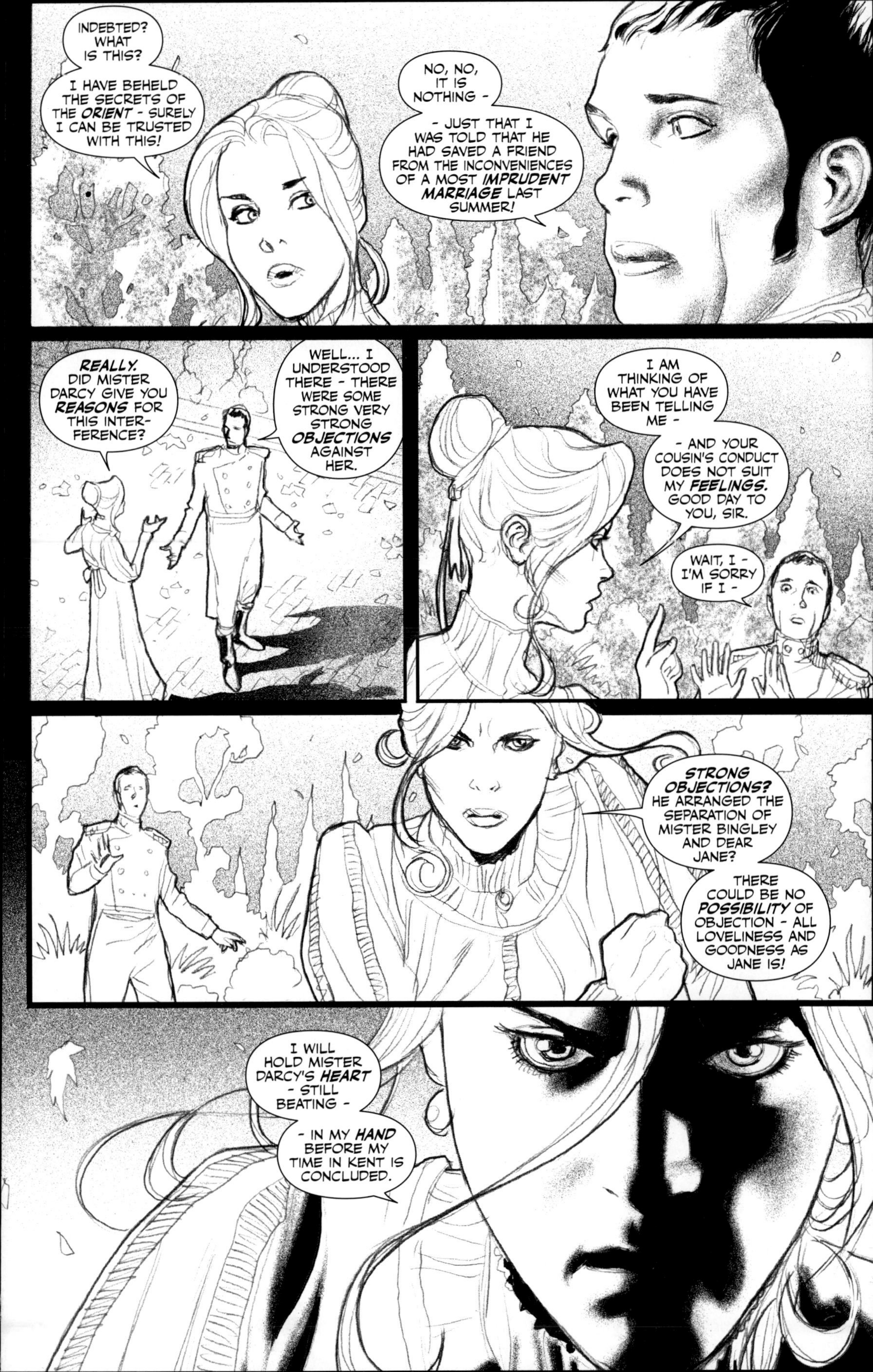
INDEBTED? WHAT IS THIS?
I HAVE BEHELD THE SECRETS OF THE ORIENT - SURELY I CAN BE TRUSTED WITH THIS!
NO, NO, IT IS NOTHING -
- JUST THAT I WAS TOLD THAT HE HAD SAVED A FRIEND FROM THE INCONVENIENCES OF A MOST IMPRUDENT MARRIAGE LAST SUMMER!
REALLY. DID MISTER DARCY GIVE YOU REASONS FOR THIS INTER-FERENCE?
WELL... I UNDERSTOOD THERE - THERE WERE SOME STRONG VERY STRONG OBJECTIONS AGAINST HER.
I AM THINKING OF WHAT YOU HAVE BEEN TELLING ME -
- AND YOUR COUSIN'S CONDUCT DOES NOT SUIT MY FEELINGS. GOOD DAY TO YOU, SIR.
WAIT, I - I'M SORRY IF I -
STRONG OBJECTIONS? HE ARRANGED THE SEPARATION OF MISTER BINGLEY AND DEAR JANE?
THERE COULD BE NO POSSIBILITY OF OBJECTION - ALL LOVELINESS AND GOODNESS AS JANE IS!
I WILL HOLD MISTER DARCY'S HEART - STILL BEATING -
- IN MY HAND BEFORE MY TIME IN KENT IS CONCLUDED.

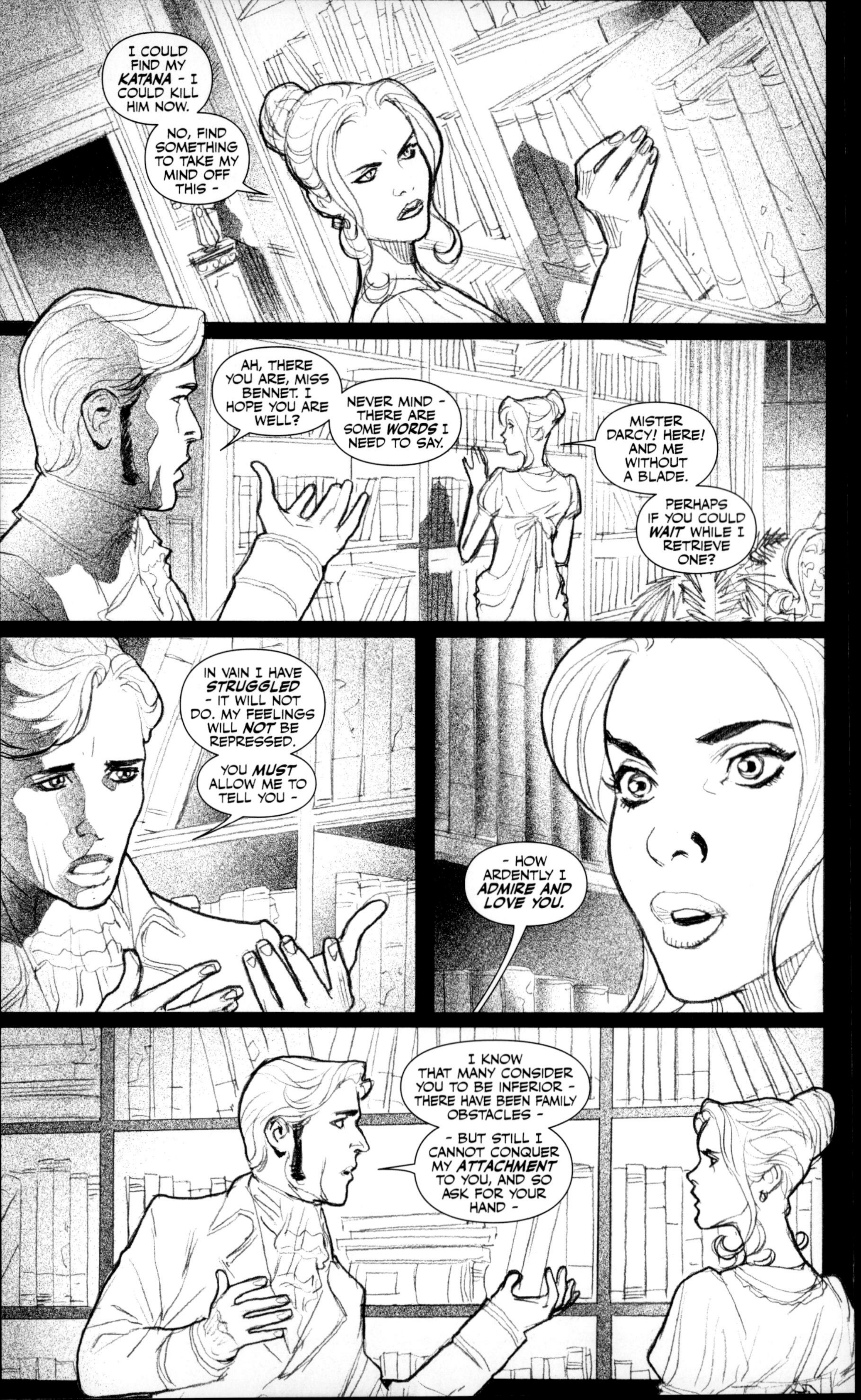
I COULD FIND MY *KATANA* - I COULD KILL HIM NOW.
NO, FIND SOMETHING TO TAKE MY MIND OFF THIS -
AH, THERE YOU ARE, MISS BENNET. I HOPE YOU ARE WELL?
NEVER MIND - THERE ARE SOME *WORDS* I NEED TO SAY.
MISTER DARCY! HERE! AND ME WITHOUT A BLADE.
PERHAPS IF YOU COULD *WAIT* WHILE I RETRIEVE ONE?
IN VAIN I HAVE *STRUGGLED* - IT WILL NOT DO. MY FEELINGS WILL *NOT* BE REPRESSED.
YOU *MUST* ALLOW ME TO TELL YOU -
- HOW ARDENTLY I *ADMIRE AND LOVE YOU.*
I KNOW THAT MANY CONSIDER YOU TO BE INFERIOR - THERE HAVE BEEN FAMILY OBSTACLES -
- BUT STILL I CANNOT CONQUER MY *ATTACHMENT* TO YOU, AND SO ASK FOR YOUR HAND -

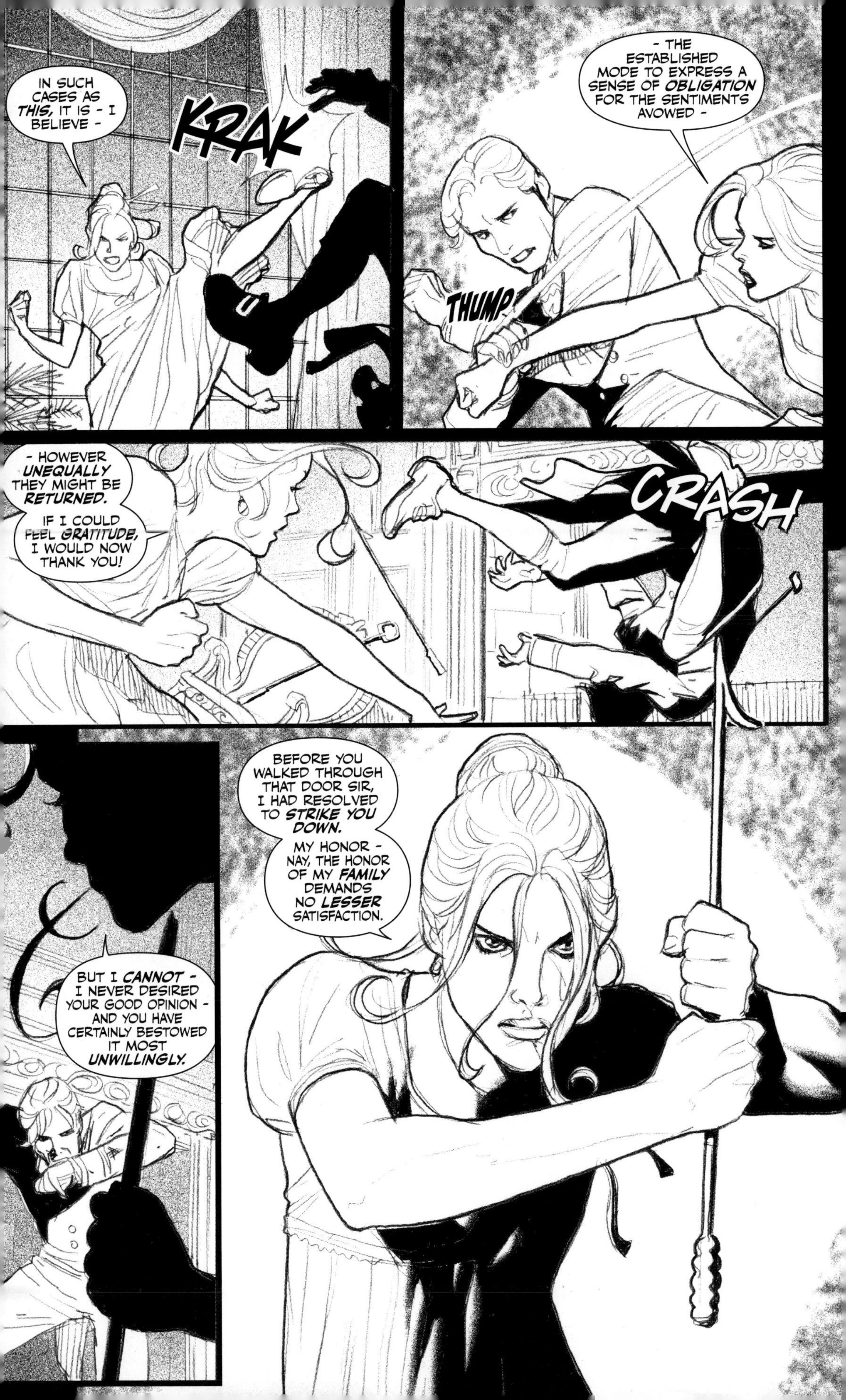
IN SUCH CASES AS THIS, IT IS - I BELIEVE -
KRAK
- THE ESTABLISHED MODE TO EXPRESS A SENSE OF OBLIGATION FOR THE SENTIMENTS AVOWED -
THUMP
- HOWEVER UNEQUALLY THEY MIGHT BE RETURNED.
IF I COULD FEEL GRATITUDE, I WOULD NOW THANK YOU!
CRASH
BUT I CANNOT - I NEVER DESIRED YOUR GOOD OPINION - AND YOU HAVE CERTAINLY BESTOWED IT MOST UNWILLINGLY.
BEFORE YOU WALKED THROUGH THAT DOOR SIR, I HAD RESOLVED TO STRIKE YOU DOWN.
MY HONOR - NAY, THE HONOR OF MY FAMILY DEMANDS NO LESSER SATISFACTION.

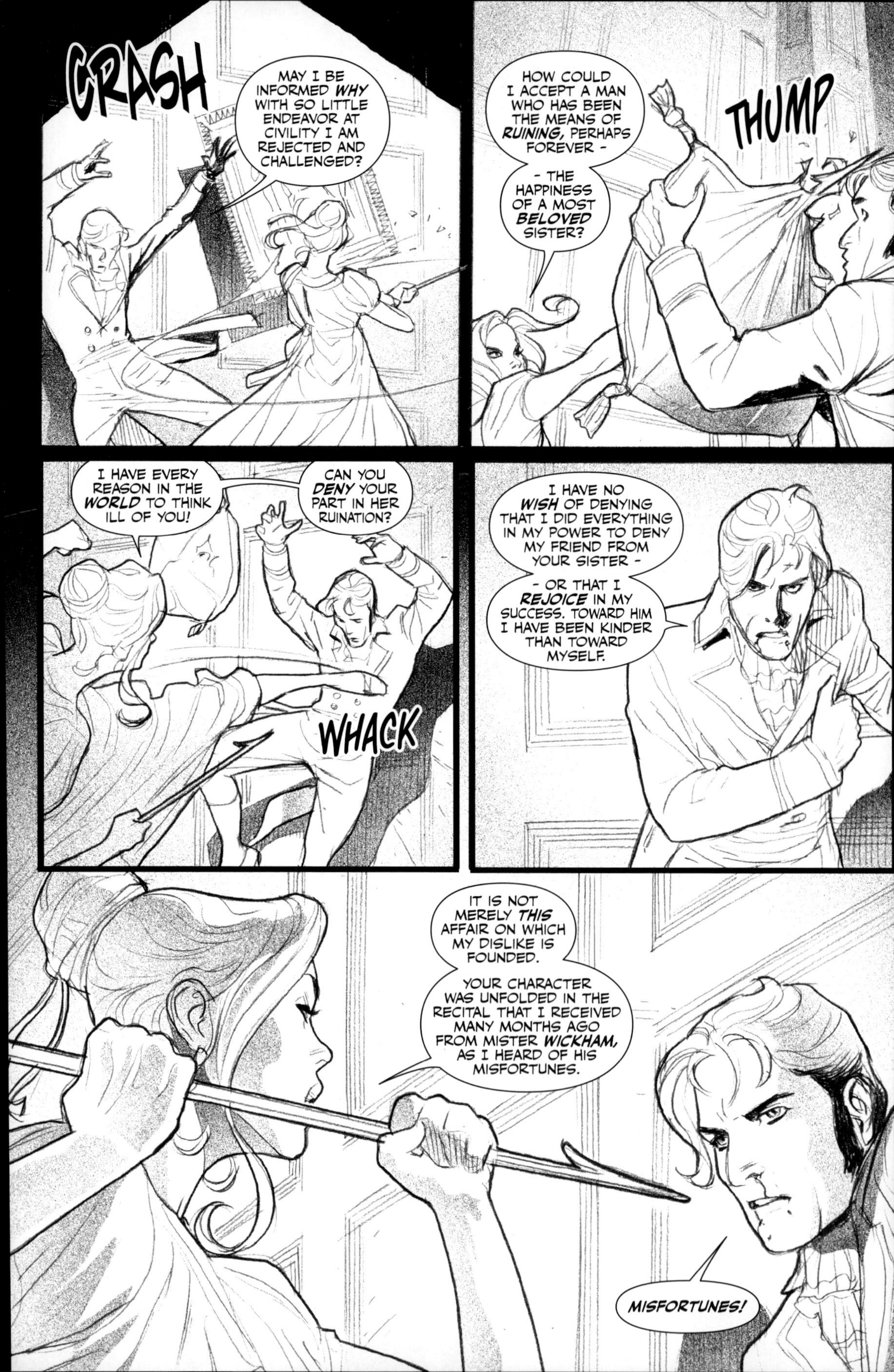
CRASH
MAY I BE INFORMED WHY WITH SO LITTLE ENDEAVOR AT CIVILITY I AM REJECTED AND CHALLENGED?
HOW COULD I ACCEPT A MAN WHO HAS BEEN THE MEANS OF RUINING, PERHAPS FOREVER -
- THE HAPPINESS OF A MOST BELOVED SISTER?
THUMP
I HAVE EVERY REASON IN THE WORLD TO THINK ILL OF YOU!
CAN YOU DENY YOUR PART IN HER RUINATION?
WHACK
I HAVE NO WISH OF DENYING THAT I DID EVERYTHING IN MY POWER TO DENY MY FRIEND FROM YOUR SISTER -
- OR THAT I REJOICE IN MY SUCCESS. TOWARD HIM I HAVE BEEN KINDER THAN TOWARD MYSELF.
IT IS NOT MERELY THIS AFFAIR ON WHICH MY DISLIKE IS FOUNDED.
YOUR CHARACTER WAS UNFOLDED IN THE RECITAL THAT I RECEIVED MANY MONTHS AGO FROM MISTER WICKHAM, AS I HEARD OF HIS MISFORTUNES.
MISFORTUNES!

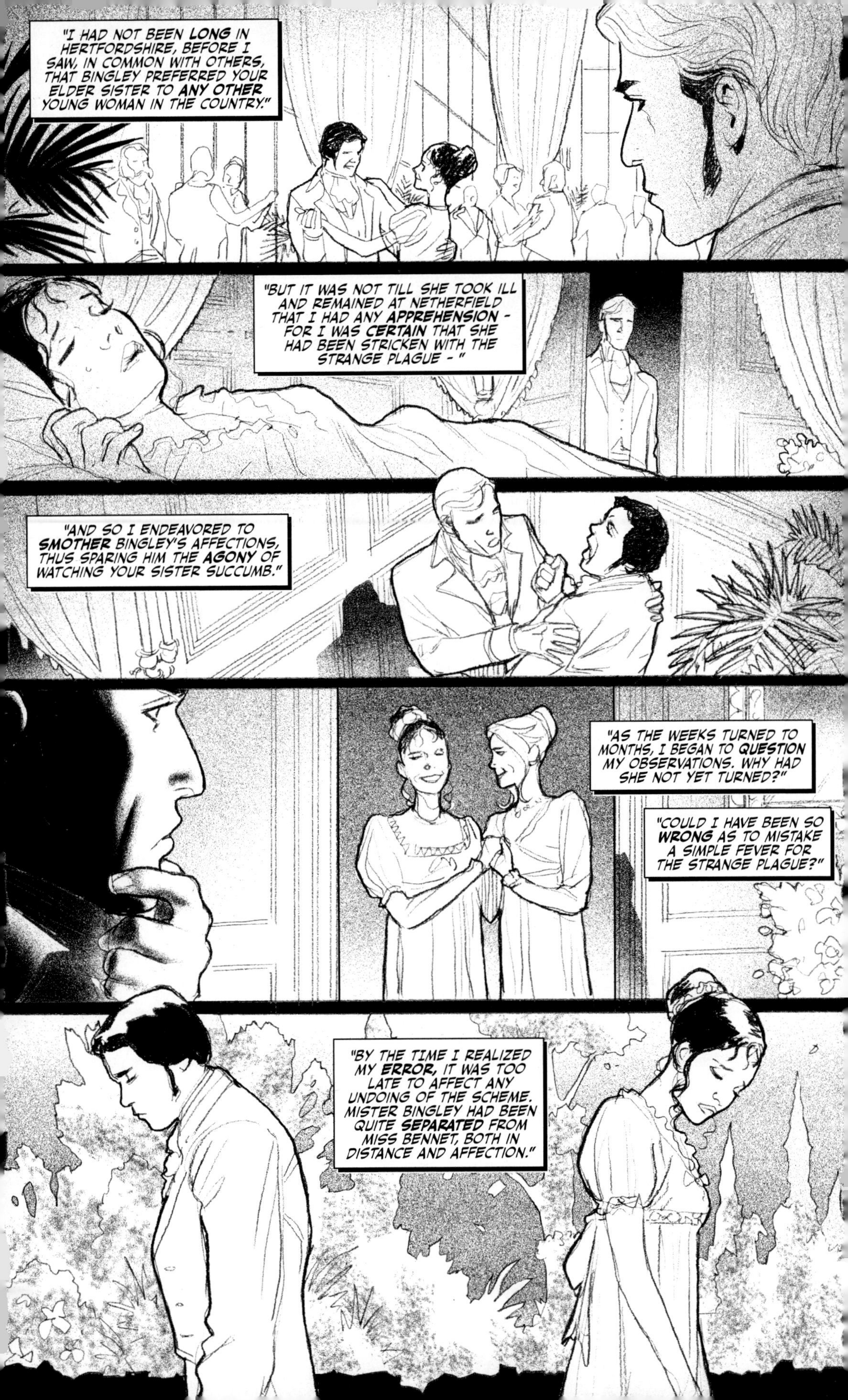
"I HAD NOT BEEN LONG IN HERTFORDSHIRE, BEFORE I SAW, IN COMMON WITH OTHERS, THAT BINGLEY PREFERRED YOUR ELDER SISTER TO ANY OTHER YOUNG WOMAN IN THE COUNTRY."
"BUT IT WAS NOT TILL SHE TOOK ILL AND REMAINED AT NETHERFIELD THAT I HAD ANY APPREHENSION - FOR I WAS CERTAIN THAT SHE HAD BEEN STRICKEN WITH THE STRANGE PLAGUE - "
"AND SO I ENDEAVORED TO SMOTHER BINGLEY'S AFFECTIONS, THUS SPARING HIM THE AGONY OF WATCHING YOUR SISTER SUCCUMB."
"AS THE WEEKS TURNED TO MONTHS, I BEGAN TO QUESTION MY OBSERVATIONS. WHY HAD SHE NOT YET TURNED?"
"COULD I HAVE BEEN SO WRONG AS TO MISTAKE A SIMPLE FEVER FOR THE STRANGE PLAGUE?"
"BY THE TIME I REALIZED MY ERROR, IT WAS TOO LATE TO AFFECT ANY UNDOING OF THE SCHEME. MISTER BINGLEY HAD BEEN QUITE SEPARATED FROM MISS BENNET, BOTH IN DISTANCE AND AFFECTION."

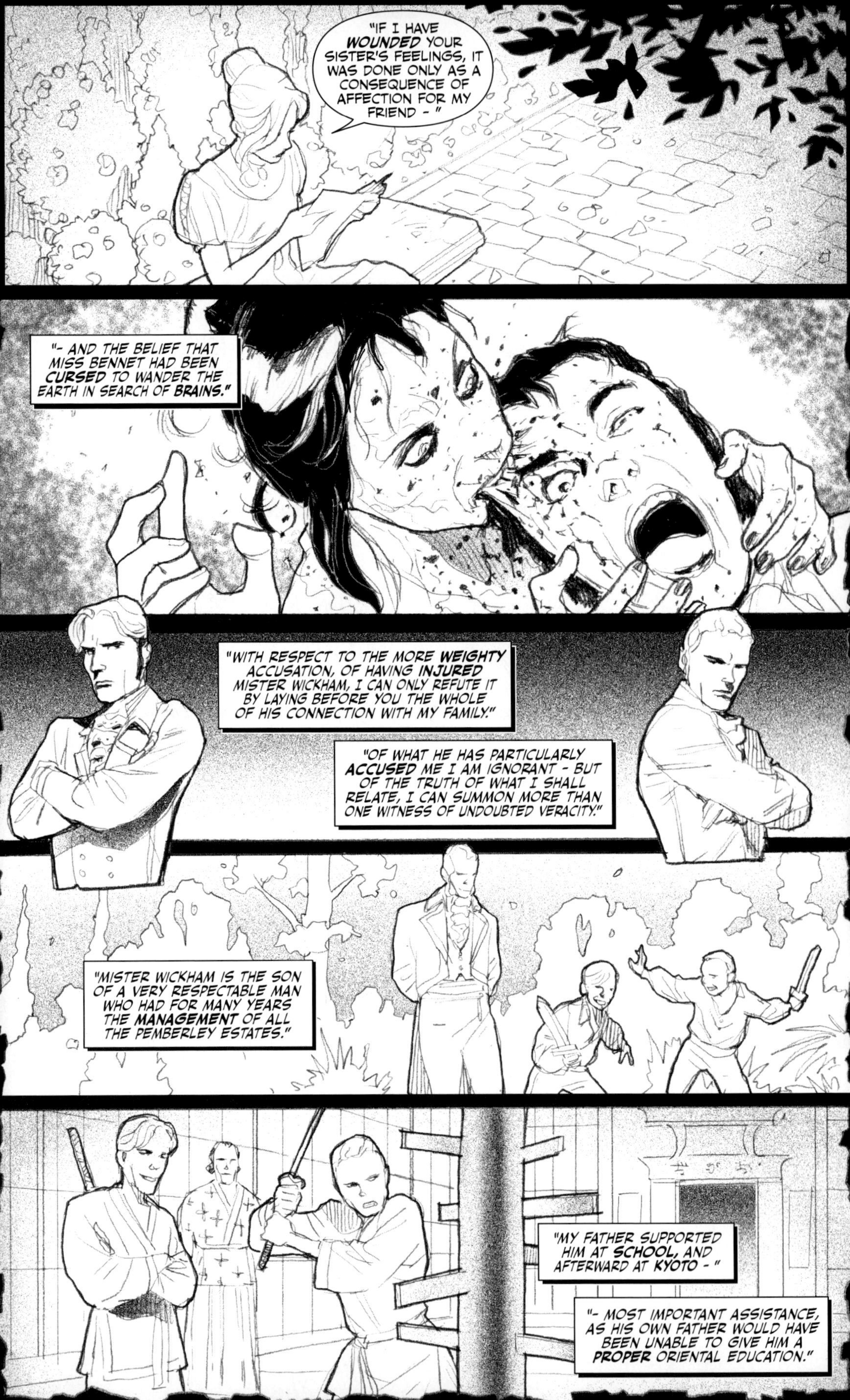

"IF I HAVE WOUNDED YOUR SISTER'S FEELINGS, IT WAS DONE ONLY AS A CONSEQUENCE OF AFFECTION FOR MY FRIEND - "
"- AND THE BELIEF THAT MISS BENNET HAD BEEN CURSED TO WANDER THE EARTH IN SEARCH OF BRAINS."
"WITH RESPECT TO THE MORE WEIGHTY ACCUSATION, OF HAVING INJURED MISTER WICKHAM, I CAN ONLY REFUTE IT BY LAYING BEFORE YOU THE WHOLE OF HIS CONNECTION WITH MY FAMILY."
"OF WHAT HE HAS PARTICULARLY ACCUSED ME I AM IGNORANT - BUT OF THE TRUTH OF WHAT I SHALL RELATE, I CAN SUMMON MORE THAN ONE WITNESS OF UNDOUBTED VERACITY."
"MISTER WICKHAM IS THE SON OF A VERY RESPECTABLE MAN WHO HAD FOR MANY YEARS THE MANAGEMENT OF ALL THE PEMBERLEY ESTATES."
"MY FATHER SUPPORTED HIM AT SCHOOL, AND AFTERWARD AT KYOTO - "
"- MOST IMPORTANT ASSISTANCE, AS HIS OWN FATHER WOULD HAVE BEEN UNABLE TO GIVE HIM A PROPER ORIENTAL EDUCATION."

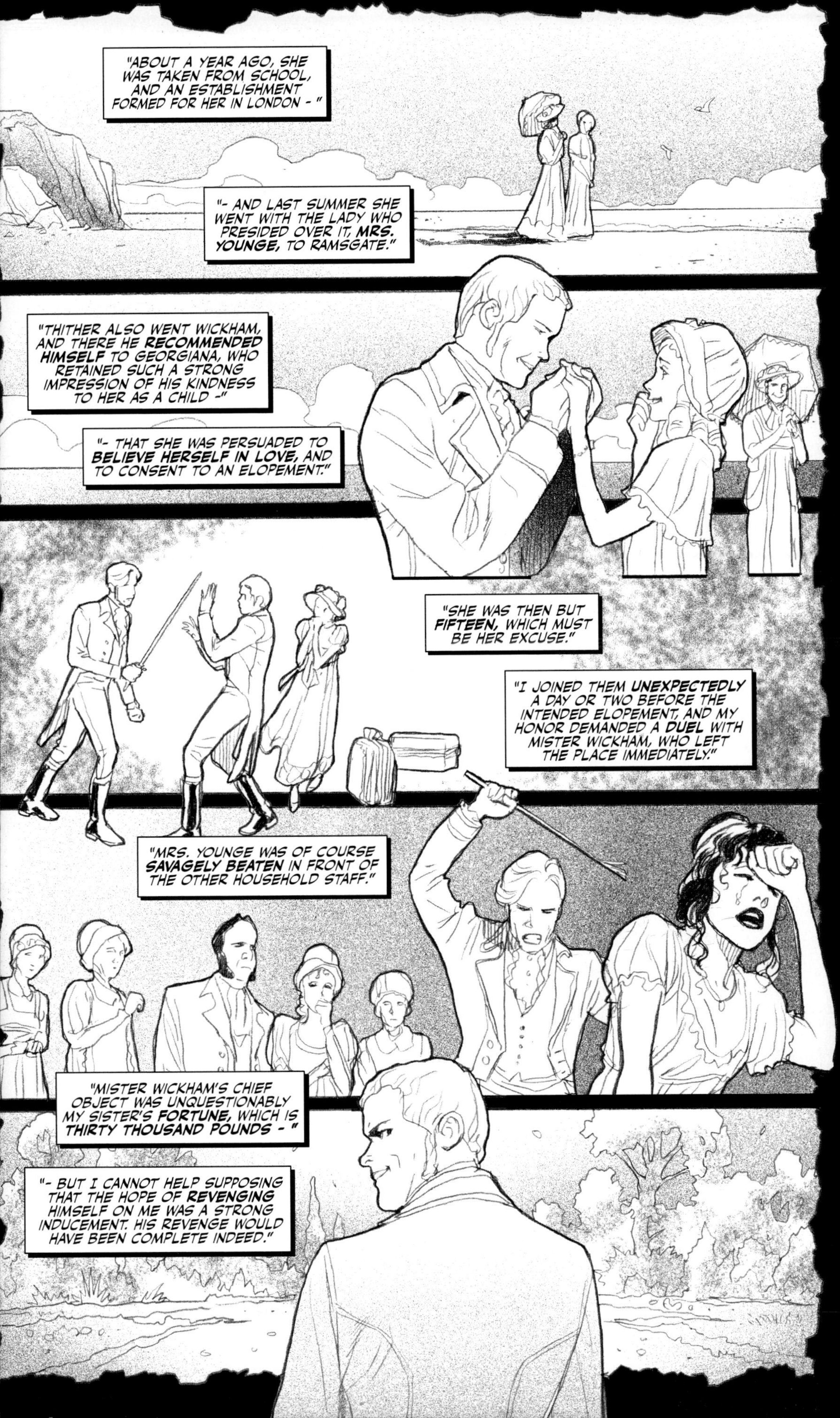
"ABOUT A YEAR AGO, SHE WAS TAKEN FROM SCHOOL, AND AN ESTABLISHMENT FORMED FOR HER IN LONDON - "
"- AND LAST SUMMER SHE WENT WITH THE LADY WHO PRESIDED OVER IT, MRS. YOUNGE, TO RAMSGATE."
"THITHER ALSO WENT WICKHAM, AND THERE HE RECOMMENDED HIMSELF TO GEORGIANA, WHO RETAINED SUCH A STRONG IMPRESSION OF HIS KINDNESS TO HER AS A CHILD -"
"- THAT SHE WAS PERSUADED TO BELIEVE HERSELF IN LOVE, AND TO CONSENT TO AN ELOPEMENT."
"SHE WAS THEN BUT FIFTEEN, WHICH MUST BE HER EXCUSE."
"I JOINED THEM UNEXPECTEDLY A DAY OR TWO BEFORE THE INTENDED ELOPEMENT, AND MY HONOR DEMANDED A DUEL WITH MISTER WICKHAM, WHO LEFT THE PLACE IMMEDIATELY."
"MRS. YOUNGE WAS OF COURSE SAVAGELY BEATEN IN FRONT OF THE OTHER HOUSEHOLD STAFF."
"MISTER WICKHAM'S CHIEF OBJECT WAS UNQUESTIONABLY MY SISTER'S FORTUNE, WHICH IS THIRTY THOUSAND POUNDS - "
"- BUT I CANNOT HELP SUPPOSING THAT THE HOPE OF REVENGING HIMSELF ON ME WAS A STRONG INDUCEMENT. HIS REVENGE WOULD HAVE BEEN COMPLETE INDEED."

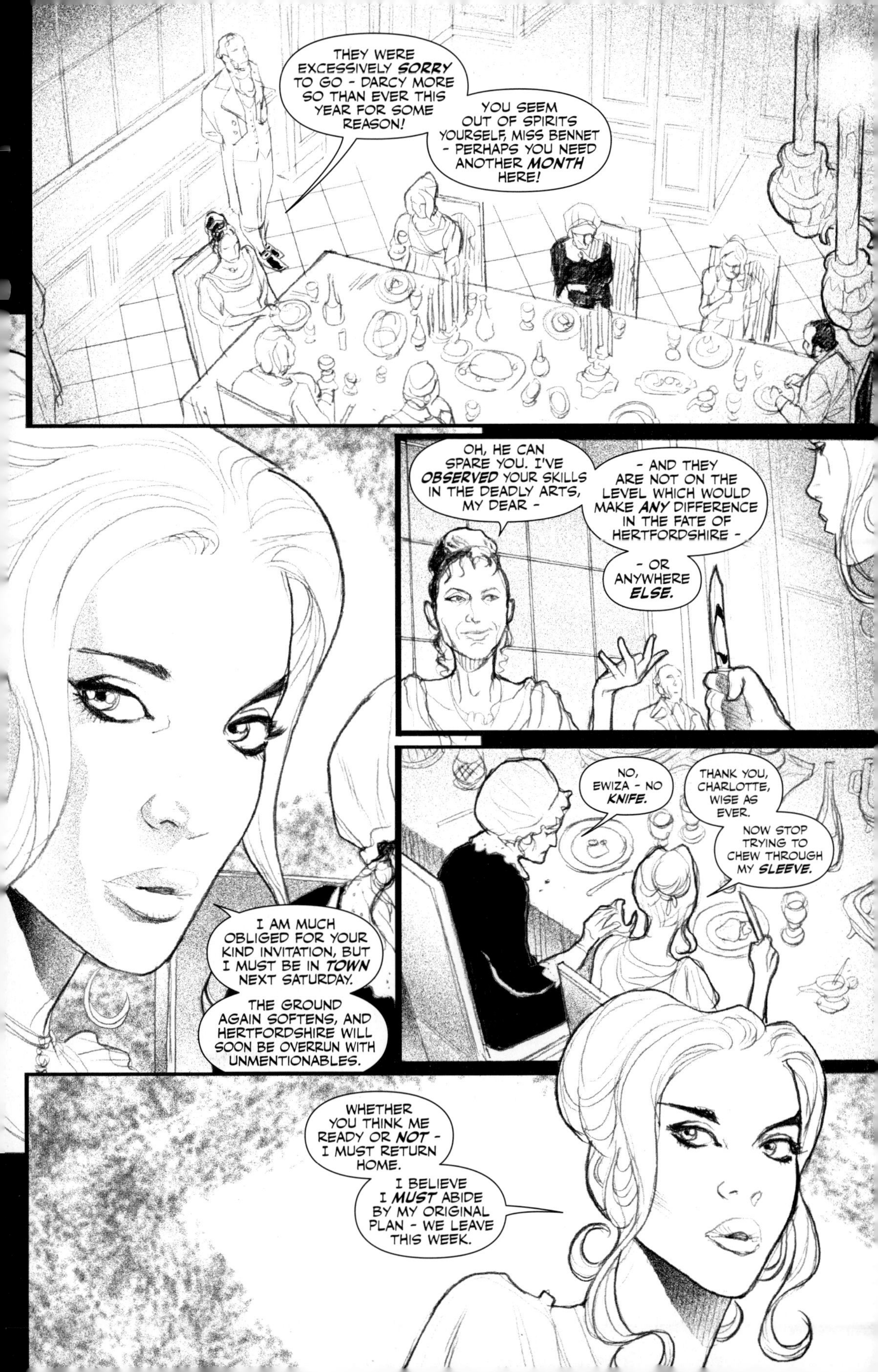
THEY WERE EXCESSIVELY SORRY TO GO - DARCY MORE SO THAN EVER THIS YEAR FOR SOME REASON!
YOU SEEM OUT OF SPIRITS YOURSELF, MISS BENNET - PERHAPS YOU NEED ANOTHER MONTH HERE!
OH, HE CAN SPARE YOU. I'VE OBSERVED YOUR SKILLS IN THE DEADLY ARTS, MY DEAR -
- AND THEY ARE NOT ON THE LEVEL WHICH WOULD MAKE ANY DIFFERENCE IN THE FATE OF HERTFORDSHIRE -
- OR ANYWHERE ELSE.
I AM MUCH OBLIGED FOR YOUR KIND INVITATION, BUT I MUST BE IN TOWN NEXT SATURDAY.
THE GROUND AGAIN SOFTENS, AND HERTFORDSHIRE WILL SOON BE OVERRUN WITH UNMENTIONABLES.
NO, EWIZA - NO KNIFE.
THANK YOU, CHARLOTTE, WISE AS EVER.
NOW STOP TRYING TO CHEW THROUGH MY SLEEVE.
WHETHER YOU THINK ME READY OR NOT - I MUST RETURN HOME.
I BELIEVE I MUST ABIDE BY MY ORIGINAL PLAN - WE LEAVE THIS WEEK.

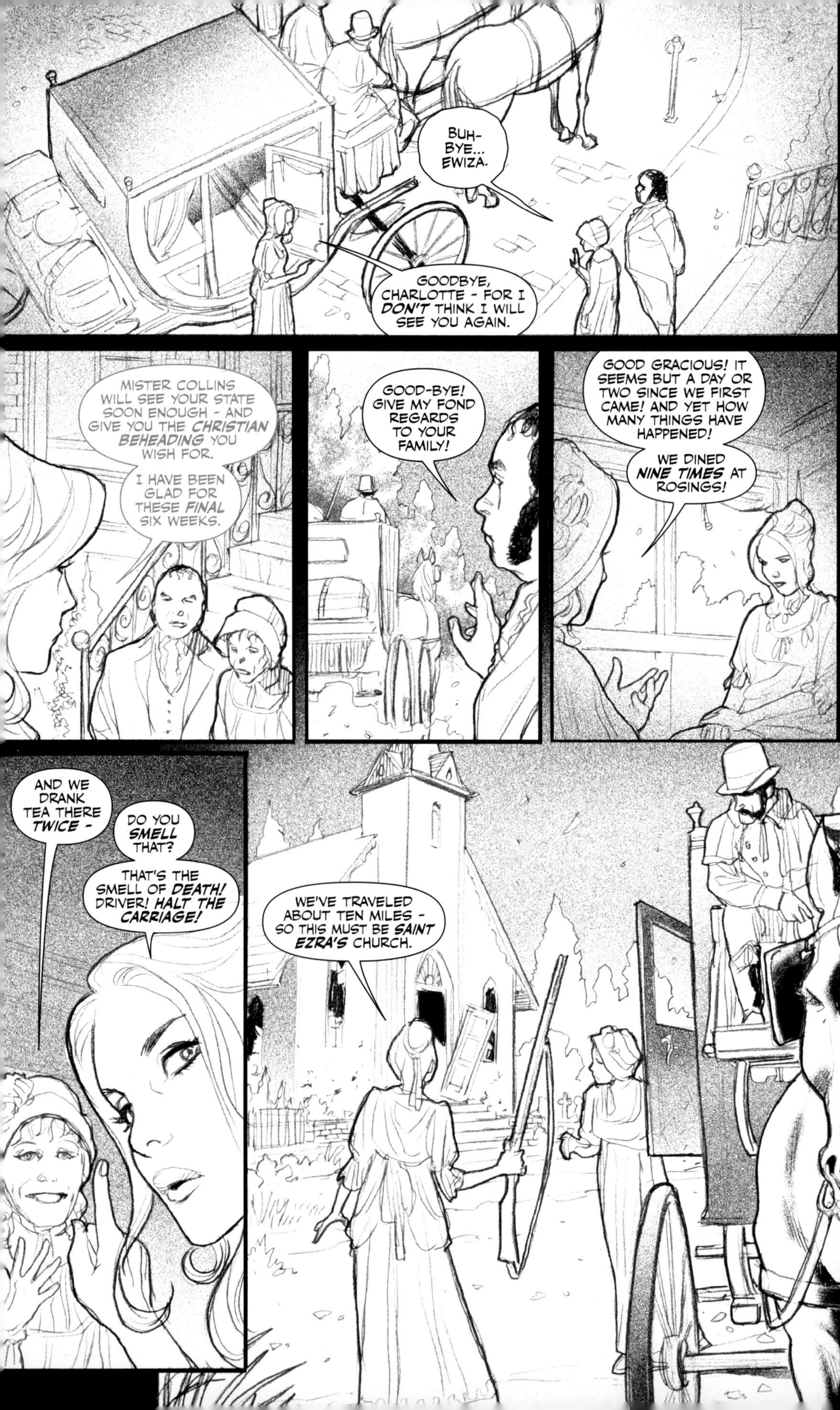
BUH-BYE... EWIZA.
GOODBYE, CHARLOTTE - FOR I DON'T THINK I WILL SEE YOU AGAIN.
MISTER COLLINS WILL SEE YOUR STATE SOON ENOUGH - AND GIVE YOU THE CHRISTIAN BEHEADING YOU WISH FOR.
I HAVE BEEN GLAD FOR THESE FINAL SIX WEEKS.
GOOD-BYE! GIVE MY FOND REGARDS TO YOUR FAMILY!
GOOD GRACIOUS! IT SEEMS BUT A DAY OR TWO SINCE WE FIRST CAME! AND YET HOW MANY THINGS HAVE HAPPENED!
WE DINED NINE TIMES AT ROSINGS!
AND WE DRANK TEA THERE TWICE -
DO YOU SMELL THAT?
THAT'S THE SMELL OF DEATH! DRIVER! HALT THE CARRIAGE!
WE'VE TRAVELED ABOUT TEN MILES - SO THIS MUST BE SAINT EZRA'S CHURCH.

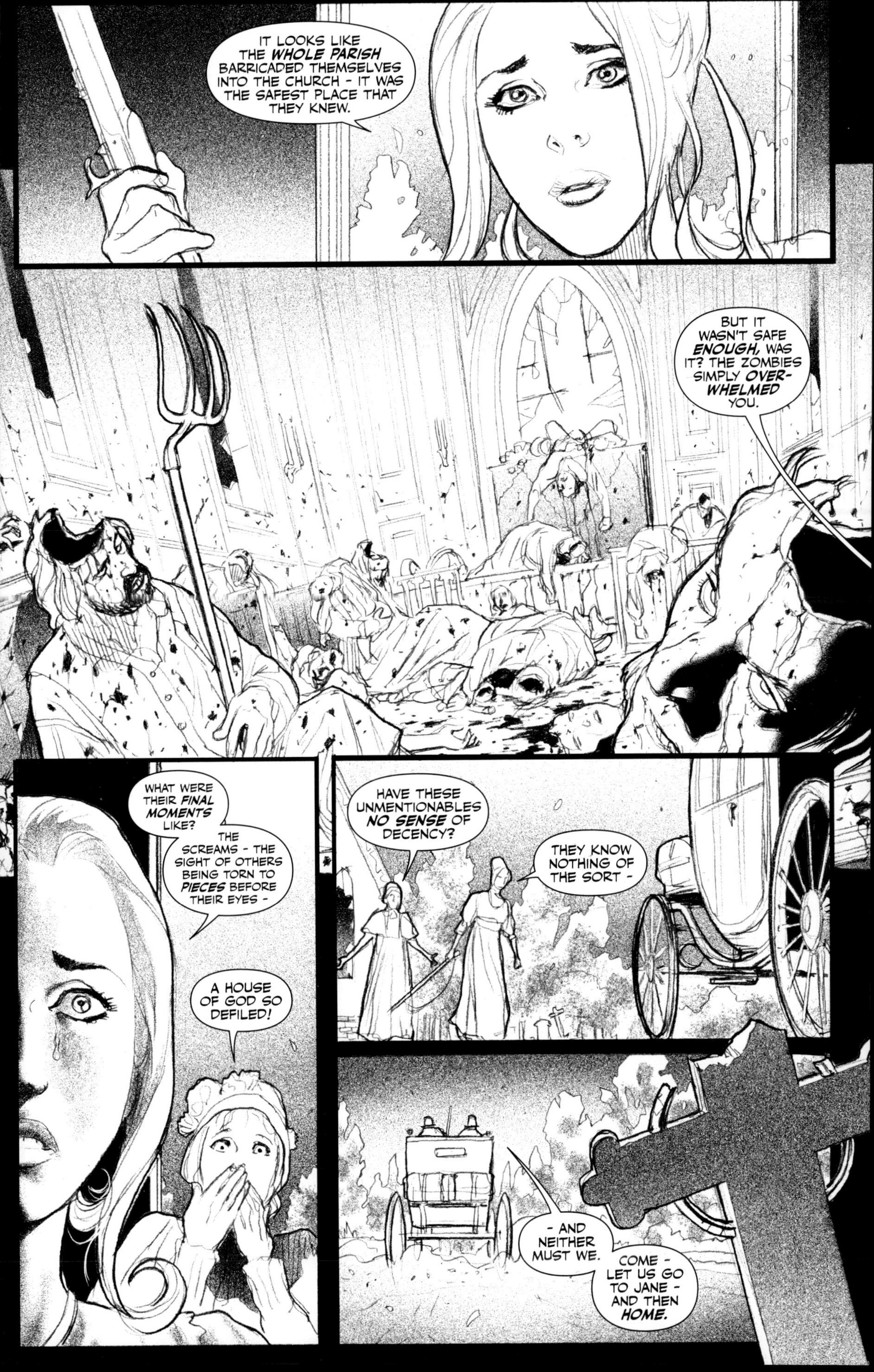
IT LOOKS LIKE THE WHOLE PARISH BARRICADED THEMSELVES INTO THE CHURCH - IT WAS THE SAFEST PLACE THAT THEY KNEW.
BUT IT WASN'T SAFE ENOUGH, WAS IT? THE ZOMBIES SIMPLY OVER-WHELMED YOU.
WHAT WERE THEIR FINAL MOMENTS LIKE?
THE SCREAMS - THE SIGHT OF OTHERS BEING TORN TO PIECES BEFORE THEIR EYES -
A HOUSE OF GOD SO DEFILED!
HAVE THESE UNMENTIONABLES NO SENSE OF DECENCY?
THEY KNOW NOTHING OF THE SORT -
- AND NEITHER MUST WE.
COME - LET US GO TO JANE - AND THEN HOME.

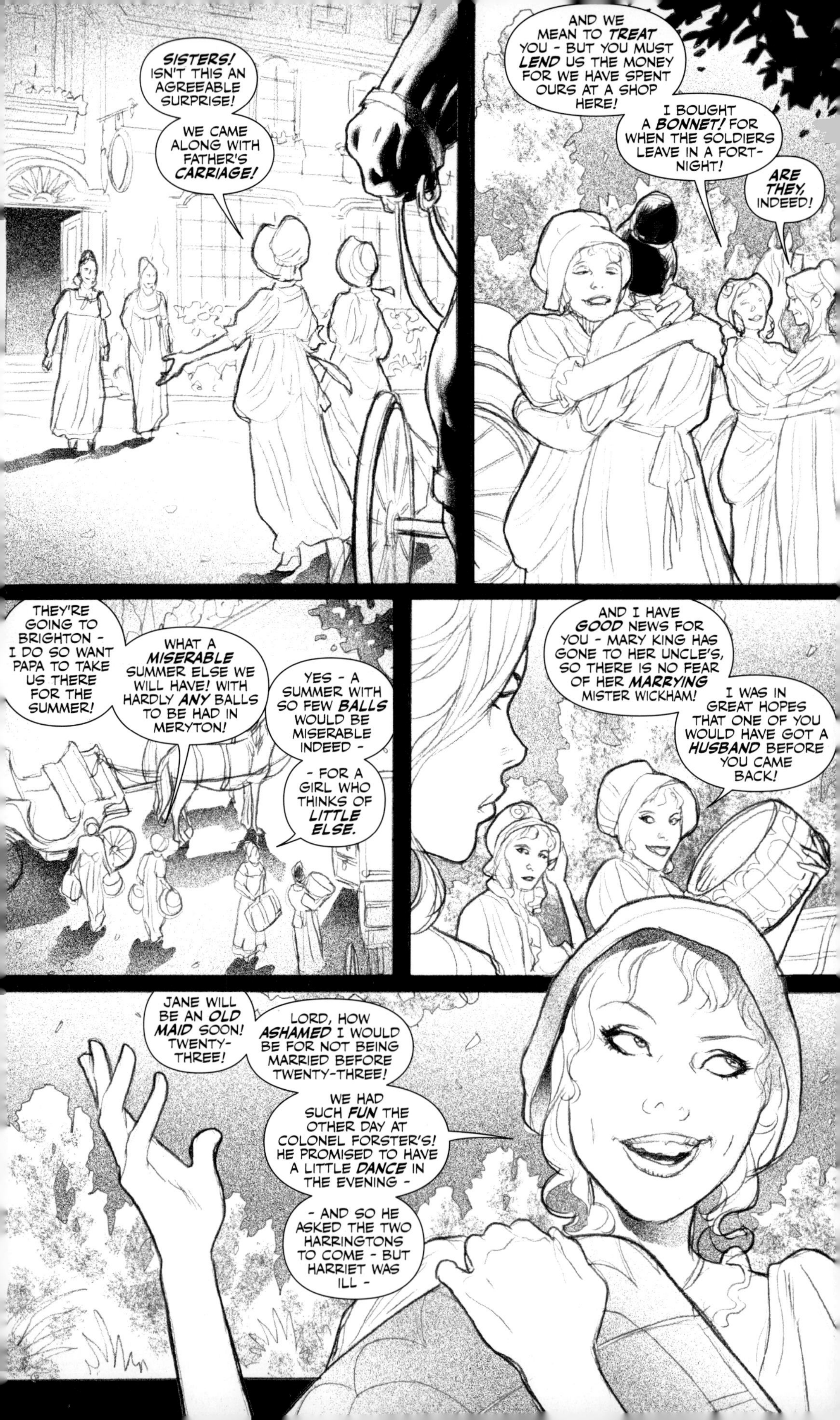
SISTERS! ISN'T THIS AN AGREEABLE SURPRISE!
WE CAME ALONG WITH FATHER'S CARRIAGE!
AND WE MEAN TO TREAT YOU - BUT YOU MUST LEND US THE MONEY FOR WE HAVE SPENT OURS AT A SHOP HERE!
I BOUGHT A BONNET! FOR WHEN THE SOLDIERS LEAVE IN A FORT-NIGHT!
ARE THEY, INDEED!
THEY'RE GOING TO BRIGHTON - I DO SO WANT PAPA TO TAKE US THERE FOR THE SUMMER!
WHAT A MISERABLE SUMMER ELSE WE WILL HAVE! WITH HARDLY ANY BALLS TO BE HAD IN MERYTON!
YES - A SUMMER WITH SO FEW BALLS WOULD BE MISERABLE INDEED -
- FOR A GIRL WHO THINKS OF LITTLE ELSE.
AND I HAVE GOOD NEWS FOR YOU - MARY KING HAS GONE TO HER UNCLE'S, SO THERE IS NO FEAR OF HER MARRYING MISTER WICKHAM!
I WAS IN GREAT HOPES THAT ONE OF YOU WOULD HAVE GOT A HUSBAND BEFORE YOU CAME BACK!
JANE WILL BE AN OLD MAID SOON! TWENTY-THREE!
LORD, HOW ASHAMED I WOULD BE FOR NOT BEING MARRIED BEFORE TWENTY-THREE!
WE HAD SUCH FUN THE OTHER DAY AT COLONEL FORSTER'S! HE PROMISED TO HAVE A LITTLE DANCE IN THE EVENING -
- AND SO HE ASKED THE TWO HARRINGTONS TO COME - BUT HARRIET WAS ILL -

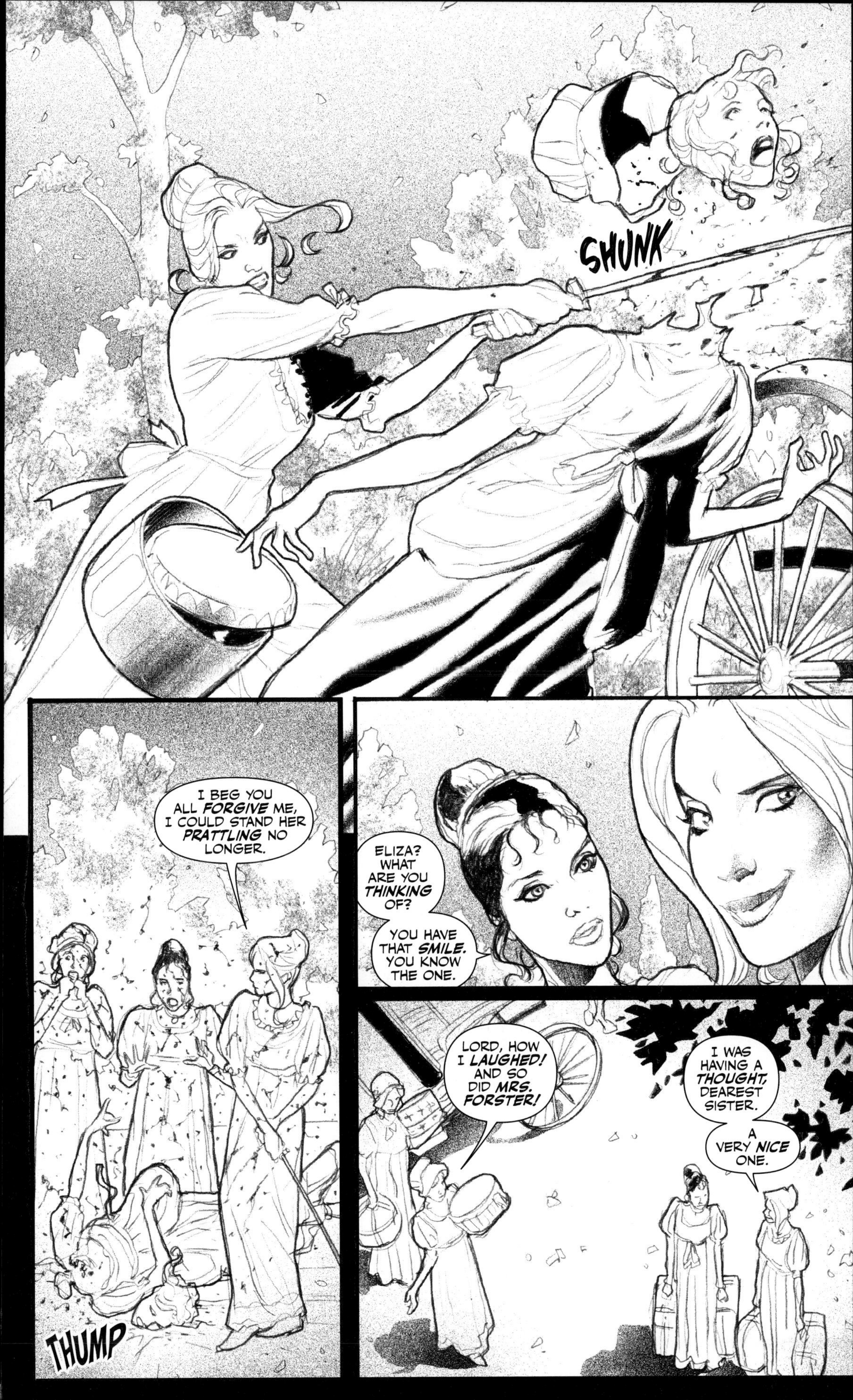
SHUNK
I BEG YOU ALL FORGIVE ME, I COULD STAND HER PRATTLING NO LONGER.
THUMP
ELIZA? WHAT ARE YOU THINKING OF?
YOU HAVE THAT SMILE. YOU KNOW THE ONE.
LORD, HOW I LAUGHED! AND SO DID MRS. FORSTER!
I WAS HAVING A THOUGHT, DEAREST SISTER.
A VERY NICE ONE.

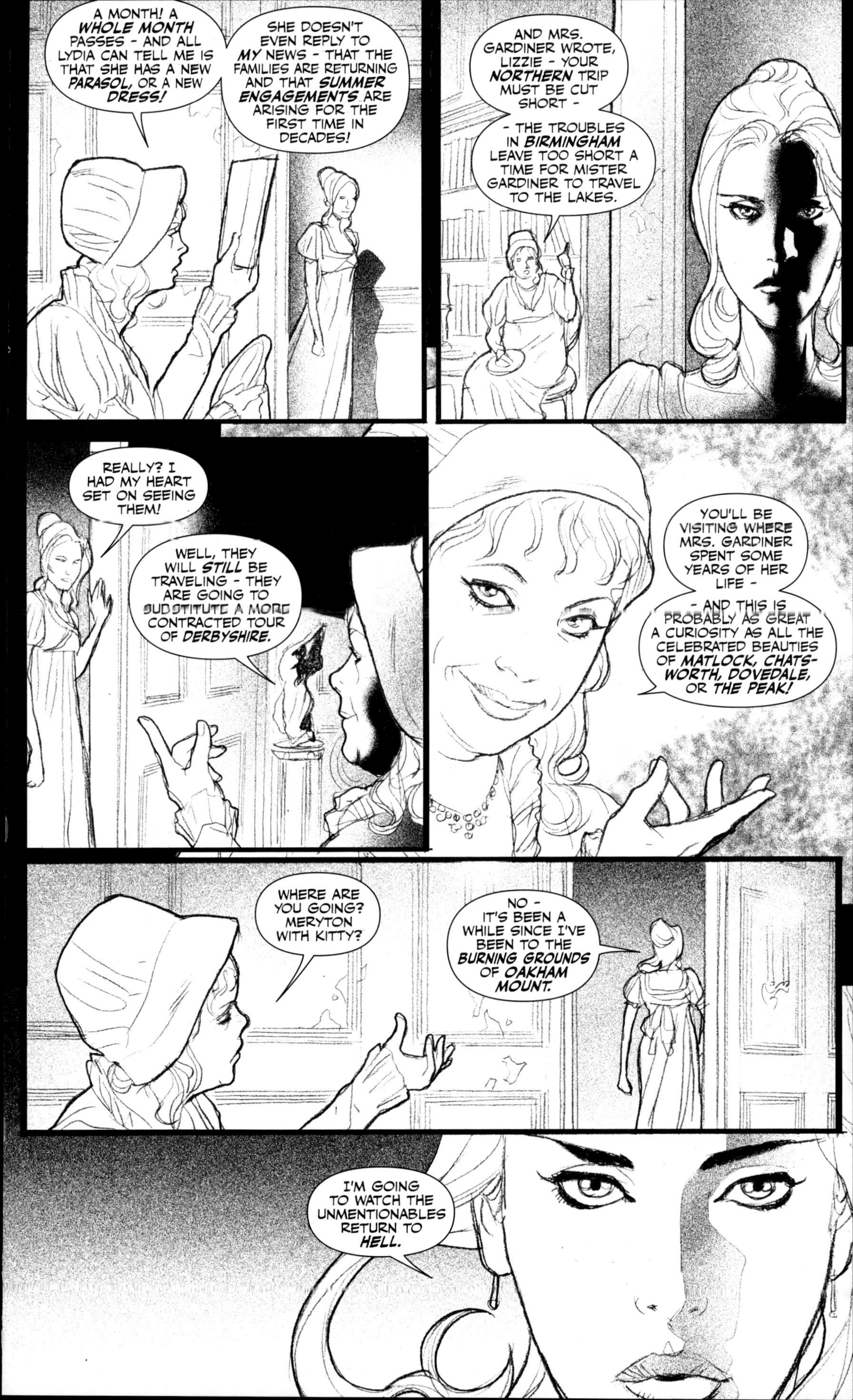
A MONTH! A WHOLE MONTH PASSES - AND ALL LYDIA CAN TELL ME IS THAT SHE HAS A NEW PARASOL, OR A NEW DRESS!
SHE DOESN'T EVEN REPLY TO MY NEWS - THAT THE FAMILIES ARE RETURNING AND THAT SUMMER ENGAGEMENTS ARE ARISING FOR THE FIRST TIME IN DECADES!
AND MRS. GARDINER WROTE, LIZZIE - YOUR NORTHERN TRIP MUST BE CUT SHORT -
- THE TROUBLES IN BIRMINGHAM LEAVE TOO SHORT A TIME FOR MISTER GARDINER TO TRAVEL TO THE LAKES.
REALLY? I HAD MY HEART SET ON SEEING THEM!
WELL, THEY WILL STILL BE TRAVELING - THEY ARE GOING TO SUBSTITUTE A MORE CONTRACTED TOUR OF DERBYSHIRE.
YOU'LL BE VISITING WHERE MRS. GARDINER SPENT SOME YEARS OF HER LIFE -
- AND THIS IS PROBABLY AS GREAT A CURIOSITY AS ALL THE CELEBRATED BEAUTIES OF MATLOCK, CHATSWORTH, DOVEDALE, OR THE PEAK!
WHERE ARE YOU GOING? MERYTON WITH KITTY?
NO - IT'S BEEN A WHILE SINCE I'VE BEEN TO THE BURNING GROUNDS OF OAKHAM MOUNT.
I'M GOING TO WATCH THE UNMENTIONABLES RETURN TO HELL.

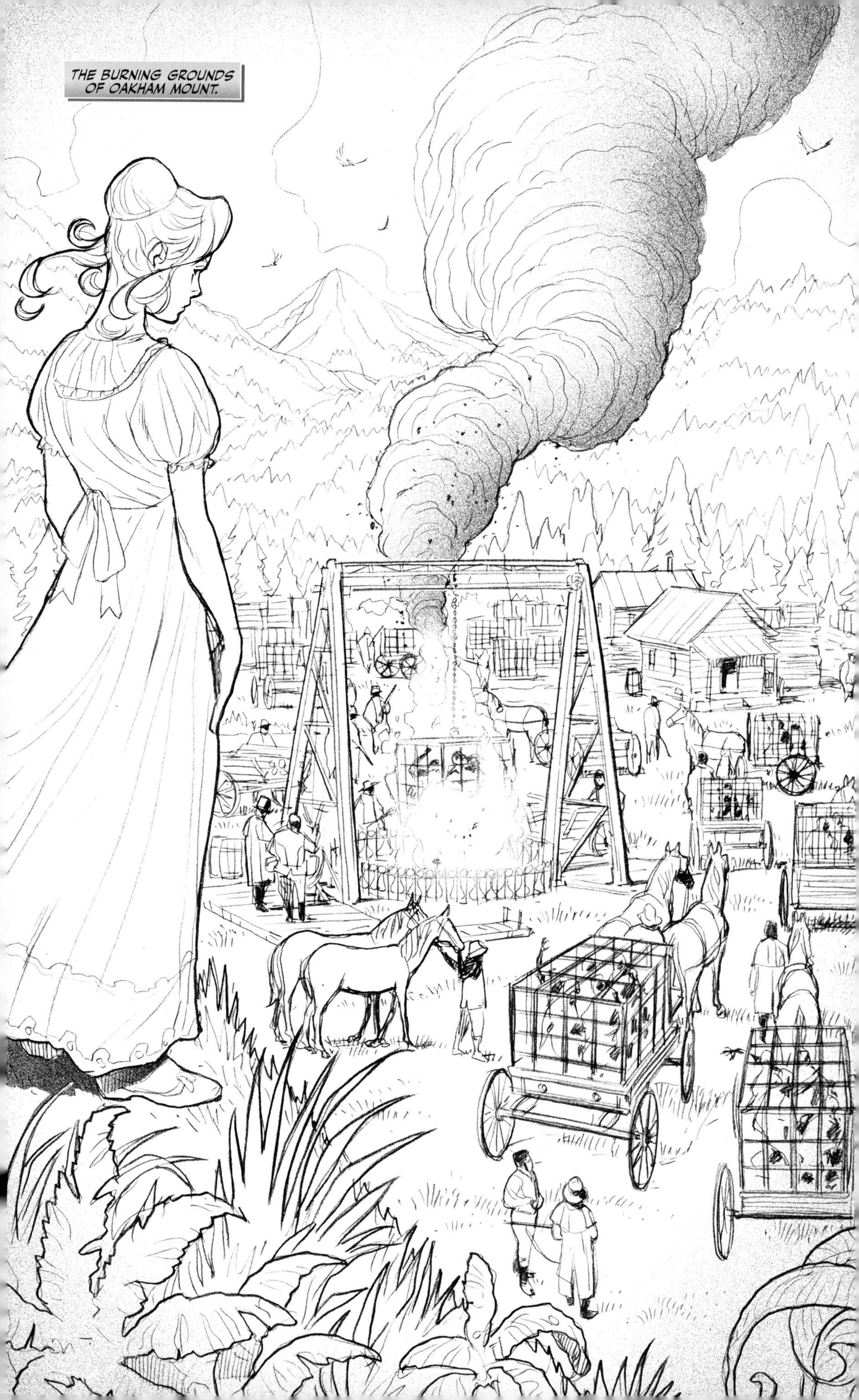
THE BURNING GROUNDS OF OAKHAM MOUNT.

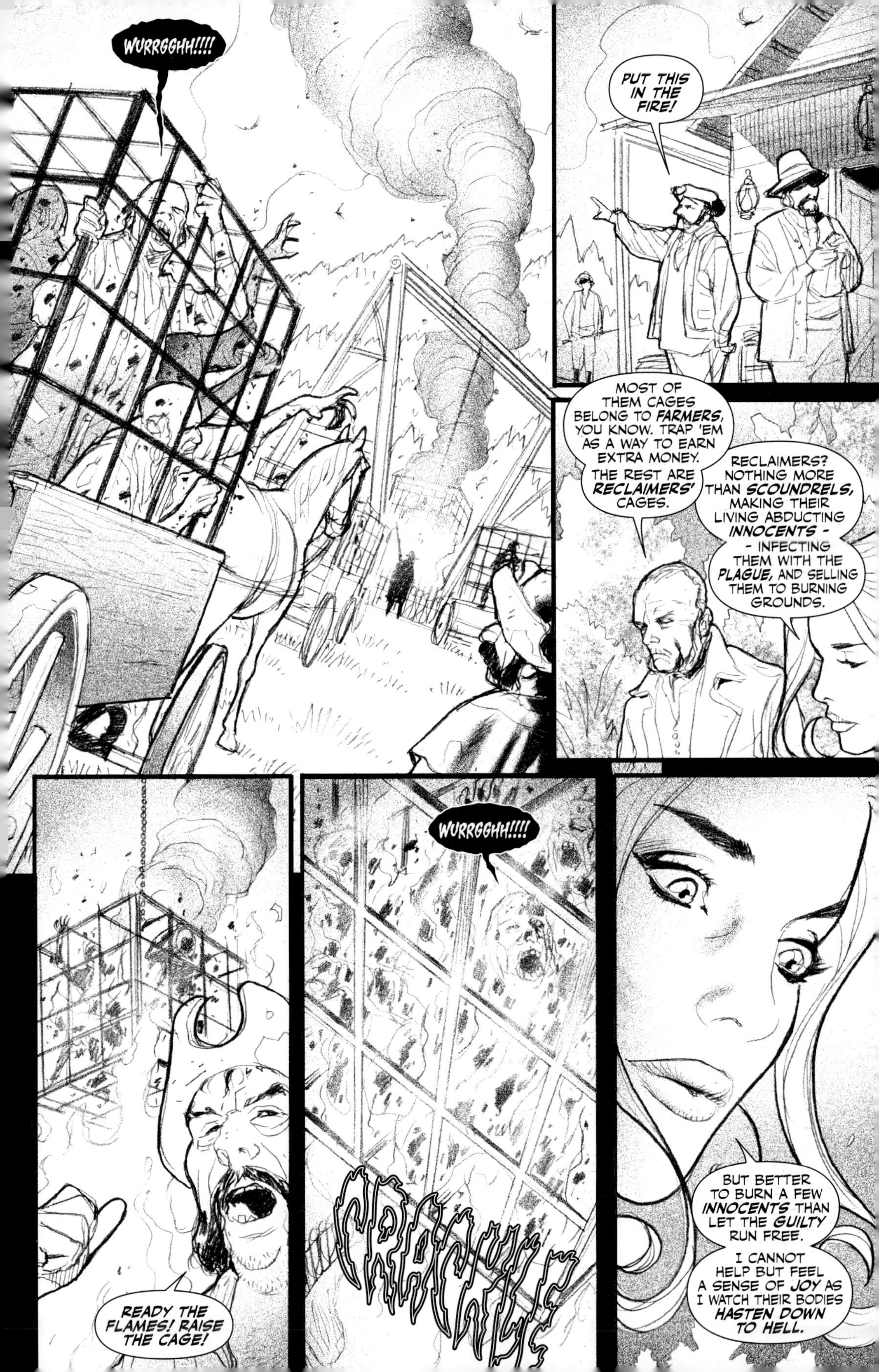
WURRGGHH!!!!
PUT THIS IN THE FIRE!
MOST OF THEM CAGES BELONG TO FARMERS, YOU KNOW. TRAP 'EM AS A WAY TO EARN EXTRA MONEY.
THE REST ARE RECLAIMERS' CAGES.
RECLAIMERS? NOTHING MORE THAN SCOUNDRELS, MAKING THEIR LIVING ABDUCTING INNOCENTS -
- INFECTING THEM WITH THE PLAGUE, AND SELLING THEM TO BURNING GROUNDS.
READY THE FLAMES! RAISE THE CAGE!
WURRGGHH!!!!
BUT BETTER TO BURN A FEW INNOCENTS THAN LET THE GUILTY RUN FREE.
I CANNOT HELP BUT FEEL A SENSE OF JOY AS I WATCH THEIR BODIES HASTEN DOWN TO HELL.

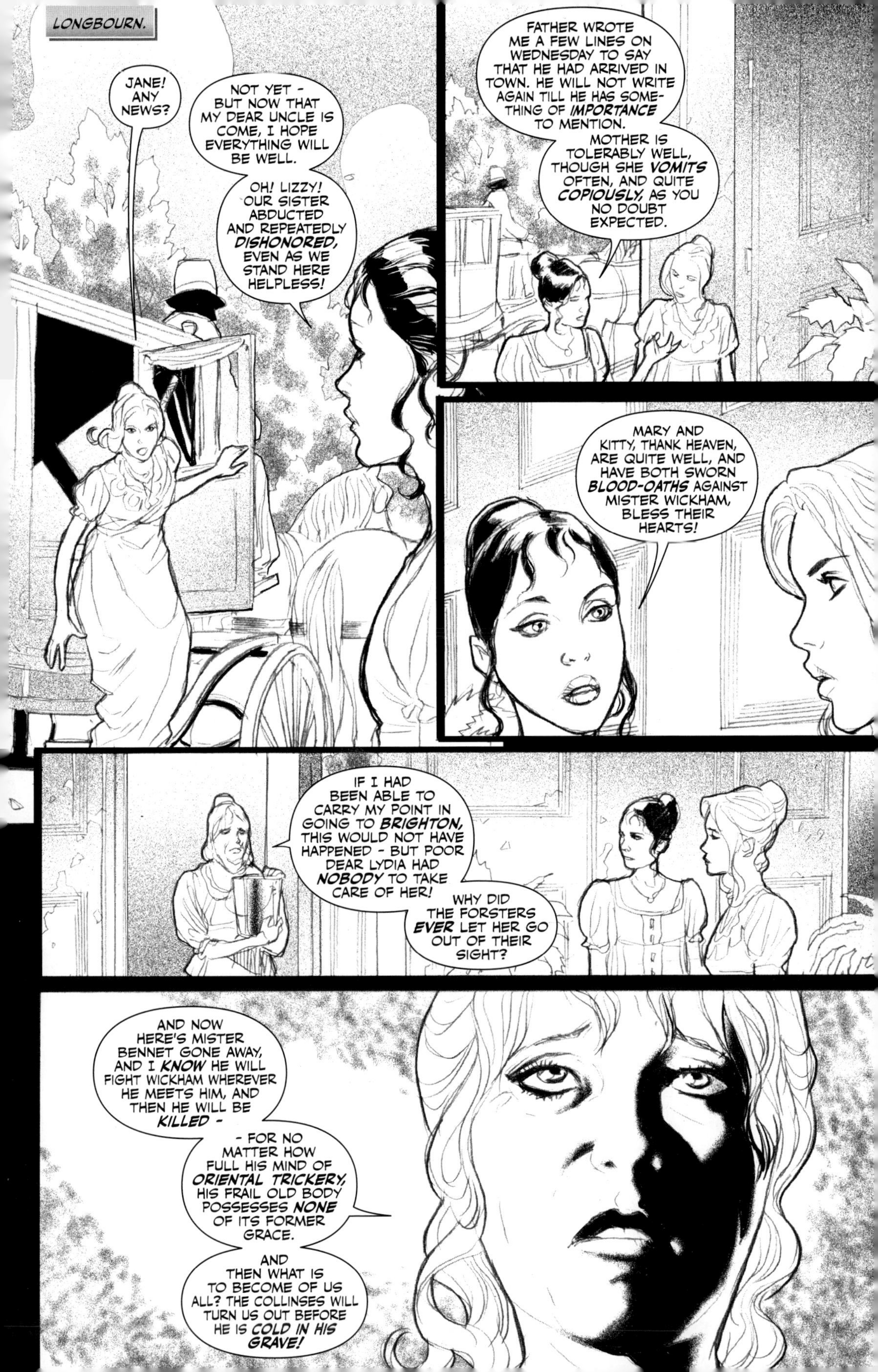
LONGBOURN.
JANE! ANY NEWS?
NOT YET - BUT NOW THAT MY DEAR UNCLE IS COME, I HOPE EVERYTHING WILL BE WELL.
OH! LIZZY! OUR SISTER ABDUCTED AND REPEATEDLY DISHONORED, EVEN AS WE STAND HERE HELPLESS!
FATHER WROTE ME A FEW LINES ON WEDNESDAY TO SAY THAT HE HAD ARRIVED IN TOWN. HE WILL NOT WRITE AGAIN TILL HE HAS SOMETHING OF IMPORTANCE TO MENTION.
MOTHER IS TOLERABLY WELL, THOUGH SHE VOMITS OFTEN, AND QUITE COPIOUSLY, AS YOU NO DOUBT EXPECTED.
MARY AND KITTY, THANK HEAVEN, ARE QUITE WELL, AND HAVE BOTH SWORN BLOOD-OATHS AGAINST MISTER WICKHAM, BLESS THEIR HEARTS!
IF I HAD BEEN ABLE TO CARRY MY POINT IN GOING TO BRIGHTON, THIS WOULD NOT HAVE HAPPENED - BUT POOR DEAR LYDIA HAD NOBODY TO TAKE CARE OF HER!
WHY DID THE FORSTERS EVER LET HER GO OUT OF THEIR SIGHT?
AND NOW HERE'S MISTER BENNET GONE AWAY, AND I KNOW HE WILL FIGHT WICKHAM WHEREVER HE MEETS HIM, AND THEN HE WILL BE KILLED -
- FOR NO MATTER HOW FULL HIS MIND OF ORIENTAL TRICKERY, HIS FRAIL OLD BODY POSSESSES NONE OF ITS FORMER GRACE.
AND THEN WHAT IS TO BECOME OF US ALL? THE COLLINSES WILL TURN US OUT BEFORE HE IS COLD IN HIS GRAVE!

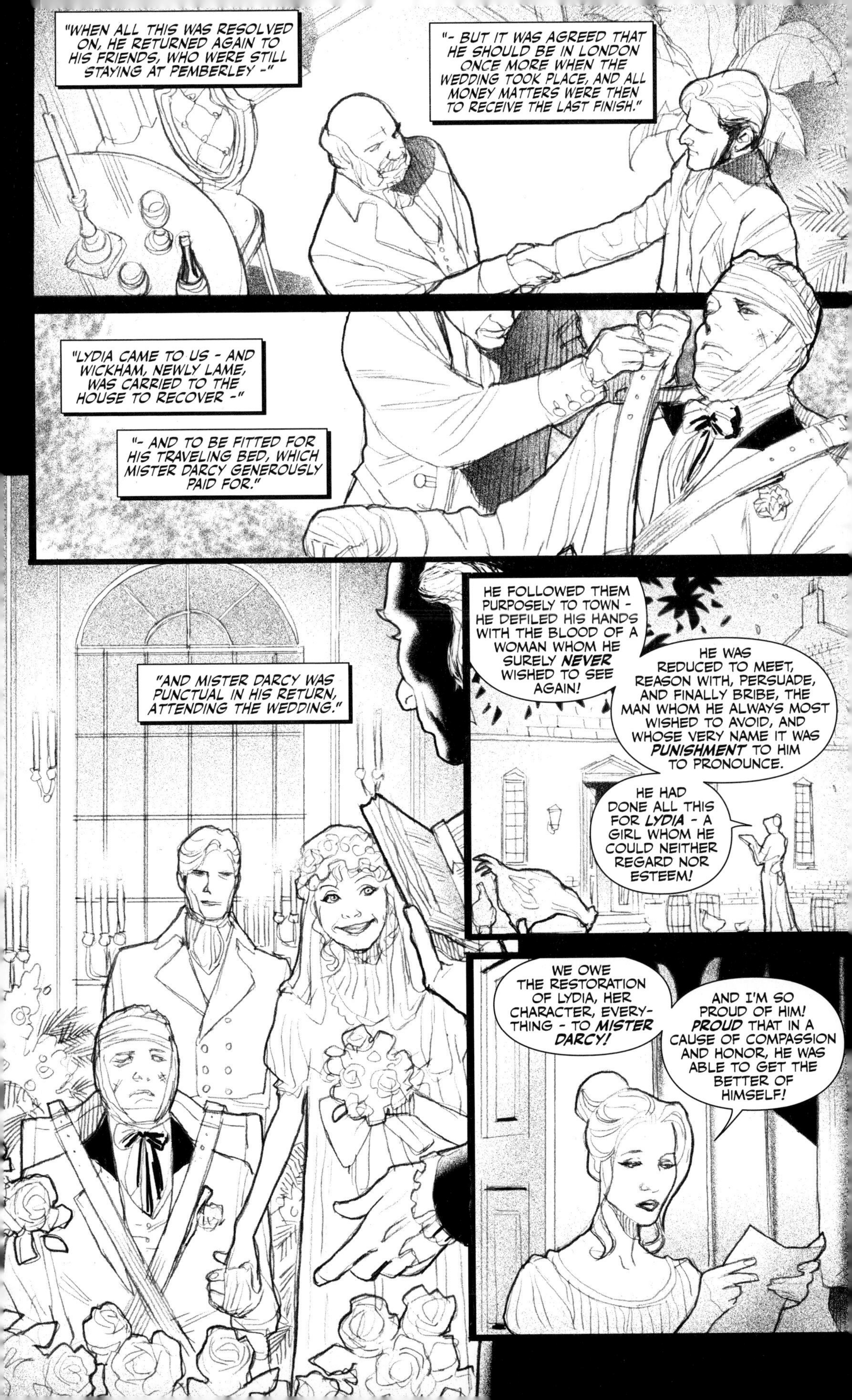
"WHEN ALL THIS WAS RESOLVED ON, HE RETURNED AGAIN TO HIS FRIENDS, WHO WERE STILL STAYING AT PEMBERLEY -"
"- BUT IT WAS AGREED THAT HE SHOULD BE IN LONDON ONCE MORE WHEN THE WEDDING TOOK PLACE, AND ALL MONEY MATTERS WERE THEN TO RECEIVE THE LAST FINISH."
"LYDIA CAME TO US - AND WICKHAM, NEWLY LAME, WAS CARRIED TO THE HOUSE TO RECOVER -"
"- AND TO BE FITTED FOR HIS TRAVELING BED, WHICH MISTER DARCY GENEROUSLY PAID FOR."
"AND MISTER DARCY WAS PUNCTUAL IN HIS RETURN, ATTENDING THE WEDDING."
HE FOLLOWED THEM PURPOSELY TO TOWN - HE DEFILED HIS HANDS WITH THE BLOOD OF A WOMAN WHOM HE SURELY **NEVER** WISHED TO SEE AGAIN!
HE WAS REDUCED TO MEET, REASON WITH, PERSUADE, AND FINALLY BRIBE, THE MAN WHOM HE ALWAYS MOST WISHED TO AVOID, AND WHOSE VERY NAME IT WAS **PUNISHMENT** TO HIM TO PRONOUNCE.
HE HAD DONE ALL THIS FOR *LYDIA* - A GIRL WHOM HE COULD NEITHER REGARD NOR ESTEEM!
WE OWE THE RESTORATION OF LYDIA, HER CHARACTER, EVERY-THING - TO ***MISTER DARCY!***
AND I'M SO PROUD OF HIM! ***PROUD*** THAT IN A CAUSE OF COMPASSION AND HONOR, HE WAS ABLE TO GET THE BETTER OF HIMSELF!

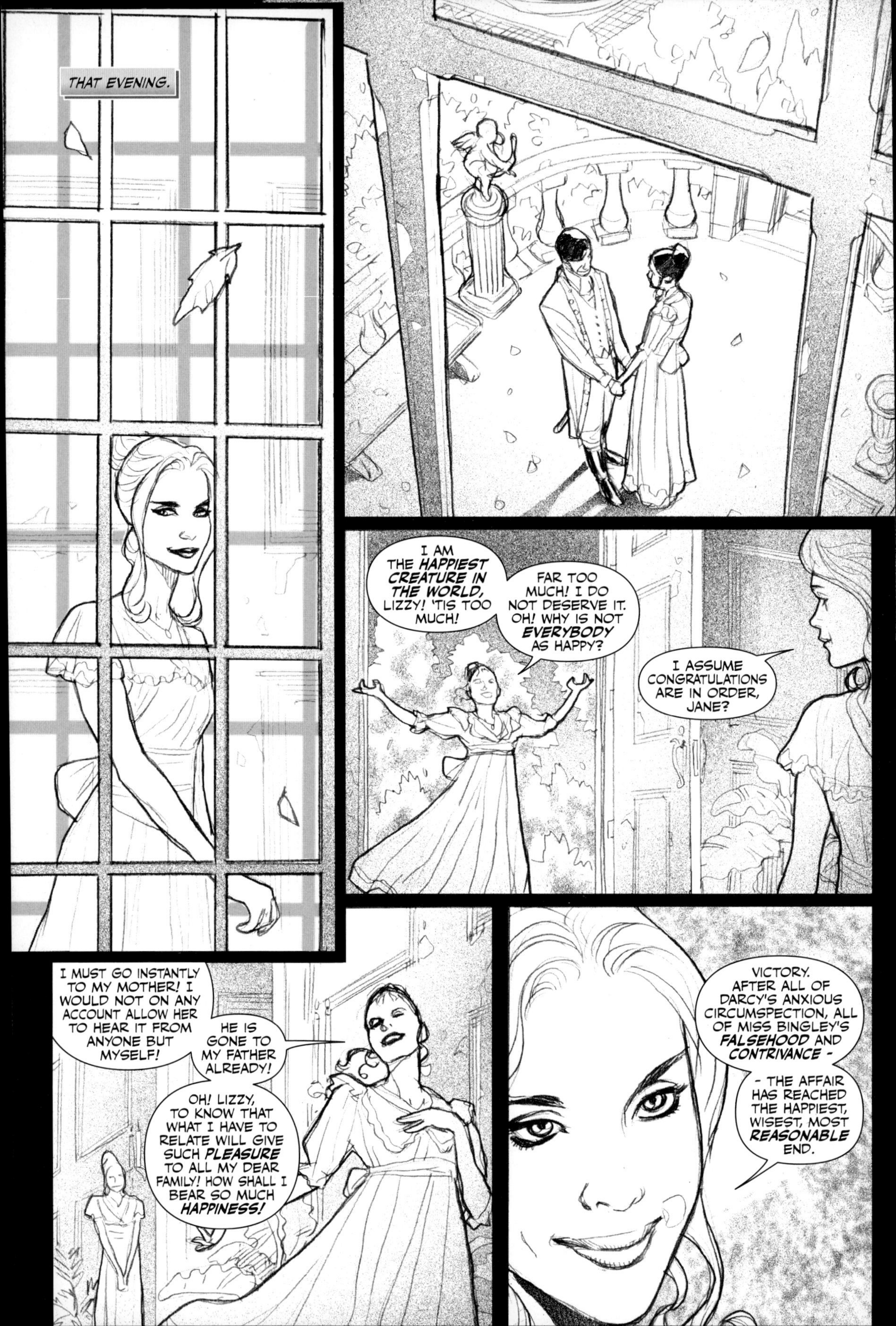
THAT EVENING.
I AM THE HAPPIEST CREATURE IN THE WORLD, LIZZY! 'TIS TOO MUCH!
FAR TOO MUCH! I DO NOT DESERVE IT. OH! WHY IS NOT EVERYBODY AS HAPPY?
I ASSUME CONGRATULATIONS ARE IN ORDER, JANE?
I MUST GO INSTANTLY TO MY MOTHER! I WOULD NOT ON ANY ACCOUNT ALLOW HER TO HEAR IT FROM ANYONE BUT MYSELF!
HE IS GONE TO MY FATHER ALREADY!
OH! LIZZY, TO KNOW THAT WHAT I HAVE TO RELATE WILL GIVE SUCH PLEASURE TO ALL MY DEAR FAMILY! HOW SHALL I BEAR SO MUCH HAPPINESS!
VICTORY. AFTER ALL OF DARCY'S ANXIOUS CIRCUMSPECTION, ALL OF MISS BINGLEY'S FALSEHOOD AND CONTRIVANCE -
- THE AFFAIR HAS REACHED THE HAPPIEST, WISEST, MOST REASONABLE END.

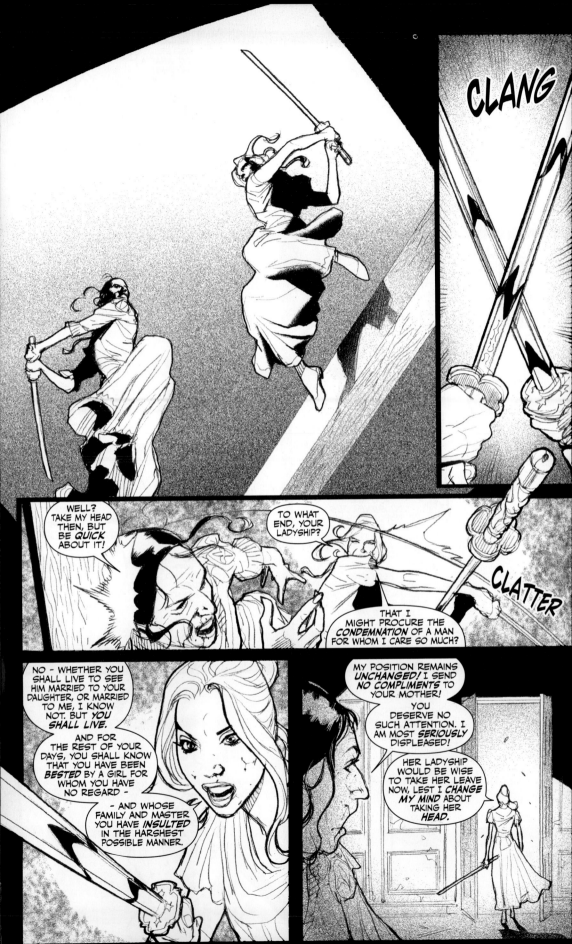

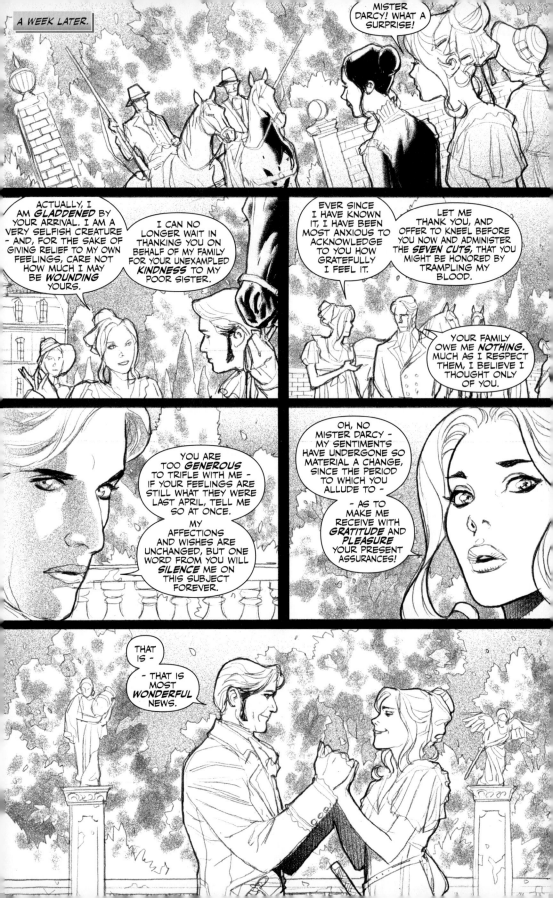

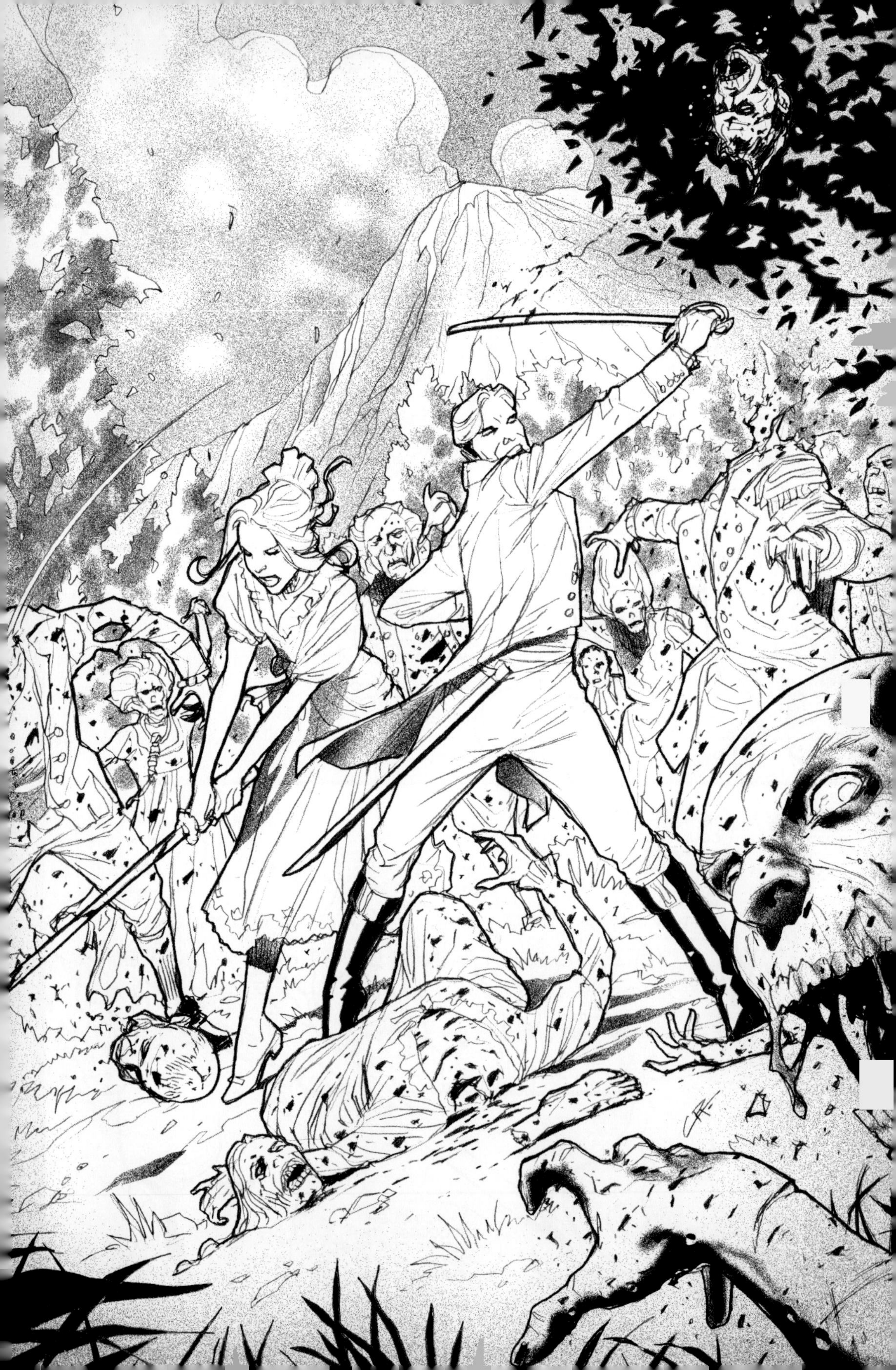

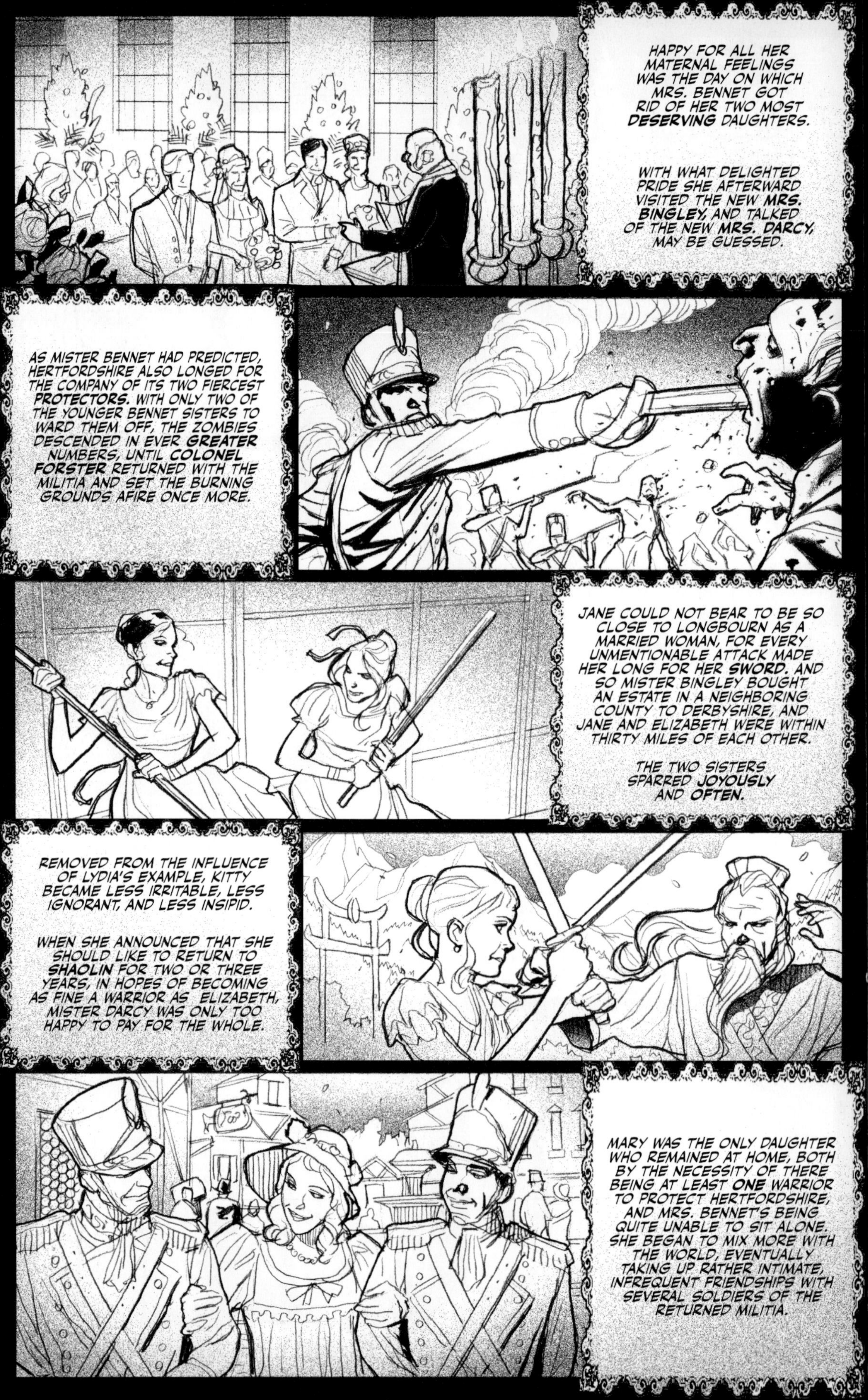

HAPPY FOR ALL HER MATERNAL FEELINGS WAS THE DAY ON WHICH MRS. BENNET GOT RID OF HER TWO MOST **DESERVING** DAUGHTERS.
WITH WHAT DELIGHTED PRIDE SHE AFTERWARD VISITED THE NEW **MRS. BINGLEY**, AND TALKED OF THE NEW **MRS. DARCY**, MAY BE GUESSED.
AS MISTER BENNET HAD PREDICTED, HERTFORDSHIRE ALSO LONGED FOR THE COMPANY OF ITS TWO FIERCEST **PROTECTORS.** WITH ONLY TWO OF THE YOUNGER BENNET SISTERS TO WARD THEM OFF, THE ZOMBIES DESCENDED IN EVER **GREATER** NUMBERS, UNTIL **COLONEL FORSTER** RETURNED WITH THE MILITIA AND SET THE BURNING GROUNDS AFIRE ONCE MORE.
JANE COULD NOT BEAR TO BE SO CLOSE TO LONGBOURN AS A MARRIED WOMAN, FOR EVERY UNMENTIONABLE ATTACK MADE HER LONG FOR HER **SWORD.** AND SO MISTER BINGLEY BOUGHT AN ESTATE IN A NEIGHBORING COUNTY TO DERBYSHIRE, AND JANE AND ELIZABETH WERE WITHIN THIRTY MILES OF EACH OTHER.
THE TWO SISTERS SPARRED **JOYOUSLY** AND **OFTEN.**
REMOVED FROM THE INFLUENCE OF LYDIA'S EXAMPLE, KITTY BECAME LESS IRRITABLE, LESS IGNORANT, AND LESS INSIPID.
WHEN SHE ANNOUNCED THAT SHE SHOULD LIKE TO RETURN TO **SHAOLIN** FOR TWO OR THREE YEARS, IN HOPES OF BECOMING AS FINE A WARRIOR AS ELIZABETH, MISTER DARCY WAS ONLY TOO HAPPY TO PAY FOR THE WHOLE.
MARY WAS THE ONLY DAUGHTER WHO REMAINED AT HOME, BOTH BY THE NECESSITY OF THERE BEING AT LEAST **ONE** WARRIOR TO PROTECT HERTFORDSHIRE, AND MRS. BENNET'S BEING QUITE UNABLE TO SIT ALONE. SHE BEGAN TO MIX MORE WITH THE WORLD, EVENTUALLY TAKING UP RATHER INTIMATE, INFREQUENT FRIENDSHIPS WITH SEVERAL SOLDIERS OF THE RETURNED MILITIA.

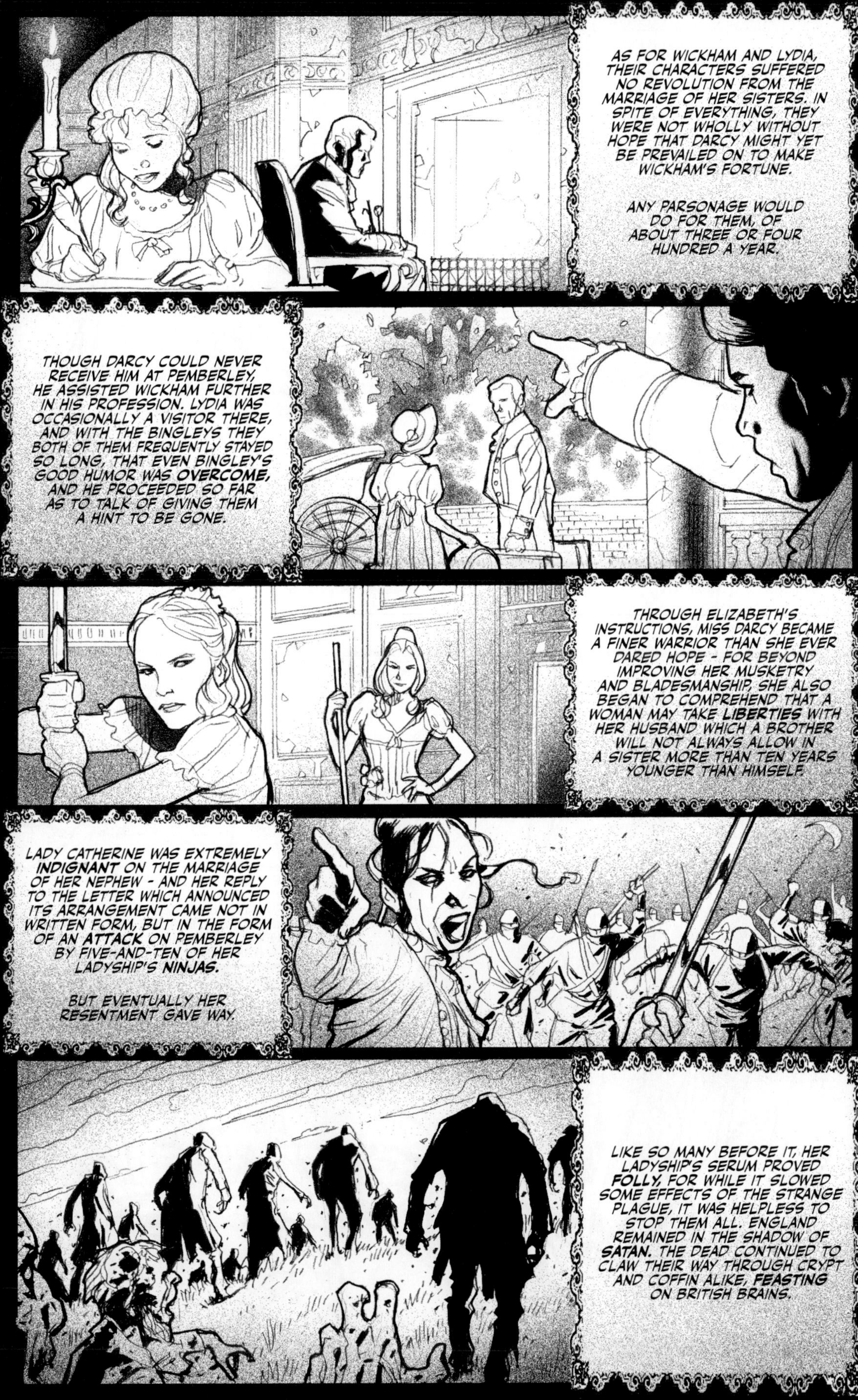
AS FOR WICKHAM AND LYDIA, THEIR CHARACTERS SUFFERED NO REVOLUTION FROM THE MARRIAGE OF HER SISTERS. IN SPITE OF EVERYTHING, THEY WERE NOT WHOLLY WITHOUT HOPE THAT DARCY MIGHT YET BE PREVAILED ON TO MAKE WICKHAM'S FORTUNE.
ANY PARSONAGE WOULD DO FOR THEM, OF ABOUT THREE OR FOUR HUNDRED A YEAR.
THOUGH DARCY COULD NEVER RECEIVE HIM AT PEMBERLEY, HE ASSISTED WICKHAM FURTHER IN HIS PROFESSION. LYDIA WAS OCCASIONALLY A VISITOR THERE, AND WITH THE BINGLEYS THEY BOTH OF THEM FREQUENTLY STAYED SO LONG, THAT EVEN BINGLEY'S GOOD HUMOR WAS **OVERCOME,** AND HE PROCEEDED SO FAR AS TO TALK OF GIVING THEM A HINT TO BE GONE.
THROUGH ELIZABETH'S INSTRUCTIONS, MISS DARCY BECAME A FINER WARRIOR THAN SHE EVER DARED HOPE - FOR BEYOND IMPROVING HER MUSKETRY AND BLADESMANSHIP, SHE ALSO BEGAN TO COMPREHEND THAT A WOMAN MAY TAKE **LIBERTIES** WITH HER HUSBAND WHICH A BROTHER WILL NOT ALWAYS ALLOW IN A SISTER MORE THAN TEN YEARS YOUNGER THAN HIMSELF.
LADY CATHERINE WAS EXTREMELY **INDIGNANT** ON THE MARRIAGE OF HER NEPHEW - AND HER REPLY TO THE LETTER WHICH ANNOUNCED ITS ARRANGEMENT CAME NOT IN WRITTEN FORM, BUT IN THE FORM OF AN **ATTACK** ON PEMBERLEY BY FIVE-AND-TEN OF HER LADYSHIP'S **NINJAS.**
BUT EVENTUALLY HER RESENTMENT GAVE WAY.
LIKE SO MANY BEFORE IT, HER LADYSHIP'S SERUM PROVED **FOLLY,** FOR WHILE IT SLOWED SOME EFFECTS OF THE STRANGE PLAGUE, IT WAS HELPLESS TO STOP THEM ALL. ENGLAND REMAINED IN THE SHADOW OF **SATAN.** THE DEAD CONTINUED TO CLAW THEIR WAY THROUGH CRYPT AND COFFIN ALIKE, **FEASTING** ON BRITISH BRAINS.

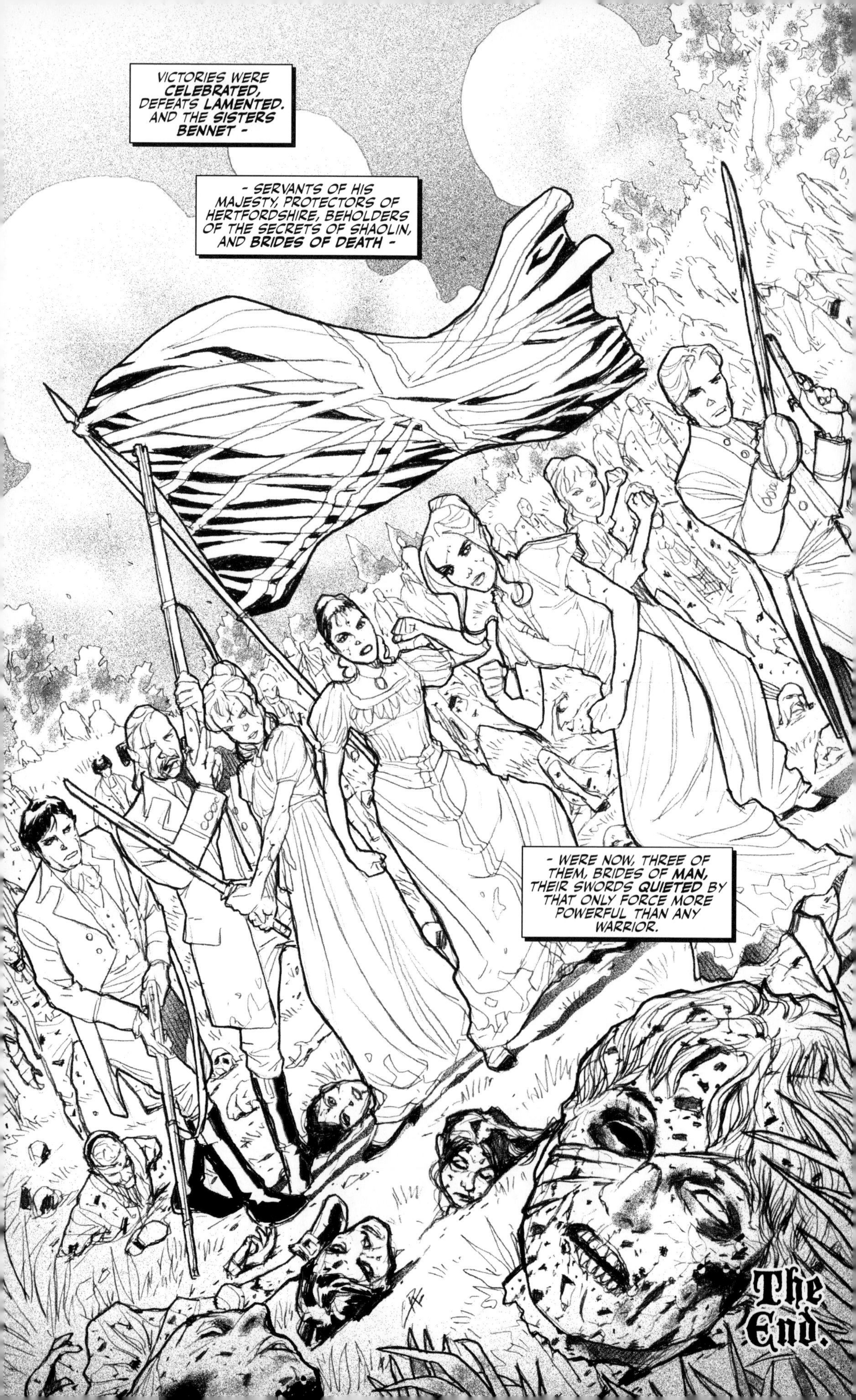
VICTORIES WERE CELEBRATED, DEFEATS LAMENTED. AND THE SISTERS BENNET -
- SERVANTS OF HIS MAJESTY, PROTECTORS OF HERTFORDSHIRE, BEHOLDERS OF THE SECRETS OF SHAOLIN, AND BRIDES OF DEATH -
- WERE NOW, THREE OF THEM, BRIDES OF MAN, THEIR SWORDS QUIETED BY THAT ONLY FORCE MORE POWERFUL THAN ANY WARRIOR.
The End.

About the Creators

TONY LEE

A writer for over twenty years in television, radio and magazines, for the last six Lee has worked extensively in comics, writing for such licences as *X-Men, Spider Man, Starship Troopers, Wallace & Gromit, Shrek* and *Doctor Who*. His critically acclaimed graphic novel *Outlaw: The Legend of Robin Hood* was announced as a Junior Library Guild Selection for 2009.

In addition, he has adapted books by a variety of bestselling authors including Anthony Horowitz and G.P Taylor, and has continued both *Oliver Twist* and *Dracula* in graphic novel format. He lives in London.

CLIFF RICHARDS

Cliff Richards, a veteran artist best known for his five-year run on the *Buffy the Vampire Slayer* comics series, illustrates this graphic novel. He has also worked on several projects for other comics publishers, including *Birds of Prey, Huntress*, and *Wonder Woman* for DC Comics, and *Rogue, Excalibur,* and *New Thunderbolts* for Marvel Comics.

FICTION AVAILABLE NOW FROM TITAN BOOKS

DRAGON AGE
The Calling - David Gaider
ISBN: 9781848567542

The Stolen Throne - David Gaider
ISBN: 9781848567535

IRON MAN
Femmes Fatales – Robert Greenberger
ISBN: 9781845769185

The Movie Novelisation - Peter David
ISBN: 9781845769178

Virus - Alex Irvine
ISBN: 9781845769192

PRIMEVAL
Extinction Event - Dan Abnett
ISBN: 9781845766931

Fire and Water - Simon Guerrier
ISBN: 9781845766955

The Lost Island - Paul Kearney
ISBN: 9781845766948

Shadow of the Jaguar - Steven Savile
ISBN: 9781845766924

THE FURTHER ADVENTURES OF
SHERLOCK HOLMES
Dr Jekyll and Mr Holmes - Loren D. Estleman
ISBN: 9781848567474

The Ectoplasmic Man - Daniel Stashower
ISBN: 9781848564923

The Man From Hell - Barrie Roberts
ISBN: 9781848565081

The Scroll of the Dead - David Stuart Davies
ISBN: 9781848564930

Séance for a Vampire - Fred Saberhagen
ISBN: 9781848566774

The Seventh Bullet - Daniel D. Victor
ISBN: 9781848566767

The Stalwart Companions - H. Paul Jeffers
ISBN: 9781848565098

The Veiled Detective - David Stuart Davies
ISBN: 9781848564909

The War of the Worlds - Manly Wade Wellman
ISBN: 9781848564916

WWW.TITANBOOKS.COM

FICTION AVAILABLE NOW FROM TITAN BOOKS

SUPERNATURAL
Bone Key - Keith R. A. DeCandido
ISBN: 9781845769475

Heart of the Dragon - Keith R. A. DeCandido
ISBN: 9781848566002

Nevermore - Keith R. A. DeCandido
ISBN: 9781845769451

The Unholy Cause - Joe Schreiber
ISBN: 9781848565289

Witch's Canyon - Jeff Mariotte
ISBN: 9781845769468

SOLOMAN KANE
The Official Movie Novelisation - Ramsey Campbell
ISBN: 9781848567269

STAR WARS
The Force Unleashed - Sean Williams
ISBN: 9781848563377

TERMINATOR
Cold War – Greg Cox
ISBN: 9781848560871

From the Ashes – Timothy Zahn
ISBN: 9781848560864

Terminator Salvation
(The Official Movie Novelisation) – Alan Dean Foster
ISBN: 9781848560857

Trial By Fire – Timothy Zahn
ISBN: 9781848560888

THE X-FILES
Antibodies - Kevin J. Anderson
ISBN: 9781848560758

Goblins - Charles Grant
ISBN: 9781848560765

Ground Zero - Kevin J. Anderson
ISBN: 9781848560772

I Want to Believe - Max Allan Collins
ISBN: 9781848560666

Ruins - Kevin J. Anderson
ISBN: 9781848560789

Skin - Ben Mezrich
ISBN: 9781848560796

Whirlwind - Charles Grant
ISBN: 9781848560802

WWW.TITANBOOKS.COM